Translated Documents of Greece ar

Robert K. Sherk, Editor

VOLUME 3

**The Hellenistic Age from the battle of Ipsos
to the death of Kleopatra VII**

The Hellenistic Age from the battle of Ipsos to the death of Kleopatra VII

EDITED AND TRANSLATED BY
STANLEY M. BURSTEIN
Professor of History,
California State University, Los Angeles

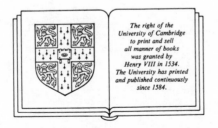

The right of the
University of Cambridge
to print and sell
all manner of books
was granted by
Henry VIII in 1534.
The University has printed
and published continuously
since 1584.

CAMBRIDGE UNIVERSITY PRESS

CAMBRIDGE

LONDON   NEW YORK   NEW ROCHELLE

MELBOURNE   SYDNEY

Published by the Press Syndicate of the University of Cambridge
The Pitt Building, Trumpington Street, Cambridge CB2 1RP
32 East 57th Street, New York, NY 10022, USA
10 Stamford Road, Oakleigh, Melbourne 3166, Australia

First published 1985

Printed in Great Britain at the University Press, Cambridge

Library of Congress catalogue card number: 84–29251

British Library Cataloguing in Publication Data
The Hellenistic age: from the battle of Ipsos
to the death of Kleopatra VII – (Translated
documents of Greece and Rome, 3)
1. Near East – History – to 30 BC
I. Title II. Series
939'.4   DS62.23

ISBN 0 521 23691 6 hard covers
ISBN 0 521 28158 X paperback

WD

Translated Documents of Greece and Rome

SERIES EDITOR'S INTRODUCTION

Greek and Roman history has always been in an ambivalent position in American higher education, having to find a home either in a Department of History or in a Department of Classics, and in both it is usually regarded as marginal. Moreover, in a History Department the subject tends to be taught without regard to the fact that the nature of the evidence is, on the whole, very different from that for American, English, or French history, while in a Classics Department it tends to be viewed as a 'philological' subject and taught by methods appropriate to Greek and Latin authors. Even on the undergraduate level the difference may be important, but on the graduate level, where future teachers and scholars, who are to engage in original research, are trained, it becomes quite clear that neither of these solutions is adequate.

One problem is the standard of proficiency that should be required in Greek and Latin – both difficult languages, necessitating years of study; and few students start the study, even of Latin, let alone Greek, before they come to college. The editor recognizes that for the student aiming at a Ph.D. in the subject and at advancing present knowledge of it there can be no substitute for a thorough training in the two languages. Nevertheless, it is possible to extend serious instruction at a high level to graduate students aiming at reaching the M.A. level and to make them into competent teachers. It is also possible to bring about a great improvement in the standard of undergraduate courses not requiring the ancient languages – courses that instructors themselves usually find unsatisfactory, since much of the source material cannot be used.

In order to use this material, at both graduate and serious undergraduate levels, the instructor must, in fact, be able to range far beyond the standard authors who have been translated many times. Harpocration, Valerius Maximus, and the *Suda* are often necessary tools, but they are usually unknown to anyone except the advanced scholar. Inscriptions, papyri, and scholia can be baffling even to the student who does have a grounding in the ancient languages.

It is the aim of the series to supply that need – which colleagues have often discussed with the editor – for translations of materials not readily available in English. The principal historical authors (authors like Herodotus, Thucydides, Livy, and Tacitus) are not included; they are easy enough to find in adequate translations, and the student will have to read far more of them than could be provided in a general source book. References to important passages in the works of those authors have been given at suitable points, but it is assumed that the instructor will direct the student's reading in them. While doing that reading, the student will now be able to have at his side a comprehensive reference book. Occasionally a passage from an otherwise accessible author (not a main historical source) has been included, so that the student may be spared the temptation of failing to search for it. But most of the material collected in this series would be hard for him to find anywhere in English, and much of it has never been translated at all.

Such translations of documentary sources as exist (and there are some major projects in translation among them, e.g. in the field of legal texts, which are intended to be far more than source books for students) tend to be seriously misleading in that they offer continuous texts where the original is (so often) fragmentary. The student cannot be aware of how much actually survives on the document and how much is modern conjecture – whether quite certain or mere guesswork. This series aims at presenting the translation of fragmentary sources in something like the way in which original documents were presented to the scholar: a variety of type fonts and brackets (which will be fully explained) have been used for this, and even though the page may at first sight appear forbidding to one unaccustomed to this, he will learn to differentiate between text and restoration and (with the instructor's help and the use of the notes provided) between the dubious, the probable, and the certain restoration. Naturally, the English can never correspond perfectly to the Greek or Latin, but the translation aims at as close a correspondence as can be achieved, so that the run of the original and (where necessary) the amount surviving can be clearly shown. Finer points of English idiom have deliberately been sacrificed in order to produce this increased accuracy, though it is hoped that there will be nothing in the translation so unnatural as to baffle the student. In the case of inscriptions (except for those with excessively short lines) line-by-line correspondence has been the aim, so that the student who sees a precise line reference in a modern work will be able to find it in the translation.

Translation is an art as well as a science; there are bound to be differing opinions on the precise interpretation and on the best rendering of any given passage. But there is always room for improvement, and a need for it. Suggestions and corrections from users of the series will always be welcome.

The general editor sincerely hopes that the present volume will make a major contribution to raising the standard of ancient history teaching in the U.S.A. and, indeed, wherever English is the medium of instruction, and that it will help to convey to students not fully proficient in Greek or Latin, or even entirely ignorant of those languages, some of the immediacy and excitement of real (as distinct from textbook) history. Perhaps some will be encouraged to develop their skill in the two languages so as to go on to a fuller understanding of the ancient world, or even to professional study of it.

State University of New York at Buffalo   R.K.S.

TO MY FAMILY
FOR THEIR PATIENCE AND SUPPORT

CONTENTS

Contents

Contents

Contents

VOLUME EDITOR'S INTRODUCTION

The purpose of this volume is to provide students and scholars with a selection of documents in translation intended to supplement standard histories dealing with the Hellenistic period from 300 to 30 BC (unless otherwise noted, all dates are BC).

The criteria for the selection of the texts translated are essentially the same as those for the other volumes in the series. Passages from authors readily available in English translation have been avoided except in those cases where they provide the only or best evidence for events or trends too important to be omitted. A few texts are drawn from secondary sources, some of which, such as the *Suda* or Photius' *Bibliotheca*, date from the Byzantine period, but contain information derived from earlier sources or fragments – quotations or summaries – of the works of now lost historians. The primary source for the latter is F. Jacoby's incomplete *Die Fragmente der griechischen Historiker*, which contains collections of the fragments of over eight hundred lost Greek historians together with a critical commentary on them in German (except for the two volumes which deal with the historians of Athens). The majority of the documents translated in this volume consist, however, of contemporary non-literary epigraphical and papyrological texts.

The special problems presented by the study of Hellenistic history have determined the arrangement and selection of the documents translated. The single most striking fact of the Hellenistic period is the existence for varying periods of time of a plethora of Greek and Macedonian states throughout the whole area from the western Mediterranean to India. In other words, Hellenistic history is not the history of a single political or cultural entity but the sum of the histories of a number of distinct regions each of which experienced its own unique development. Unlike the other volumes in the series, therefore, the documents in it are not organized chronologically but are instead divided into a number of topical chapters each of which, after Chapter 1, deals with the history of a specific region. The documents within each chapter, however, have been arranged chronologically according to the earliest date proposed by scholars for each text. The few exceptions to this rule are documents which are clearly later copies of earlier texts and those in which the earliest proposed dates are based on chronological systems that have been shown to be incorrect. In the former case the few such texts have been placed in the context suggested by their content, and in the latter case the discredited dates have been ignored. If the breadth of the geographical background against which the events of Hellenistic history took place is the most significant characteristic of the period, the lack of even one comprehensive ancient narrative source for the three centuries covered by this volume is the single most important and frustrating problem faced by the Hellenistic historian. As a result, modern studies and textbooks for the period rest to a considerably greater degree than those concerned with periods dealt with by other volumes in this series on inferences and reconstructions based on combinations of frequently isolated epigraphical and/or papyrological documents and often allusive and unclear references in the few surviving literary sources. For this reason, while an attempt has been made to include in the volume a representative selection of sources dealing with a variety of aspects of Hellenistic social and cultural history, particular emphasis has been placed on including as many as space permits of those documents most often referred to by modern scholars so as to permit students to evaluate critically the accounts found in the various textbooks and studies encountered by them.

The format in which the translations are presented follows that established for all the series' volumes. Each text is preceded by a heading containing in order a descriptive title for the document, its place of origin and date; the physical character (stele, statue base, wall block, etc.) and notation of any special peculiarities of its lettering. A brief selection of previous editions of the text follows, together with an indication of which edition has served as the basis for the translation, a list of related ancient sources and a brief bibliography of relevant modern scholarly studies of the text and its historical context. The bibliographies are not intended to be exhaustive but instead to contain works which will serve as starting points for further study in addition to those used in the preparation of the notes which follow each translation. The purpose of the notes is severely limited. They are intended solely to provide the student with sufficient background information to enable him to evaluate intelligently the significance of the text translated and the use made of it by modern scholars, and to that end the contents of the notes are limited to brief summaries of scholarly views concerning the texts and their dates and significance and relevant factual information about their contents and, where necessary, reports of differing readings and restorations by previous editors.

In accordance with the guidelines established for the series a particu-

lar effort has been made to produce translations that are accurate
reflections of their originals. Wherever possible, a line for line corre-
spondance between the translations and the texts being translated has
been aimed at even at the expense of some awkwardness and depar-
tures from normal idiomatic English usage in the resulting versions.
Line endings and every fifth line have been marked. Brackets ([ ])
indicate missing letters in personal and geographical names and titles.
Elsewhere restorations of missing letters are indicated by italics except
where the restoration is absolutely certain, as in the case of portions of
standard formulae or so obvious and trivial that no useful purpose
would be served by marking them.

A list of abbreviations of books and journals frequently mentioned
in the bibliographies, a concordance of texts translated, kinglists of the
principal Hellenistic dynasties, a glossary and indexes of names and
subjects have been provided. The indexes are keyed to the numbers of
the translations and not to the pages, while the glossary is limited to
definitions of terms and explanations of institutions encountered in
several documents. All others are dealt with in the notes. Finally, a
word about the treatment of Greek personal and geographical names.
In both the translations and the notes the Greek forms have been used
with two exceptions. In cases of Latin texts the Latin forms of Greek
names have usually been employed and the same is true for the names
of Greek authors cited in the bibliographies since their general use in
scholarly and popular literature means that to do otherwise would
cause users of the volume needless inconvenience.

At this point there remains only the pleasant task of acknowledging
those people whose help was instrumental in bringing this volume to a
successful conclusion. First and foremost, I would like to express my
gratitude to the present and former Series Editors for inviting me to
undertake the volume and to Professor R. Sherk for his seemingly
endless patience and the tireless efforts he expended in the thankless
task of editing my manuscript. Thanks are also due to Professor
Christian Habicht and the staff of the Institute for Advanced Study for
making it possible for me to exploit the riches of the Institute's
epigraphical library under the most pleasant of conditions, and to
California State University, Los Angeles, for the award of a grant in aid
which allowed me to visit Princeton. Finally, I would like to
acknowledge the kind assistance of Professors J. Puhvel and K. Bolle of
the University of California, Los Angeles, and A. K. Narain of the
University of Wisconsin with the texts dealing with Baktria and India.

ABBREVIATIONS

AJA	*American Journal of Archaeology*
AJAH	*American Journal of Ancient History*
AJP	*American Journal of Philology*
Allen, *Attalid Kingdom*	R. E. Allen, *The Attalid Kingdom: A Constitutional History* (Oxford 1983)
ANRW	*Aufstieg und Niedergang der römischen Welt* (Berlin 1972–)
ANS-MN	*American Numismatic Society Museum Notes*
Ath. Mitt.	*Mitteilungen des deutschen Archäologischen Instituts, Athenische Abteilung*
Bagnall, *Administration*	R. S. Bagnall, *The Administration of the Ptolemaic Possessions Outside Egypt* (Leiden 1976)
BCH	*Bulletin de Correspondance Hellénique*
Bengtson, *Strategie*	H. Bengtson, *Die Strategie in der hellenistischen Zeit*, 3 vols. (Munich 1937–52)
Bevan, *Ptolemy*	E. R. Bevan, *The House of Ptolemy* (London 1927)
Bevan, *Seleucus*	E. R. Bevan, *The House of Seleucus*, 2 vols. (London 1902)
Burstein, 'Arsinoe II'	S. M. Burstein, 'Arsinoe II Philadelphos: A Revisionist View', in *Philip II, Alexander the Great and the Macedonian Heritage* (Washington, D.C. 1982)
Busolt-Swoboda, *Staatskunde*	G. Busolt and H. Swoboda, *Griechische Staatskunde*, 2 vols. (Munich 1920–6)
CAH[1]	*The Cambridge Ancient History*, vols. 7 and 8 (Cambridge 1928, 1930)
CAH[2]	*The Cambridge Ancient History*, vol. 7.1[2] (Cambridge 1984)
Cerfaux and Tondriau, *Culte des Souverains*	L. Cerfaux and J. Tondriau, *Le culte des souverains dans la civilisation gréco-romaine* (Paris 1957)
Choix	J. Pouilloux, *Choix d'inscriptions grecques* (Paris 1960)
C. Ord. Ptol.[2]	Marie-Thérèse Lenger, *Corpus des Ordonnances des Ptolémées*[2] (Brussels 1980)
CP	*Classical Philology*
CRAI	*Comptes Rendus de l'Académie des Inscriptions et Belles-Lettres*
CSCA	*California Studies in Classical Antiquity*
Das ptolemäische Aegypten	*Das ptolemäische Aegypten: Akten des internationalen Symposions, 27–29 September 1976 in Berlin*, ed. H. Maehler and V. M. Strocka (Mainz 1976)
Daux, *Delphes*	G. Daux, *Delphes au IIe et au Ier siècle* (Paris 1936)
Epigraphica 2	H. W. Pleket, *Epigraphica*, vol. 2 (Leiden 1969)
Ehrenberg, *Greek State*	V. Ehrenberg, *The Greek State* (New York 1960)
Errington, *Philopoemen*	R. M. Errington, *Philopoemen* (Oxford 1969)
Ferguson, *Athens*	W. S. Ferguson, *Hellenistic Athens* (London 1911)
Flacelière, *Aitoliens*	R. Flacelière, *Les Aitoliens à Delphes* (Paris 1937)
FGrHist	F. Jacoby, *Die Fragmente der griechischen Historiker* (Berlin and Leiden 1923–)

Abbreviations

Fraser, *Ptolemaic Alexandria*	P. M. Fraser, *Ptolemaic Alexandria*, 3 vols. (Oxford 1972)
Geagan, *Athenian Constitution*	D. J. Geagan, *The Athenian Constitution after Sulla, Hesperia* Supp. 12 (1967)
GGA	*Göttingische gelehrte Anzeigen*
M. Guarducci, *Epigrafia greca*	M. Guarducci, *Epigrafia greca*, 4 vols. (Rome 1967–74)
Günther, *Orakel*	W. Günther, *Das Orakel von Didyma in hellenistischer Zeit, Istanbuler Mitteilungen* 4 (Tübingen 1971)
Habicht, *Gottmenschentum*	C. Habicht, *Gottmenschentum und griechische Städte*[2], *Zetemata* 14 (Munich 1970)
Habicht, *Studien*	C. Habicht, *Studien zur Geschichte Athens in hellenistischer Zeit, Hypomnemata* 73 (Göttingen 1982)
Habicht, *Untersuchungen*	C. Habicht, *Untersuchungen zur politischen Geschichte Athens im 3. Jahrhundert v. Chr.*, *Vestigia* 30 (Munich 1979)
Hansen, *Attalids*[2]	E. V. Hansen, *The Attalids of Pergamon*[2] (Ithaca, N.Y. 1971)
Hauben, *Callicrates*	H. Hauben, *Callicrates of Samos: A Contribution to the Study of the Ptolemaic Admiralty, Studia Hellenistica* 18 (Louvain 1970)
Haussoulier, *Études*	B. C. L. M. Haussoulier, *Études sur l'histoire de Milet et du Didymeion* (Paris 1902)
Heinen, *Untersuchungen*	H. Heinen, *Untersuchungen zur hellenistischen Geschichte des 3. Jahrhunderts v. Chr.*, *Historia Einzelschriften* 20 (Wiesbaden 1972)
Historia	*Historia: Zeitschrift für Alte Geschichte*
Holleaux, *Études*	Maurice Holleaux, *Études d'épigraphie et d'histoire grecques*, 6 vols., ed. L. Robert (Paris 1938–68)
Hopp, *Untersuchungen*	J. Hopp, *Untersuchungen zur Geschichte der letzten Attaliden, Vestigia* 25 (Munich 1977)
HSCP	*Harvard Studies in Classical Philology*
HTR	*Harvard Theological Review*
Hutmacher, *Ehrendekret*	R. Hutmacher, *Das Ehrendekret für den Strategen Kallimachos, Beiträge zur klassischen Philologie* 17 (Meisenheim am Glan 1965)
I. Delphi	*Fouilles de Delphes*, vol. 3, *Épigraphie* (Paris 1910–)
I. Didyma	A. Rehm, *Die Inschriften*, *Milet*, vol. 3 (Berlin 1914)
I. Ephesos	H. Wankel *et al.*, *Die Inschriften von Ephesos*, 7 vols., *Inschriften griechischer Städte aus Kleinasien* (= *IGSK*) 11–17 (Bonn 1979–81)
I. Erythrae	H. Engelmann and R. Merkelbach, *Die Inschriften von Erythrai und Klazomenai*, 2 vols., *IGSK* 1–2 (Bonn 1972–3)
IG	*Inscriptiones Graecae* (Berlin 1873–)
I. Kyme	H. Engelmann, *Die Inschriften von Kyme*, *IGSK* 5 (Bonn 1976)
I. Ilion	R. Frisch, *Die Inschriften von Ilion*, *IGSK* 3 (Bonn 1975)
I. Labraunda	J. Crampa, *Labraunda*, vol. 3.1, *The Greek Inscriptions* (Lund 1969)
I. Magnesia	O. Kern, *Die Inschriften von Magnesia am Maeander* (Berlin 1900)
I. Olympia	W. Dittenberger and K. Purgold, *Die Inschriften von Olympia* (Berlin 1896)
I. Pergamum	M. Frankel *et al.*, *Die Inschriften von Pergamon, Die Altertümer von Pergamon* VIII (Berlin 1890–1969)

Abbreviations

I. Philae	E. Bernard, *Les inscriptions grecques de Philae*, 2 vols. (Paris 1969)
I. Priene	F. Hiller von Gaertringen, *Inschriften von Priene* (Berlin 1906)
I. Samothrace	P. M. Fraser, *Samothrace*, vol. 2.1, *The Inscriptions on Stone* (Princeton 1960)
ISE	L. Moretti, *Iscrizioni Storiche Ellenistiche* (Florence 1967–75)
JEA	*Journal of Egyptian Archaeology*
JHS	*Journal of Hellenic Studies*
JOAI	*Jahreshefte des Oesterreichischen Archäologischen Instituts*
MacDowell and Taddei, *Afghanistan*	D. W. MacDowell and M. Taddei, *The Archaeology of Afghanistan*, ed. F. R. Allchin and N. Hammond (London 1978), 233–99
McShane, *Foreign Policy*	R. B. McShane, *The Foreign Policy of the Attalids of Pergamum* (Urbana 1964)
Magie, *RRAM*	D. Magie, *Roman Rule in Asia Minor*, 2 vols. (Princeton 1950)
Mastrocinque, *Caria*	A. Mastrocinque, *La Caria e la Ionia meridionale in epoca ellenistica* (Rome 1979)
Mørkholm, *Antiochus IV*	O. Mørkholm, *Antiochus IV of Syria* (Copenhagen 1966)
Narain, *Indo-Greeks*	A. K. Narain, *The Indo-Greeks* (Oxford 1957)
Nouveau Choix	*Nouveau choix d'inscriptions grecques* (Paris 1971)
OGIS	W. Dittenberger, *Orientis Graeci Inscriptiones Selectae* (Leipzig 1903)
Orth, *Machtanspruch*	W. Orth, *Königlicher Machtanspruch und städtische Freiheit*, *Münchener Beiträge zur Papyrusforschung und antiken Rechtsgeschichte* 71 (Munich 1977)
Parke, *Festivals*	H. W. Parke, *Festivals of the Athenians* (Ithaca, NY 1977)
Pomeroy, *Goddesses*	S. B. Pomeroy, *Goddesses, Whores, Wives, and Slaves* (New York 1975)
P. Oxy.	*The Oxyrhynchus Papyri* (London 1898–)
P. Tebt.	*The Tebtunis Papyri*, ed. B. P. Grenfell *et al.*, 3 vols. (London 1902–38)
RA	*Revue Archéologique*
REA	*Revue des Études Anciennes*
REG	*Revue des Études Grecques*
REJ	*Revue des Études Juives*
RFIC	*Rivista di Filologia e di Istruzione Classica*
Rhodes, *Boule*	P. J. Rhodes, *The Athenian Boule* (Oxford 1972)
Rhodes, *Commentary*	P. J. Rhodes, *Commentary on the Aristotelian* Athenaion Politeia (Oxford 1981)
RHR	*Revue de l'Histoire des Religions*
Rostovtzeff, *SEHHW*	M. Rostovtzeff, *The Social and Economic History of the Hellenistic World*, 3 vols. (Oxford 1941)
RPhil.	*Revue de Philologie, de Littérature et d'Histoire Anciennes*
Schmitt, *Antiochos*	H. Schmitt, *Untersuchungen zur Geschichte Antiochos des Grossen und seiner Zeit*, *Historia Einzelschriften* 6 (Wiesbaden 1964)
Schmitt, *Staatsverträge*	H. Schmitt, *Die Staatsverträge des Altertums*, vol. 3 (Munich 1969)

Abbreviations

SEG	*Supplementum Epigraphicum Graecum*
Sherk, *RDGE*	R. K. Sherk, *Roman Documents from the Greek East* (Baltimore 1969)
Sherk, *TDGR*	R. K. Sherk, *Translated Documents of Greece and Rome*, vol. 4, *Rome and the Greek East to the Death of Augustus* (Cambridge 1984)
SIG^3	W. Dittenberger, *Sylloge Inscriptionum Graecarum*^{3} (Leipzig 1915–24)
TAM	*Tituli Asiae Minoris* (Vienna 1901–)
TAPA	*Transactions of the American Philological Association*
Tarn, *Bactria*	W. W. Tarn, *The Greeks in Bactria and India*^{2} (Cambridge 1951)
Tarn, *Gonatas*	W. W. Tarn, *Antigonos Gonatas* (Oxford 1913)
Tscherikower, *Städtegründungen*	V. Tscherikower, *Die hellenistischen Städtegründungen von Alexander dem Grossen bis auf die Römerzeit, Philologus* Supp. 19.1 (Leipzig 1927)
Walbank, *Commentary*	F. W. Walbank, *A Historical Commentary on Polybius*, 3 vols. (Oxford 1957–79)
Walbank, *Philip V*	F. W. Walbank, *Philip V of Macedon* (Cambridge 1939)
Welles, *RC*	C. Bradford Welles, *Royal Correspondence in the Hellenistic Period* (London 1934)
Will, *Histoire*	Édouard Will, *Histoire politique du monde hellénistique (323–30 av. J.-C.)*, 2 vols., vol. 1^2 (Nancy 1979); vol. 2 (Nancy 1967)
ZPE	*Zeitschrift für Papyrologie und Epigraphik*

SYMBOLS

*	indicates the edition on which a translation is based.
( )	indicates an explanatory addition to the text.
[ ]	enclose letters or words no longer extant but restored by modern scholars.
[---]	indicate an unknown number of letters missing.
{ }	indicate probably superfluous ancient letters.
< >	indicate letters or words thought to have been accidentally omitted at the time the original document was prepared.
[[ ]]	enclose letters or words deliberately erased in antiquity.
|	indicates the end of a line in an inscription or papyrus.
||	indicates the beginning of every fifth line in an inscription or papyrus.
/	indicates the end of a line of verse.
//	indicate the beginning of every fifth line of verse.
v	indicates a blank space in an inscription.
vv	indicate more than one blank space in an inscription.
vacat	indicates that a line or space between lines was left blank.
Italics	indicate that part of the original word is extant on the document.

Chapter 1
FROM IPSOS TO KORUPEDION (301–281)

1 Ephesos honors Nikagoras, son of Aristarchos, from Rhodes, ambassador of Demetrios Poliorketes and Seleukos. Ephesos, 300/299. Wall block from the temple of Artemis.

OGIS 10; **I. Ephesos* 5.1453; cf. Plutarch, *Demetrios* 31.2.

Tarn, *Gonatas* 11–12; Will, *Histoire* 1².87–9; J. Seibert, *Historische Beiträge zu den dynastischen Verbindungen in hellenistischer Zeit* (Wiesbaden 1967) 48–50.

Resolved by the Boule and the People. Philainetos, son of Philophron, introduced the motion. Since | Nikagoras, son of Aristarchos, a Rhodian, having been sent by the kings, Demetrios | and Seleukos (I),[1] to both the Ephesian people and the other Greeks | and having been brought before the People, spoke about the relationship existing
5 ‖ between them and about the *good will* which they continue to have for | the Greeks, and (since) *he renewed* the friendship which he previously had | with the city, it has been resolved by the Boule and the People | that they *praise* Nikagoras for the good will which he continues to have for the | *kings* and the People and crown him with a gold wreath
10 ‖ *and* announce (it) at the *Ephesia*[2] in the theatre. They shall also grant citizenship to him | [on an equal] and like (basis) just as to the other benefactors, and he shall also have | a *front seat* at the contests and the right of import and export both in war | [and in] *peace* and exemption from taxation for whatever he imports or exports {or} to his own home | [and the right of access to] the Boule and People immediately
15 after the sacred business. These (rights) shall belong ‖ [also to his descendants]. The neopoioi[3] *shall record* the gifts that have been given to him | [on the temple] *of Artemis,*[4] and he shall be assigned by lot to a tribe and to | [a chiliastys[5] by the Essenes][6] in order that all may know that the Ephesian people | [honors those who are zealous for the interests of the Greeks][7] and of itself | [with suitable gifts]. Gifts of
20 hospitality shall also be sent to him by the ‖ [oikonomos.[8] He obtained by lot] the tribe Epheseus,[9] the chiliastys Lebedios.

1 Seleukos I and Demetrios became allies about 299.
2 Festival of Artemis Ephesia.
3 'Temple builders'. Originally officials in charge of temple building and repairs, their functions often expanded to cover the whole field of temple administration. Their responsibility for registering gifts and honors resulted from the practice at Ephesos of recording such awards in the sanctuary of Artemis (cf. *SIG*³ 353, line 8).

4   Restored by Borker and Merkelbach on the basis of other similar Ephesian decrees
    such as *I. Ephesos* 1408, line 15.
5   The chiliastys or thousand was a subdivision of a tribe at Ephesos and, therefore,
    presumably a kinship unit. Twenty are attested at Ephesos.
6   Most likely a priestly college. Its origin and function are unknown, but the title
    Essen, 'king', suggests a connection with the archaic Ephesian monarchy.
7   Restored by Borker and Merkelbach. Dittenberger: '[confer benefits on it]'.
8   Restored by Dittenberger on the basis of *SIG*[3] 352, line 8. He was probably the chief
    financial officer of the city.
9   The first of the five tribes so far attested at Ephesos.

**2   Miletos honors the future Antiochos I for providing funds for a
stoa. Miletos, 299.** Three fragments of a white marble stele, early
third-century lettering.

Haussoulier, *Études* 34–5; *OGIS* 213; *I. Didyma* 479; *Günther, Orakel* 29–30.

Haussoulier, *Études* 33–48; W. W. Tarn, *JHS* 60 (1940) 92–4; F. Schel, *TAPA* 82 (1951)
111–13, 118; Tarn, *Bactria* 83–4; *FGrHist* 3b, pp. 252–4; Günther, *Orakel* 23–9, 36–8;
H. Müller, *Milesische Volksbeschlüsse* (Göttingen 1976) 20–39; D. Musti, *CAH*[2] 207.

Resolved by the People; decree of the synedroi;[1] Demodamas, son | of
Aristeides,[2] introduced the motion. Since Antiochos, the eldest
<son> | of King Seleukos (I), previously displayed *great* | good will and
5   zeal *continuously* || *for* the Milesian people and now, *seeing* | *his own* father
    exerting every effort | on behalf of the sanctuary at Didyma,[3] (and)
    ju|*dging* that it would be good to follow his father's [po|licy], *promises to*
10 *construct* a stoa [one stad||ion[4] (in length) for the] *god*[5] in the city from
    which there shall be (derived) *every* [year | income, which] he thinks
    ought to be spent for works | *undertaken* in the sanctuary at Didyma, and
    the structures | built *with* [these (revenues)] shall be his own
    dedi|*cations*;[6] it has been resolved by the Milesians that they praise
15 || [Antiochos] for his reverence for the god and his | good will [toward
    the] *Greeks*;[7] and that there shall be given to him | [for the stoa]
    whichever spot the architect, | *who is chosen*, and the men *ap*|*pointed* by
20 Antiochos may designate; and the treasurers [---||---] *and* those [in the
    future] holding (the office of) Prytanis[8] | *shall receive* [the] *income* derived
    [from] it | [and] *deposit* it separately, and the *lease* | is to be let [just] as
    the People decides; | and *when* what has been authorized *is completed*,
25 || let them inscribe (on it): | '*Antiochos*, the eldest son of King Seleukos
    (I), | has *dedicated*'. And in order that others also will choose *to exert* |
    themselves on behalf of the sanctuary at *Didyma* and of [the People] | of
30 the Milesians, seeing *the sanctuary's benefac*||*tors* being honored by the
    People, [it has been resolved] | by the Milesians that they will set up a

bronze [statue] of Antiochos | on a horse at whichever spot the [Boule] decides *to desig|nate*. The expenditure for [the statue] | shall be paid out by the anataktai[9] [in the year of the] stephanephoros [after

35   Athenaios][10] ‖ when also (the money for) the [other expenditures] *is allo|cated* by them; and he shall be invited to [a front seat in Miletos] | at the Dionysia and at Didyma | [at the Didymeia], (both) periodic games;[11] [and] there shall be granted [to him also the right of main-tenance] | in the prytaneion[12] and exemption [from all taxes and per-

40   sonal security] ‖ both in peace and in war, *inviolate* [and without treaty, and he shall have] | the right of *first consultation* (of the oracle) [in the sanctuary at] | Didyma; and these rights [also | shall belong to the descendants of] *Antiochos*; and in order that the statue *be com|pleted* [as

45   soon as possible], *there shall be chosen* ‖ by the People three *men* [immediately, and] *they shall supervise the manufacture* [---].

1   Commission chosen by the assembly at Miletos to draft decrees for submission to it.
2   He is probably to be identified with the Seleucid general who, sometime between 293 and 281, led an army across the Jaxartes River where he set up altars to Apollo of Didyma (Pliny, *HN* 6.49). In 299 he was a member of the Boule at Miletos and recommended to it the honoring of Apama, the wife of Seleukos I and mother of Antiochos I, as well as being a member of the commission charged with supervis-ing the manufacture of her statue. The fragments of his books on Halikarnassos and India are collected in *FGrHist* 428.
3   Cf. Günther, *Orakel* 23, lines 7–10.
4   Approximately 183 m (200 yards) in length.
5   Apollo.
6   The restorations concerning the stoa are based on lines 11–14 of the decree honoring Apama for her influence with Seleukos I and Antiochos I (cf. above n. 3). The reference to revenues indicates that it was a commercial stoa, that is, one in which space could be leased from the city for shops, etc. An architrave block from it preserves part of the dedicatory inscription (*I. Didyma* 193a): '[Antiochos, of King] *Seleukos* [the eldest son, | to Apollo] in *Didyma*.'
7   Dittenberger suggests: '[toward the] *citizens*'.
8   Clearly a body of officials with executive power. Müller considers them a college of magistrates; Schel suggests a committee of the Boule. Their number in the Hellenistic period is unknown, although there were five in the Roman imperial period. See Glossary.
9   Financial officials who managed Miletos' annual revenues and allocated them to the various magistrates.
10   299/8. The restoration is based on Günther, *Orakel* 23–4, lines 17–18.
11   Interval unknown.
12   The office of the college of prytaneis.

3   Dedication of Arsinoe (II) to the Great Gods. Samothrace, about 300–281. Marble fragments of six blocks from the frieze of the Arsinoeion.

IG XII 8, 227; *OGIS* 15; **I. Samothrace* 10 with photograph; cf. Plutarch, *Demetrios* 31.3.

Tarn, *Gonatas* 11; P. M. Fraser, *I. Samothrace* pp. 48–50; G.Longega, *Arsinoe* II (Rome 1968) 39–42; K. Lehmann, *Samothrace*[4] (Locust Valley 1975) 54–8; Burstein, 'Arsinoe II', 198–200.

Queen Arsinoe, [of King] *Ptolemaios* (I) *the daughter,*[1] | *of King* [Lysimachos][2] *the wife*[3] [---],[4] *to the Great Gods.*

1   316–270. Daughter of Ptolemaios I and Berenike I.
2   Restoration proposed by Wilamowitz because Ptolemaios I was still alive at the time of the dedication.
3   About 300.
4   The lacuna probably contained the ancient name of the Arsinoeion, a round building whose function is unknown.

4   Athens honors Poseidippos for aiding an embassy to Kassandros. Athens, 299/8. Marble stele, stoichedon.

IG II[2] 641; **SIG*[3] 362.

Ferguson, *Athens* 131; W. B. Dinsmoor, *The Archons of Athens in the Hellenistic Age* (Cambridge, Mass. 1931) 3–16; M. Fortina, *Cassandro, Re di Macedonia* (Turin 1965) 114–15; Will, *Histoire* 1[2].86–7.

In the archonship of E[uktem]on,[1] in | the prytany of Antigo[nis][2] (which is) the second, | in which Theophilos, son of Xeno[phon], | from
5   Kephale was secretar‖y, Metageitnion's twenty-first·| day,[3] twenty-first day of the p|rytany; (regular) assembly; | the motion was put to the vote by (the chairman) of the proedroi, Lysimachos, son of Na|usistratos,
10   from Prospalta, and ‖ by his fellow proedroi. Resolved by the Peopl|e; Philippides, son of Philomelos,[4] from Paia|nia, introduced the motion.
15   Since the ambassado|rs sent to K|ing Kassandros[5] decla‖re that Poseidippos, who made the jour|ney with them, was useful | to them, demonstrating | the good will which he has for the p|eople of the
20   Athenians, it has been resolved by t‖he People that it praise Poseidip|pos, son of Bakchios, from Kothokide, and cr|own him with a palm leaf wrea|th in order that as many men as possible | may be
25   zealous in furnishing aid t‖oward (the accomplishment of) matters advantageous to the People. | This decree shall be inscribed by th|e secretary for the prytan|y on a stone stele and set | up on the Akropolis,

30   and for the in‖scribing of the stele there shall be paid out by th|e
     exetastes[6] and the trittya|rchs 20 drachmas.

1   Two tribes, Antigonis and Demetrias (numbers 11 and 12 in the secretary cycle)
    were created in 307/6 in honor of Antigonos Monophthalmos and Demetrios
    Poliorketes because of their role in the expulsion of Demetrios of Phaleron. Both
    tribes were abolished in 200 because of the enmity then existing between Athens
    and Philippos V.
2   299/8.
3   Second month of the Athenian calendar, approximately equivalent to August–
    September.
4   A prominent Athenian politician in the 290s. *IG* II[2] 649 contains a biographical
    decree proposed in his honor by the pro-Macedonian orator Stratokles in 293.
5   Ruler of Macedon from 316–297.
6   Between 299/8 and 295/4 the exetastes, 'inspector', and the trittyarchs, the chief
    officials of the trittyes, replaced the treasurer of the People as the officials respon-
    sible for paying for the inscribing and erection of stelae containing public docu-
    ments.

5   Papyrus containing excerpts from an Olympiad chronicle.
Oxyrhynchus, second century AD.

P. Oxy. 2082; **FGrHist* 275a with supplements proposed by G. de Sanctis and W. S.
Ferguson; cf. Pausanias 1.25.5; Polyaenus 3.7, 4.7.5.

Ferguson, *Athens* 130–5; G. de Sanctis, *RFIC* n.s. 6 (1928) 53–77; Ferguson, *CP* 24 (1929)
1–31; G. de Sanctis, *RFIC* n.s. 14 (1936) 134–44, 263–4; M. Fortina, *Cassandro, Re di
Macedonia* (Turin 1965) 115–16.

I

      [---] *Stasis* broke out between the | Athenian generals, the | hoplite
5   general Charias and ‖ *Lachares*,[1] the commander of the mercenaries. |
      Charias seized the Akropolis | [---] after | [the] campaign,[2] but *he did not*
10   *cause the* | *People* to be fed, *and previously,* ‖ during the *war* [he had paid no]
      attention [to the city]. And *Lachares* with *the* | *mercenaries* to [whose com-
      mand] *he had been elected* [---].

II

      [---] having *seized the Museion hill,* | *the garrison* that *Charias* had installed |
5   he,[3] with the aid of the *soldiers* from Piraeus, ‖ expelled. Those who had
      occupied with Charias *the* | *Akropolis* he overcame and | released *under truce.*
      As for *Chari*|*as and* Peithias and Lysander, | *the son of Kalliphon,* and
10   <A>meinias, ‖ who had taken refuge [in the] temple of | *Athena,* (the

People) *convened* an assembly | and *condemned* them all to death [by a single] vote | *on the motion of Apollodoros.* | [The] *soldiers from Piraeus seized,*
15 *however,* || *Munichia*[4] [unbeknownst][5] to those from *city* [---].

III

[---|---] and [by means of a] *palisade* he[6] besieged those in Piraeus.
15 || Also *Kassandros,* [the] king [of the] Macedonians, died, after having taken | sick in Pella, on the *twenty-first* day of the intercalary *month* of |
20 Artemisios,[7] | and the *kingdom* was || taken over by *Philippos, his eldest* | son, *who ruled* | [4] months.[8] [And] Diyllos,[9] *the son of Phanodemos, the Athenian,* [ended his work,| which encompassed a] period [of? years in]
25 the year *Phi*||*lippos,* [the king of the] Macedonians, [---] died.

IV

15 [---][10] and the golden [image] of *Athena,* and from || [these] he paid [the] mercenaries. | 121[11]

The text translated contains the sections dealing with the tyranny of Lachares at Athens from the first two columns of a fragmentary papyrus that is believed to contain excerpts from the Olympiad chronicle of the second-century AD scholar, Phlegon of Tralles.

1   Tyrant of Athens during the first half of the 290s.
2   Presumably dealt with in a lost portion of the chronicle. De Sanctis suggested a campaign against Kassandros, Ferguson military action in Attika aimed at recovering Piraeus and the Long Walls.
3   Lachares.
4   Jacoby: '*Piraeus*'.
5   Hunt: '[those from the city | holding similar] *views*'.
6   Lachares. Forces allied with Demetrios Poliorketes had occupied Piraeus.
7   Late spring 297. Intercalary month refers to the practice of adding one or more months to the calendar, in this case a second Artemisios (the seventh month of the Macedonian calendar), in order to reconcile the discrepancies between lunar and solar years.
8   The restoration is based on Eusebius, *Chronicle* 1.242 (Schoene).
9   Athenian historian, author of a history of Greece from 357/6 to 297/6 (Diodorus 16.14.4, 76.6; cf. *FGrHist* 73 for the surviving fragments).
10 Thirteen lines too fragmentary for any restoration precede the reference to Lachares' looting of the gold from the Athena Parthenos to pay his mercenaries.
11 The heading of the next section of the chronicle which dealt with events of the 121st olympiad (296–292), thus tending to support Pausanias' claim that Lachares became tyrant with the aid of Kassandros.

6   Athens honors Herodoros, a courtier of Demetrios Poliorketes. Athens, April 294. Right half of a marble stele, stoichedon.

IG II² 646; cf. Plutarch, *Demetrios* 33–4.

W. S. Ferguson, *CP* 24 (1929) 1–31; G. de Sanctis, *RFIC* 64 (1936) 134–53, 253–73; S. Dow, *HSCP* 67 (1963) 81–6; M. J. Osborne, *Ancient Society* 5 (1974) 83–97; Will, *Histoire* 1².89, 93; Habicht, *Untersuchungen* 1–8; H. Heinen, *GGA* 233 (1981) 180–1.

Gods. | [In the archonship of] *Nikostratos*,[1] in [Demetrias'] | prytany (which is) the *ninth, Elaphe|bolion's*[2] *ninth* (day), *fif|teenth* of the prytany.
5 [Main] assembly. ‖ The motion was put to the vote by (the chairman) of the *proedroi* [---] | [---] from Acharnai and by his *fellow pro|edroi*. [Resolved] by the People. Gorgos, *son of Phryni*‖[---] introduced the
10 motion. Since *Herodor|os*, [before], while residing with [King] *Antigo‖nos*, was sympathetic to the people | of the *Athenians* and now, being a confidant of | [King] *Demetrios*, (whatever) good he can, | [he does] *publicly* on behalf of the city an|d [privately on behalf of] *each* Athenian who at any
15 time ‖ [asks]; and, moreover, he is said by | [the ambassadors], who were sent concerning *p|eace* [to] King Demetrios, to | [have aided] the
20 People in *arr|anging* both friendship with ‖ [King] *Demetrios* and that the Peopl|e, [having been freed] from the war *as soon* | *as possible and having recovered* the city,[3] | [might continue to have] democracy; with good fortune, it has been *re|solved* [by the People] that it praise Herodoros, *son*
25 *of Ph*‖[---][4] for the good will a|nd [zeal] which he continues to have for | [the people of the] Athenians and that it crow|n [him with a] *gold* wreath
30 in accordance with the *la|w* [and that it proclaim] the wreath ‖ at the competition for tragedies in honor of *Dionysos* [in] *the city.* | [In addition, he shall be an] Athenian together with his *des|cendants*, and he shall be enrolled in whatever *tri|be* [and deme] and phratry[5] he *wish|es*, [and he
35 shall have] also the right of maintenance in the *pryt‖aneion*, [and] (likewise) the eldest of his *descendants* in each generation | [together with a] *front seat* at all *con|tests* [which the city holds]. There shall [also] be set up | [by the People] a bronze statue of him in the Agora | [next to]
40 *Harmodios and Aristogeiton* ‖ *and the Saviors*,[6] and there shall be chosen | [by the People] three men from [all the] *Athenians* | *who* shall supervise [t|he manufacture of the] statue; and there shall be allocated to *th|em by the*
45 *exetastes* and the *trittyar‖chs*[7] [for the] *statue* whatever costs are | [incurred; and the] *prytaneis* shall schedule [the vote] concerning | [him] for the next *assem|bly; and the thesmothetai*[8] shall bring | *the scrutiny* of his citizen-
50 ship ‖ [and of his gift] before the court *in* | *accordance with* [the law as] soon as the juries | [have been impaneled by them]. This *decree* shall be inscribed | [by the] *secretary* for the prytany | [on a] stone [stele] and set

55   up on ‖ [the Akropolis], and [for] the inscribing of the s|*tele* the financial
administrator shall pay.

(in wreath)   (in wreath)

[The Boule]   The People

1   295/4.
2   Ninth month of the Athenian year, i.e. April 294.
3   Following the flight of the tyrant Lachares.
4   On the basis of the letters '*KENON*' remaining from Herodoros' ethnic, an origin
from Lampsakos or Kyzikos is possible.
5   See Glossary.
6   This combination of honors is the highest awarded by Athens.
7   See no. 4 n. 6.
8   See Glossary.

7   Hymn honoring Demetrios Poliorketes as a god. Athens, 291.

*Duris, *FGrHist* 76F13 (= Athenaeus 6.253d–f); cf. Demochares, *FGrHist* 75F2
(= Athenaeus 6.253b–d); Plutarch, *Pyrrhos* 10, *Demetrios* 40–1.

Ferguson, *Athens* 143–4; Tarn, *Gonatas* 49; K. Scott, *AJP* 49 (1928) 229–33; V. Ehrenberg,
Aspects of the Ancient World (Oxford 1946) 179–98; Habicht, *Gottmenschentum* 214–16,
232–3; C. Wehrli, *Antigone et Demetrios* (Geneva 1969) 177–9; Robert B. Kebric, *In the
Shadow of Macedon: Duris of Samos* (Wiésbaden 1977) 23; Will, *Histoire* 1².91–2.

Demochares,[1] therefore, said things of this sort about the servility of
the Athenians. Duris the Samian[2] even <included> the ithyphallic
(hymn)[3] itself in the twenty-second book of his histories:

    The greatest of the gods and (those) dearest/ to the city are present;/
    <for Demeter and> Demetrios here/ the occasion has brought

5   together.// She, the holy mysteries of the Maiden,/ has come to
    perform;/ and he, gracious, as a god ought to be, and handsome/ and
    laughing, is present.[4]/ Something majestic has appeared, all his

10   friends in a circle// and he in their midst,/ his friends just like stars/
    and he the sun./ O son of the most powerful god, Poseidon,/ and of

15   Aphrodite, greeting.[5]// For the other gods either are far away/ or
    they have no ears/ or they are not or they do not heed us, not even

20   one,/ but we see you present,/ not wood, not stone but real;// so we
    pray to you./ First, make peace, dearest one,/ for you are master./

25   Not over Thebes but over all Greece/ does the Sphinx hold sway,//
    the Aitolian[6] who, seated on the rock,/ even as the old (Sphinx) did,/
    having seized all our bodies, carries them away,/ and I cannot fight./

30   For the Aitolian used to plunder the possessions of those nearby,//
    but now also those far away./ You, yourself, take special care, but if

not,/ find some Oidipous/ who will hurl down this Sphinx/ or make it SPEINOS.[7]

The 'warriors of Marathon' would sing this not only publicly but also at home, they who killed a man who performed proskynesis to the king of the Persians,[8] they who slaughtered myriads of barbarians.

1   Athenian anti-Macedonian politician, nephew of Demosthenes (about 350–271) and author of a history of Greece from which Athenaeus quotes a paraphrase of this same hymn.
2   Tyrant of Samos, Peripatetic and author of numerous works including a history of Greece entitled *Makedonika* covering the period 370 to about 281/80.
3   The hymn has been ascribed to Hermokles of Kyzikos on the basis of Athenaeus' statement (15.697a) that he won a contest at Athens by composing paians – a category of hymn appropriate to gods – in honor of Antigonos Monophthalmos and Demetrios.
4   Probably an allusion to the celebration of the Eleusinian Mysteries in Boedromion (the third month of the Athenian year, approximately equivalent to September–October). Demochares dated the episode after Demetrios' return from Leukas and Korkyra in 291 following his marriage to Lanassa.
5   No claim by Demetrios to be son of Poseidon and Aphrodite is attested in the sources, but Poseidon appeared regularly after 301 on his coins in commemoration of his naval victory over Ptolemaios I at Salamis in Cyprus in 306 (E. T. Newell, *The Coinages of Demetrius Poliorcetes* (London 1927) 29–32).
6   The Aitolian League occupied Delphi sometime between 301 and 298. No details are known concerning the war Demetrios fought with the League between 291 and 289.
7   Proposed emendations are: SPILON = 'rock', SPINOS = 'stone', and SPODON = 'ash'.
8   Prostration, the traditional ceremonial recognition of the supremacy of the Persian Great King. The reference is to Timagoras, Athenian ambassador to Artaxerxes II in 367, who was supposedly executed because of his disgraceful behavior while in Persia but actually, according to Xenophon and Plutarch, because of his failure to prevent a Theban diplomatic success in their dealings with Artaxerxes (cf. Xenophon, *Hellenika* 7.1.38; Plutarch, *Pelopidas* 30 and *Artaxerxes* 22; and Valerius Maximus 6.3).

8   The Ionian League honors Hippostratos, strategos in charge of the cities of the Ionian League. Miletos, 289/8. Marble stele.

I. Didyma 1; *SIG^3 368; cf. SIG^2 189 for a second copy of this decree from Smyrna; Diodorus 20.107.4.

C. Friedrich, *Ath. Mitt.* 25 (1900) 100–6 with photograph; Bengtson, *Strategie* 1.215–23; Magie, *RRAM* 2. 65–7; 2.921 n. 12; C. Roebuck, *CP* 50 (1955) 26–40; S. Burstein, *The Ancient World* 3 (1980) 73–9.

I

Resolved by the League of the Ionians.[1] Since Hippostratos, son of
Hippo|demos, a Milesian, being a friend of King Lysi|machos and
having been appointed strategos of the cities of the Ionians,[2] | continues
5   dealing properly and generously both privately with e‖ach of the cities
and publicly with the Ionians; | with good fortune, it has been resolved
by the League of the Io|nians that it praise Hippostratos, son of
Hippodemos, for the excel‖lence and good will which he continues to
have for | the League of the Ionians and that he be exempt from all
10   (taxes) in ‖ (the) cities of the Ionians; and that these same privileges
shall belong to Hippostra|tos himself and to his descendants; and that
it erect also a bronze | statue of him on a horse at Panionion;[3] and that
two cities be chosen | immediately that will take care that the statue |
of Hippostratos be erected as soon as possible in order that also all
15   others ‖ may know that on those fine and go|od men who furnish service
to the cities | the Ionians confer honor with appropriate gifts; and that
| each of the councillors[4] shall report the decisions of the Ionians | to
20   their own cities in order that in the public archives ‖ the decisions of the
Ionians may be entered; | and that it have this decree inscribed on the
base of the st|atue of Hippostratos at Panionion and that ea|ch of the
cities shall have it inscribed in its own (territory) on a stele of sto|ne.[5]
25   Cities that were chosen: Miletcs, Arsinoeia.[6] ‖

II

In (the year in which the stephanephoros) is Telesios (289/8), (month)
Panemos.[7] | With regard to the decree from Panionion which has been
approved, it has been resolved by the | People that it be entered in the
public register; there were chosen | also as supervisors for (the
manufacture of) the statue of Hippostratos, son of | Hippodemos, in
30   accordance with the decree voted by the Io‖nians Archidemos, son of
Aristokrates, Ameinias, son of Krateos. |
In (the year in which stephanephoros) is Telesios, (month)
Lenaion.[8] | Resolved by the Boule. Protomachos, son of Pylios, intro-
duced the motion. In order that | the honors voted to Hippostratos, son
35   of Hippodemos, | by the League of the Ionians be completed as ‖ soon
as possible, it has been resolved by the Boule that the teichopoioi[9] be |
responsible and that they hire out the manufacture of the | stele and the
inscribing of the decisions, | and that the Treasurer, who is treasurer
for the month | of Lenaion, furnish (the funds) from the wall-building
fund.

1 A confederation of the Ionian cities with primarily religious functions founded
   probably in the seventh century. The reference to the 'League of thirteen Ionian
   cities' in the Smyrna copy of this decree (lines 1-2) reflects an increase in its membership from the twelve attested in the fifth century (Herodotus 1.142) because of
   the addition of the re-founded city of Smyrna during the reign of Lysimachos
   (Strabo 14.1.4, C 633; Vitruvius 4.1.4).
2 Since 302/1 Lysimachos had treated the Ionian League as an administrative unit
   governed by a strategos appointed by himself.
3 The sanctuary of Poseidon Helikonios on the Mykale peninsula which
   functioned as the religious and political center of the Ionian League.
4 The delegates of the member cities to the council of the Ionian League.
5 For a copy at Smyrna see n. 1.
6 The new name of Ephesos which was re-founded by Lysimachos in the 290s on a
   new site and named, according to Strabo (14.1.21, C 640), for his wife Arsinoe.
7 The fourth month of the Milesian calendar, corresponding approximately to July.
8 The tenth month of the Milesian calendar, corresponding approximately to
   January.
9 'Wall builders', a regular commission in charge of the maintenance of the city walls
   and responsible for the inscribing of Milesian decrees.

9   Letter of Seleukos I informing Miletos of a dedication by him to Apollo at Didyma. Miletos, 288/7. Marble stele, early third-century lettering.

Haussoulier, *Études* 194–8; *OGIS* 214; *Welles, *RC* 5; *I. Didyma* 424; cf. *I. Didyma* 426,
lines 6–9; Appian, *Syriaka* 56; Pausanias 1.16.3, 8.46.3.

Haussoulier, *Études* 49–51, 211; Welles, *RC* pp. 33–50; Rostovtzeff, *SEHHW* 1.174, 459;
Magie, *RRAM* 1.94, 2.924; Günther, *Orakel* 43–50; S. Burstein, *The Ancient World* 3 (1980)
76–7.

King Seleukos (I)[1] to the Boule of the Milesians | and the People, greet-
ing. We have sent to | the sanctuary of Apollo at Didyma[2] | both the
5   large lampstand and drinking cups ‖ of gold and silver for dedication to
the Savior gods.[3] | They are being brought by Polianthes[4] and are
in|scribed. You, therefore, when he ar|rives, taking them, with good
fortune, | deliver (them) to the sanctuary in order that you may be able
10 to pour libations ‖ and employ them, we being in good health and
enjoying good | fortune and the city remaining safe[5] as I | wish and you
pray. Carry out the instructions | of Polianthes by making the dedi-
15 cation | of the items we have sent and performing the sacrifice ‖ which
we have enjoined on him. Take care, | therefore, that it be done
properly. Of the | gold and silver items sent | to the sanctuary I have
appended below for you a list | in order that you may know both the
20 types and weight ‖ of each. Farewell.[6]

1 The letter is preceded by a prescript dating the gift to the year in which the
   stephanephoros at Miletos was Poseidippos (288/7). The first thirteen lines of the
   inscription are known only from copies made by Cyriacus of Ancona in the fifteenth
   and Sherard in the eighteenth centuries AD.
2 According to Appian, Apollo of Didyma predicted Seleukos' kingship. Pausanias
   reports that Seleukos I also returned to Didyma from Ekbatana the statue of
   Apollo looted by the Persians in 494.
3 Identity unknown.
4 Seleukos' emissary.
5 Welles suggested that this unusual phraseology is equivalent to the common 'on
   behalf of our health and good fortune and the safety of the city'.
6 A detailed list of the objects included in the dedication follows (lines 21–52),
   concluding with a notice (lines 52–3) that Polianthes brought sacrificial animals for
   the god.

**10   Priene establishes a cult in honor of King Lysimachos. Priene,
about 286/5.** Several blocks from the antae of the temple of Athena.

I. Priene 14 with photograph; *OGIS 11; cf. Welles, *RC* 6.

Welles, *RC* pp. 40–5; Bengtson, *Strategie* 1.220–33; Rostovtzeff, *SEHHW* 1.178–9; Magie,
RRAM 1.91–2; Habicht, *Gottmenschentum* 38–9.

For King [Lysimachos].¹ | Resolved by the People; decision [of the
strategoi. Since] *Ki|ng* Lysimachos in [previous times always]² | *continued*
5 *exercising care* [for the people] *of the Prie||neans* and since now, by sending
an army by land [against the Magne|sians]³ and the other Pedieis,⁴ [he
saved | the] city, it has been resolved by the People that there shall be
chosen as *ambassadors* | [from] *all* the citizens ten men,⁵ who, *on* | *meeting*
10 with him, shall give him the decree and con||gratulate the king that he
is well and that his army⁶ | and his other affairs are faring as he wishes,
and they shall make known | *the good will* which the People continues to
have for King | *Lysimachos* and they shall crown him with a [gold]
wreath | [made] from a thousand gold (staters). [The] People shall also
15 erect || a bronze statue [of the king in the agora, and] they shall set up |
beside *it* [on the right ---] | near [---] *there shall also be establish|ed* an altar
for [him. And also sacrifices shall be made each] | year by [all] the
20 [priests and priestesses throughout] || the city and *all the* citizens shall
wear wreaths, | and both the priests and the board of magistrates shall
conduct a procession | with *all* the citizens [on the birthday of King] |
Lysimachos, [and] *there shall* [also] *be present* [---] | and the *financial*
25 *administrator shall give* [for the offerings to the] || sacrificers of the *tribes* [as
much money as is also given for the] Pana|thenaia [--- | ---] *of all* the
30 citizens | [---] sacrifices yearly | [---] shall perform the sacrifice || [---] in

the countryside each | [---] *altar shall be established* and sacrificed for *Ki|ng* ---.[7]

1   This decree was one of a number of important documents inscribed on the antae of the temple of Athena Polias. Lysimachos' reply accepting these honors is contained in Welles, *RC* 6.
2   The reference to previous concern for Priene's welfare, however formal, excludes Dittenberger's suggested date of 302/1 for this text. More probable is Welles' connection of the events alluded to in the decree with Demetrios Poliorketes' invasion of Asia in 286.
3   Restored on the basis of Welles, *RC* 6, line 14. The reference is to the city of Magnesia on the Maeander.
4   'Plainsmen', apparently the native population of the Maeander valley, some of whom are known to have formed a class of subject agricultural laborers at Priene. In connection with these events, Welles, *RC* 6,line 15 mentions soldiers, presumably those of Demetrios, instead of Pedieis.
5   Particularly interesting from the point of view of diplomatic procedure is the reference in Welles, *RC* 6, lines 19–20 to Lysimachos granting something requested orally by the ambassadors at the time they presented him with this decree.
6   In Welles, *RC* 6, lines 6–7, Lysimachos describes his government as consisting of himself, his friends and his army.
7   Lines 33 to 37 are too fragmentary for translation.

11   Athens honors Philippides, son of Philokles, from Kephale, a friend of King Lysimachos. Athens, 283/2. Marble stele with gable; third-century lettering, stoichedon.

IG II[2] 657; *SIG[3] 374. For photograph see J. Kirchner, *Imagines Inscriptionum Atticarum* (Berlin 1948) no. 78. Cf. Plutarch, *Demetrios* 12; Ps.-Plutarch, *Moralia* 851E.

Ferguson, *Athens* 136–54; T. Leslie Shear, Jr, *Hesperia* Supp. 17 (1978) 27–8, 40–4, 49, 79–89; Habicht, *Untersuchungen* 77–81; S. Burstein, *ZPE* 31 (1978) 181–5; *CSCA* 12 (1980) 39–50.

In the archonship of Euthios, in the *third prytany* (which is that) *of Akamantis,* | in which Nausimenes, son of Nausikydes, from *Cholargo|s* was secretary; on the eighteenth day of Boedromion,[1] n|ineteenth day
5   of the prytany; main assembl‖y; the motion was put to the vote by (the chairman) of the proedroi, Hieromnemon, son of Teisimach|os, from Koile, and by his fellow proedroi; resolved by the Boule a|nd by the People; Nikeratos, son of Phileos, from Kephale, introduced the motion. | Philippides[2] has continued on every occasion | to demonstrate
10   his good will toward the People and, ‖ having gone[3] to King Lysimachos | and having previously spoken with the king, he obtained for the People a gi|ft of ten thousand Attic medimnoi of wheat which was dis|tributed to all Athenians in the archonship of Euktemon

13

15 (299/8). | He also spoke about the yardarm and mast, in order that ‖ he
    (Lysimachos) might give them to the goddess for the Panathenaia for
    the peplos,[4] which (items) were bro|ught in the archonship of
    Euktemon. After the victory of King Ly|simachos in the battle that took
    place at Ipsos | against Antigonos and Demetrios, those of the citizens
20 kil|led in the *battle* he buried at his ‖ own expense; [those] who were
    prisoners | he pointed out to the *king* [and] obtained release for them;
    t|hose *wishing to serve* in the army he arranged to | have enrolled [in]
    units and those choos|ing to depart he clothed and provided with travel
25 money fro‖m his own resources and sent whither each wished, to the
    number of more | than three hundred; and he also interceded for the |
    release of all citizens who had been seized in | Asia after being
    imprisoned by Demetrios and Antigono|s. And to any Athenian meet-
30 ing him ‖ he continues to be of assistance just as each urges him; | and,
    the People having recovered its freedom,[5] he has cont|inued to say and
    do what is advantageous to the | security of the city and to urge the king
    to assi|st it with both money and grain in order that the People may
35 remain ‖ free and recover Pirae|us[6] and the | forts[7] as soon as possible,
    and to all these things | the king has often borne witness on his behalf
    to en|voys of the Athenians on mission to him.[8] Having been elected
40 agonothetes in the archonship of Isaios (284/3), he hearkened ‖ to the
    People and willingly at his own expense performed the ancestr|al
    sacrifices to the gods on behalf of the People and th|e [---][9] he gave to all
    Athenians <for> all the | [contests, and] an *additional* contest he
    arranged for *Dem|eter* [and the] *Maiden* for the first time[10] as a memorial
45 of the People's ‖ [freedom]. *He managed* also the other contests and |
    [sacrifices for the] *city*, and for all these things, | [after expending from
    his own resources much] *money*, he has presented his accounts | accord-
    ing to the laws, *and nothing* against the d|emocracy [has he] ever done
50 either [in word or] ‖ deed.[11] (Since these things are so), in order, there-
    fore, that it shall be clear [to all that the People] | knows how to return
    favors *to* [its benefactors] *wor|thy* of their benefactions, with good
    [fortune, it has been resolved by the] | Boule that the proedroi, who
    shall be chosen by lot to presi|de over the People, when [the (number of) days
55 required by the law] ‖ (to pass after the submission) of the motion shall
    have elapsed,[12] shall bring up *these matters at the* | first assembly in
    accordance with the law, and *they shall refer the opinion* | of the Boule to
    the People that it resolves | that it praise Philippides, son of Philokles,
    from Kephale, | because of his excellence and the good will he con-
60 tinues to have for ‖ the Athenian people and that it crown him with a
    g|old wreath according to the law, and that it proclaim the w|reath at
    the contest for tragedies at the greater Dionysia, | and that it also set up
    a bronze statue of him in the theat|re and that it grant public main-

65 tenance in the prytaneion to him and of his de‖scendants in each gener-
ation to the eldest, together with a front seat at all | the contests which
the city holds; and that the manufacture of t|he wreath and the procla-
mation of it shall be the concern of the financial admin|istrators; and
that this decree shall be inscribed by the secretary for the prytany on a
stone stele | and set up next to the temple of Dionysos, and that for
70 ‖the inscribing of the stele there shall be allocated by the financial |
administrators 20 drachmas [from] the monies to be spent for decrees|
by the People.

(in wreath)
The People

1 Third month of the Athenian calendar, approximately equivalent to September–
October.
2 A comic poet and friend of Lysimachos. The testimonia for his life and the fragments of his plays are collected in *The Fragments of Attic Comedy* 3A, ed. J. M.
Edmonds (Leiden 1961) 165–81.
3 Probably a euphemism for exile.
4 They were to be used as supports for the peplos (an embroidered over-life-size
dress for Athena woven by a select group of young Athenian aristocratic
maidens) which served as the sail for the Panathenaic ship during the procession
at the Panathenaic festival. The previous set had been accidentally destroyed in
302/1.
5 In 287 when Demetrios' garrison was expelled from the Museion hill.
6 The Piraeus had been occupied in 294 and remained in Macedonian hands until
229.
7 Probably the border fortresses of Rhamnous, Phyle, Panakton and Eleusis
together with Salamis, all of which had been occupied by Macedonian garrisons in
294 and retained by them after the liberation of the city.
8 The reference is probably to the two embassies led by Demochares after his return
from exile in 286/5 that resulted in gifts totaling 130 talents of silver for Athens.
9 Dittenberger restored: '*the two obol payment*'. Shear suggested a reference to the
wine and sweetmeats given to the spectators at Dionysiac festivals.
10 The reference to an additional contest for Demeter and Kore ('the Maiden')
indicates that Demochares had already recovered Eleusis for Athens.
11 The allusion is to the Macedonian dominated government that ruled Athens for
Demetrios Poliorketes from 294 to 287 and during which Philippides was probably
in exile.
12 Five days had to elapse between a motion being placed on the agenda and its
submission to the assembly.

**12   Letter of King Lysimachos to the Samians concerning a bound-
ary dispute with Priene. Samos, 283/2.** Marble stele crowned with a
gable.

OGIS 13; *Welles, *RC* 7; cf. *I. Priene* 37 and *SIG*^{3} 688.

M. N. Tod, *International Arbitration among the Greeks* (Oxford 1913) 41–3, 135–40; Welles, *RC* 46–51; Magie, *RRAM* 1.78; C. Roebuck, *CP* 50 (1955) 60–1; S. Burstein, *The Ancient World* 3 (1980) 76.

King Lysimachos to the Boule and the people of the Samians, greeting. | There appeared before us both the ambassadors from you and the *Prie|neans*, | (ambassadors) who were sent concerning the land about which they happened to *have contested* | before us previously.[1] If, there-
5   fore, we had known ‖ that you had possessed and occupied this land for so many years, | we would not have taken on the case at all, but, as it was, we thought | that your *entry* had been very recent, | for so we had been informed in their previous *speeches* by the | Prienean ambassadors.
10 But, indeed, when both your (ambassadors) were present ‖ and those of the Prieneans, it was necessary to hear through the statements *of e|ach*. The Prieneans, therefore, attempted to demonstrate *their* original | [possession] of the territory (known as) the Batinetis[2] both from his- tories [and] | *other* proofs and documents including the Six Years *Truce*.[3] | But they conceded that *later*, when Lygdamis[4] invaded *Ionia*
15 ‖ [with] his *army*, the rest left the territory and the *Sami|ans* withdrew [to the] *island. Lygdamis*, having occupied it for [three (?) | years],[5] returned these same possessions [to them], and the *Prie|neans* [took possession] and no Samian was present *at all* | then [unless one]
20 happened to have settled among them, and he ‖ contributed [his har- vest] to the Prieneans;[6] *but* later | the Samians, [returning with] *force*, seized the territory; | Bias,[7] therefore, [was sent] by the Prieneans to effect a reconciliation with the *Samians* [with | full authority, and he] reconciled the cities, and the *settlers* [with|drew] from the territory
25 (known as) [the] Batinetis. Previously, then, they [said] that ‖ [their affairs] remained in this situation, and that until the most recent *ti|me* [they controlled the territory]; and now they asked that we, in accord- ance with their original [possess|ion, return to them] the territory; but the [ambassadors] sent | by you [said] that [possession of the terri- tory] (known as) the Batinetis | had been received by you [from your
30 ancestors]; but after the [invasion] of Lygdamis ‖ *they conceded* that, just as the others, they also [left | the territory and withdrew to] the island, but later [--- | --- | ---] a thousand *Samians settled* [---].

1 This letter deals with an early phase of a long series of boundary disputes between Samos and Priene that was finally settled in 135 when the Roman senate confirmed (*SIG*[3] 688) the results of the arbitration decision rendered the parties by the Rhodians at the beginning of the second century and of which a large portion is preserved in *I. Priene* 37.
2 The southern portion of the plain of Anaia, just north of the Mykale peninsula.
3 This is probably to be dated to the mid sixth century and followed a battle in which

the Prieneans are said to have killed one thousand Samians (Plutarch, *Moralia* 296A).
4   King of the Kimmerians. He captured Sardis, the capital of Lydia, and killed Gyges about 652 (Strabo 1.3.21, C 61).
5   Welles notes that seven or ten years are possible restorations.
6   The interpretation of this is not clear. Dittenberger thought a tax was intended, Welles some sort of restriction on the sale of their crops.
7   One of the so-called Seven Wise Men (Diogenes Laertius 1.82–8) and, according to Plutarch (*Moralia* 296A), responsible for reconciling Samos and Priene by negotiating the Six Years Truce.

13   Athens honors the archon Euthios. Athens, February 281.
Marble stele crowned with gable, third-century lettering, stoichedon.

B. D. Meritt, *Hesperia* 7 (1938) 100–9 with photograph; **ISE* 14.

Habicht, *Untersuchungen* 95–107; P. Gauthier, *REG* 92 (1979) 348–99.

Gods. | In the archonship of Nikias,[1] in the prytany of Oineis, | (which is) the seventh, in which Theophilos, son of Theod|otos, from
5   Acharnai, was secretary. Gamelion's[2] || ninth day, twenty-third day | of the prytany; (regular) assembly; | the motion was put to the vote by (the chairman) of the proedroi Oinokrates, son of Oinobi|os, from Eleusis, and by his fellow proedroi. *vv* Resol|ved by the People;[3] Agyrrhios, son
10   of Kallimedon, || from Kollytos, introduced the motion. Since Euthios, while archon (283/2), | performed the sacrifices to the | gods in accordance with the ancestral customs and managed the procession in honor of | Dionysos with zeal and | carried out all the other (responsibilities)
15   connected with his office j||ustly, obeying both the laws and | the decrees of the Boule and the Peo|ple, and for these reasons also previously the | People praised him and crowned him in t|he assembly (that met in
20   the theatre) of Dionysos[4] in order that || it might be clear to all that the People both now | and in the future shall honor those | who perform their offices justly and in accordance with | the laws; with good fortune, it has been resolved by the | People that it praise Euthios, son of
25   Antiphon, || from Teithrasios, for his zeal and the good | will which he continues to have for the People a|nd that it crown him with a gold wreath | in accordance with {these} the law; and that it shall also be
30   possible for him | to obtain another reward from the People of || which he seems to be worthy when the Piraeu|s and the city shall be together;[5] and that it praise | also his assessors, Mei|dogenes, son of Meidon, from Athmonon, Sokrates, | son of Sodamos, from Paiania, for their
35   justice a||nd zeal and that it crown each | of them with a gold wreath in accordance with the law. | This decree is to be inscribed by the | sec-

retary for the prytany on a stele | of stone and placed in front of the
40   syne‖drion.[6] For the inscribing of the stele | the financial administrators
are to allocate 10 | drachmas. (in wreath) The People; (in wreath) The
People of the Salaminians;[7] (in wreath) The Tribesmen.

1   Nikias II, archon in 282/1.
2   Seventh month of the Attic calendar, approximately equivalent to January–
    February.
3   The phraseology indicates that the motion originated in the assembly and not in the
    Boule.
4   By law the assembly met in the theatre of Dionysos immediately after the city
    Dionysia in Elaphebolion/March–April.
5   The wording indicates that the Piraeus was still in Macedonian hands at the time of
    the passage of the decree, but that the Athenians had hopes, hopes that would be
    frustrated, of recovering it in the near future.
6   Location unknown, possibly the meeting place of the nine archons at the
    Thesmotheteion; cf. R. E. Wycherley, *JHS* 75 (1955) 118–211.
7   The inclusion of the wreath for the People of the Salaminians indicates that the
    Macedonian garrison had withdrawn from Salamis and that the Athenian kleruchs
    on the island were again united with the rest of the Athenians.

14   A letter of Epicurus concerning the ransoming of Mithres, dioiketes of Lysimachos. About 282–277. Papyrus from Herculaneum.

*C. Diano, *Lettere di Epicuro e dei suoi* (Florence 1946) no. 14; cf. Plutarch, *Moralia*
1097A, 1126E; Diogenes Laertius 2.10, 10.4, 10.28.

A. Vogliano & G. Beloch, *RFIC* 54 (1926) 310–35; G. de Sanctis, *RFIC* 55 (1927)
491–5; Habicht, *Untersuchungen* 99 n. 28; P. Gauthier, *REG* 92 (1979) 374–8.

[---] Epicurus to [He]r[o]dotos;[1] pre|viously, *he says*,[2] a servant of the
5   strategoi was sent bearing ‖ letters | from Olympiodoros[3] | and m<e
and> not having *been in tim*(e to find) ei|ther of you with
10   Antipater,[4] | he said that he gave the letter to Ant[ip]a‖ter as he was
present. Know | that originally he[5] | was held in Corinth *by*
Krat|eros,[6] and is now being held under guard in Piraeus | by one
15   Lysias,[7] who, with regard to his *release*, ‖ has *refused* the ten talents |
[on the ground that] twenty talents had been agreed |[upon] with
Krateros.

1   An Epicurean, the recipient of Epicurus' first letter (Diogenes Laertius 10.29), who
    later defected and wrote a book critical of Epicurus.
2   Epicurus. The editorial comment is by Philodemos of Gadara (about 110–about
    40/45) in whose book entitled *Pragmateia* this letter is preserved.
3   Athenian politician and general, archon in 294/3 and 293/2, who was responsible

for the expulsion of the Macedonian garrison from the Museion hill in 287 (Pausanias 1.26.1–3).

4 Identification uncertain. Suggested alternatives are either Antipater Etesias, nephew of Kassandros and briefly king of Macedon in 279, or the Macedonian garrison commander in the Piraeus.

5 Mithres, Lysimachos' dioiketes, that is, finance minister (see Glossary), and Epicurus' friend and patron. The *terminus ante quem* for the events of this letter is 277/6, the date of the death of Epicurus' disciple Metrodoros of Lampsakos who was involved in arranging Mithres' ransom.

6 Half-brother of Antigonos Gonatas and his representative in Corinth. He may also be the editor of a collection of Athenian inscriptions (for the fragments see *FGrHist* 342).

7 An otherwise unknown Macedonian officer.

Chapter 2
THE SELEUCID KINGDOM

15 A decree of Ilion honoring Antiochos I. Sigeum, about 280–278. Marble stele, early third-century lettering.

OGIS 219; *I. Ilion* 32; cf. Memnon, *FGrHist* 434F9.1; Justin 25.1.1.

Bevan, *Seleucus* 1.127–35; Tarn, *Gonatas* 168; Magie, *RRAM* 1.95 and 2.925–6; L. Robert, *Essays in Honor of C. B. Welles* (New Haven 1966) 175–92 with photograph; Habicht, *Gottmenschentum* 83–5; Orth, *Machtanspruch* 43–51; 61–72; Will, *Histoire* 1².140; Mastrocinque, *Caria* 72–3; F. Piejko, *Gnomon* 52 (1980) 258.

Nymphis, son of Diotrephes, being epimenios,[1] and the epistates[2] being Dionysios, son of | Hippomedon, Demetrios, son of Dies, introduced the motion. Since King Antiochos (I), son of King | Seleukos (I), at the beginning (of his reign), after having taken over the kingdom and manifested an hon|orable and good policy, sought to bring the cities in

5 Se||leukis,[3] which were hard pressed by harsh circumstances because of those who had rebelled against | his regime, back to peace and their old prosperity, | and, having advanced against those attacking his regime,[4] as was just, (he sought) to re|gain his ancestral realm; wherefore, acting with a good and just purpose | and taking not only his friends and his

10 army, who were zealous for the struggle for || his regime, but also the divinity as a benevolent hel|per, he restored the cities to peace and his kingdom to its old condition; | and now, having arrived in the districts on this side of the Tauros (mountains) | with all haste and zeal, at the same time he has arranged peace[5] for the cities, | and he has raised up his regime and kingdom to a better and more flourishing condition,

15 || particularly through his own excellence, then also through his friends' and his | army's good will; in order, therefore, that the People, since it previously, when | he took over the kingdom, continued to offer prayers and sacrifices on his behalf to all the gods, | may now also appear to the king as being well intentioned and having the same policy, | it has been

20 resolved by the *Boule* and the || People that the priestess and the Hieronomoi[6] and the Prytaneis shall pray | to Athena Ilias together with the | ambassadors that his visit shall be <for the good>[7] of the king and of his sister,[8] and of his friends | and of his army, and that all other good things shall belong to the king and queen, | and that the regime and kingdom shall remain in their possession, having

25 || increased just as they desire; and prayer shall also be offered by the other priests and | priestesses together with the priest of King

Antiochos to Apollo, the *founder*[9] | of his family and to Victory and to Zeus and to all the other gods and goddesses.[10]

1   Probably the priest in charge of monthly sacrifices.
2   Possibly the chairman of the assembly as at Athens.
3   The area of Syria that includes the four cities of Antioch, Seleukeia, Apameia and Laodikeia (Strabo 16.2.4,C 749).
4   The 'enemies' cannot be identified, but they probably included Ptolemaios II who occupied portions of Karia and Ionia shortly after the death of Seleukos I in 281.
5   If not a general allusion to current conditions, this may be a reference to the peace concluded between Antiochos I and Antigonos Gonatas in 278.
6   'Temple wardens', magistrates in charge of temple treasures.
7   This supplement was proposed by A. Boeckh.
8   If, as is generally assumed, 'sister' is to be understood as an honorary appellation, then the reference is to Stratonike, daughter of Demetrios Poliorketes, whom Antiochos I married about 294/3 after her divorce from his father Seleukos I (cf. Plutarch, *Demetrios* 32, and Appian, *Syriaka* 59). It should be noted, however, that F. Piejko has dated this inscription to the reign of Antiochos III on the ground that no queen is known to have borne the title 'sister' before Laodike III.
9   Justin 15.4.2–4; Appian, *Syriaka* 56; Welles, *RC* 22, lines 2–6; cf. R. Hadley, *Historia* 18 (1969) 150–1.
10 Omitted are lines 27 to 48 which authorize: (1) the performance of sacrifices on behalf of Antiochos and the People by all the residents – citizen and alien – of Ilion, (2) the erection of a gold equestrian statue of Antiochos, (3) the proclamation of the honours awarded the king during the Panathenaia, (4) the appointment of three ambassadors to convey the decree to Antiochos and to congratulate him on his present well-being.

16   The crossing of the Galatians to Asia. 278.

*Memnon, *FGrHist* 434 F 11.1–7. Cf. Livy 38.16; Strabo 12.5.1, C 567; Pausanias 1.4.5; Justin 25.2.8–11.

Bevan, *Seleucus* 1.135–44; Tarn, *Gonatas* 164–5; Magie, *RRAM* 1.311; G. Vitucci, *Il Regno di Bitinia* (Rome 1953) 25–7; P. Moraux, *Istanbuler Mitteilungen* 7 (1957) 56–75; Schmitt, *Staatsverträge* 3.111–12; Will, *Histoire* 1².142–4; H. Heinen, *CAH²* 422–5.

(11.1) When the Galatians came to (the territory) of Byzantion and ravaged most of it, the Byzantines, having been brought low by the war, sent to their allies to ask for aid. All furnished as their strength allowed, and the Herakleotes[1] provided – for so much did the embassy request – four thousand gold (staters). (2) But not long afterwards Nikomedes (I),[2] although the Galatians who had raided Byzantion and had often tried to cross to Asia but just as often had failed because the Byzantines had not permitted the crossing, nevertheless arranged to bring them across on terms. The terms were: the barbarians would always maintain a friendly attitude toward Nikomedes and his descendants, and with-

out the approval of Nikomedes they would ally with none of those who
sent embassies to them, but they would be friends with his friends and
enemies to those who were not his friends; and also they would ally
with the Byzantines, if by chance there were need, and with the Tians
and the Herakleotes and the Kalchedonians and the citizens of Kieros
and with some other rulers of peoples.[3] (3) On these terms Nikomedes
brought the Galatian horde across to Asia. Of these there were seventeen prominent leaders and of those the most eminent and chief were
Leonnorios and Loutourios. (4) At first the crossing of the Galatians to
Asia was believed to have led to evil for the inhabitants, but the result
proved it to have been to their advantage. For, the kings[4] being eager to
deprive the cities of democracy,[5] they (i.e. the Galatians) especially
secured it by opposing those attacking it. (5) But Nikomedes, with the
Herakleotes as his allies, first armed the barbarians against the
Bithynians[6] and gained control of the country and slaughtered the
inhabitants while the Galatians divided among themselves the rest of
the booty. (6) Then, after over-running much territory, they withdrew
again, and from that seized by them, they separated what is now called
Galatia and divided it into three portions, one for those called Trogmoi,
one for the Tolostobogioi and one for the Tektosages. (7) They also
built cities, the Trogmoi Ankyra, the Tolostobogioi Tabai and the
Tektosages Pisinos.

1   Herakleia Pontika.
2   Nikomedes I of Bithynia (about 300–about 250).
3   Together with Nikomedes I of Bithynia and Mithridates I of Pontos (302/1–266/5)
    these cities made up the Northern League, which was formed in the early 270s to
    ward off Seleucid domination (cf. Tarn, *CAH*[1] 98, and Will, *Histoire* 1[2].139).
4   The Seleucids.
5   In the Hellenistic period democracy means little more than constitutional govern-
    ment.
6   The subjects of Nikomedes' brother Zipoetes who ruled the area called Thynias in
    northern Bithynia.

**17   Priene honors Sotas, son of Lykos, for valor against the Gala-
tians. Priene, about 278–270.** Marble stele, early third-century
lettering.

OGIS 765; **I. Priene* 17 with facsimile.

Magie, *RRAM* 2.730 n. 11; Orth, *Machtanspruch* 102.

[In the year in which the] stephanephoros was Pos[e]id[on]i[o]s,[1]
month [Artem]ision,[2] [it was resol|ved by the Boule] and the People.

[Sotas in] both *former* | [times] the [--- | applied] himself to [what was
5 advantageous] to the People; and now [when ‖ first the G]alatians
[arrived in the] countryside and *many* | [of those] in the countryside
[who were politically hostile] to the citizens[3] [--- | ---] lawlessly wishing
to attack [--- | ---] savagery no one resisted [--- | ---] and not only in the
10 countryside did they commit [outrages] against *their prisoners* [--- ‖ but
they also] committed sacrilege against the divinity by *ravaging* the
sacred precincts and [the | altars] and temples [---] | omitting no *dis-*
graceful act toward the divinity. [And] during their withdrawal, [---] |
they set fire to [all] the farm buildings [--- whence] *it happened* that many
15 | of *the Greeks* inhabiting Asia were killed, [since they were ‖ unable] to
resist the barbarians. But the people | [of the Priene]ans and he drew
up in opposition and warded | off the barbarians who were committing
sacrilege against the divinity and outrages against the Greeks | by
dispatching paid citizen infantry and *oth|er cavalry*[4] and *advancing* (?) in
20 full force. Sotas, moreover, having recr‖uited the [best] of the citizens
and from the country people those | [who were eager] to [join in the
fight] with the citizens against the barbarians, | and having decided to
save the *citizens* in the countryside, them|selves and their children and
wives and [property in] the countryside, in order to bri|ng them safely
25 into the city, occupied in the countryside the [most ‖ strategic] places
[--- | ---] with his comrades in danger, and many of the *citi|zens* [---]
being led away captive [by] *the Galatians* [and] some | [---] he saved, |
30 [having dared (to face)] their savagery. Having decided (?) [--- ‖ ---] for
the citizens, keeping together those who with him were risk|ing their
lives [for the sake of] the common salvation of the [People], he
remained in the countryside | [fighting against] the barbarians [--- | ---]
with himself many of the citizens, and in general [---] | against the
barbarians and coming to the rescue of the countryside. In addition, he
35 continually [acted so][5] ‖ that [the city] in no way suffered evil and that
many of the citizens [sur|vived] and that they and their children and
their wives and their land | *and possessions* were saved and brought into
the city. After these events took place, the Pe|ople applied itself boldly
to the Galatian war.[6] (Since these things are so), with good fortune, | it
has been resolved by the Boule and the People that Sotas, son of Lykos,
40 be praised ‖ for the [excellence] and bravery he displayed on behalf of
the People by nobly *fi|ghting* against the Galatians, and that he be
crowned with a wreath | of palm leaves in the theatre during the tragic
contest at the next Dionysi|a. In addition, the agonothetes shall *provide*
for [the proclamation]. In order, therefore, that [the] | attitude [of our]
45 People toward [good and noble m‖en who desire] eagerly and
unhesitatingly to aid [---] | may be [clear to all] and that the wreath
awarded to Sotas may be conspicuous, | [this decree] shall be inscribed

on a stone stele and set up in the san|ctuary of [A]then[a]. *vv* As for the expenditure for the stele and the [i|nscription of this] decree, it shall be
50   provided from the sacred mo‖nies by the neopoios,[7] Pammenes.

1   Date unknown. The lettering and content suggest a date shortly after the arrival of the Galatians in Anatolia in 270.
2   Probably the first month of the Prienean calendar, approximately equivalent to March.
3   The reference is probably to the Pedieis (cf. no. 10) and suggests that in some areas the Galatian raids were exploited by local subject populations.
4   Literally 'horsebreeders'.
5   The context seems to require a restoration with this sense.
6   Priene's initiative in conducting her own defense without aid from any king should be noted.
7   Originally, as his title, 'temple builder', suggests, he was an official responsible for construction in a sanctuary, but in the Hellenistic period the neopoios was in charge of general temple administration. Cf. no. 1 n. 3.

18   Biography of the epic poet Simonides of Magnesia. About 281–262 or 223–187.

FGrHist 163 T1 = *Suda s.v.* 'Simonides'; cf. Lucian, *Zeuxis* 8–11.

W. W. Tarn, *JHS* 46 (1926) 157; B. Bar-Kochva, *Proceedings of the Cambridge Philological Society* 199 (1973) 1–8; M. Wörrle, *Chiron* 5 (1975) 65–72; Will, *Histoire* 1².143–4.

Simonides: Magnesian <from> Sipylos; an epic poet; he flourished in the time of Antiochos surnamed the Great,[1] and he wrote the deeds of Antiochos (the Great)[2] and the battle against the Galatians, when he destroyed their cavalry with elephants.[3]

1   Probably Antiochos III, although Bar-Kochva notes that both Antiochos I and Antiochos II are called 'the Great King' in a Babylonian chronicle.
2   Probably to be deleted as a duplication of the earlier mention of the title.
3   Exact date unknown, but suggested dates range from 276 to 268.

19   A decree of the villages of Neoteichos and Kiddios. January 267. Marble stele, third-century lettering, from Denizli (near Izmir), Turkey.

*M. Wörrle, *Chiron* 5 (1975) 59–87.
J. and L. Robert, *REG* 80 (1967) 667; D. Musti, *CAH*² 195–6.

In the reign of the Kings, Antiochos and Se|leukos,[1] forty-fifth | year,

month Peritios,[2] | when Helenos was overseer of the topos,[3] an
5 assembly ‖ having been held, it was resolved by the inhabitants of
Neoteichos | and of the village of Kiddios.[4] Since Bana|belos,[5] the
steward of Achaios[6] and La|chares, son of Papos, the accountant of the
10 estate[7] | of Achaios, have been their benefactors ‖ always, and publicly
and privately | they aided each individual during the | Galatian War;[8]
and since, when ma|ny had been taken prisoner | by the Galatians, by
15 revealing it ‖ to Achaios, they brought about their *ransom*, | they shall
praise them and inscribe | their benefaction on a | stone stele and set it
20 up in the | sanctuary of Zeus in the village of Baba and ‖ in that of
Apollo in the village of Kiddios. | They shall also grant to them and
their descendants | for all time a front seat | at the public festivals | and
25 they shall sacrifice to Achaios, the master of the to‖pos and their savior,
yearly | in the sanctuary of Zeus a bull | and to Lachares and Banabelos,
their benefactors, | two rams in the sanctuary of Apollo | in the village
30 of Kiddios, three sacrificial victims (in all),[9] ‖ in order that others also
may know that the inhabitants of Neot[ei]|chos and of the village of
Kiddios, | with regard to those from whom | they have received some
benefit, under|stand how to award honors in return.

1 The eldest son and co-regent of Antiochos I until his execution for plotting against
   his father (Trogus, *Prologue* 26; John of Antioch, *Fragmenta Historicum Graecorum*, ed.
   C. Mueller (Paris 1851) 4.558F55) either later in 267 or in 266 when Babylonian
   documents record as co-regent his younger brother, the future Antiochos II.
2 Fourth month of the Seleucid calendar, equivalent to January.
3 The first reference to the existence of this post in the Seleucid kingdom. The extent
   of the topos (place) under Helenos' supervision is unclear, but it clearly included
   the villages mentioned in this inscription.
4 From its name Kiddios was clearly a non-Greek settlement while Neoteichos, by the
   same criterion, may have been inhabited by Greek immigrants. Particularly note-
   worthy, however, is the completely Greek character of the political and religious
   forms mentioned in this inscription.
5 A Hellenized form of a West Semitic name meaning 'Bel has created'.
6 The father of Antiochis, the mother of Attalos I of Pergamon (Strabo 13.4.2, C 624)
   and Laodike, wife of Antiochos II (Eusebius, *Chronicle* 251 (Schoene)), and possibly
   the grandfather of Achaios, the son of Andromachos, who was successively the
   representative and co-regent of Antiochos III in Anatolia and a rebel against him.
7 This implies that estates with full ownership, and not precarious tenure as in
   Ptolemaic Egypt, existed in the Seleucid kingdom.
8 It is not clear if the reference is to the war that ended with the so-called 'elephant
   victory' or to a new Galatian invasion in the early 260s which would suggest that the
   'elephant victory' was not as decisive as has generally been believed.
9 The villages established a benefactor cult on the model of civic cults in Greek cities.

20   Decree of Ilion honoring Metrodoros, physician to Antiochos I. Ilion, 281–266. Marble stele.

OGIS 220; *I. Ilion* 34.

K. M. T. Atkinson, *Antichthon* 2 (1968) 32–57; Orth, *Machtanspruch* 52–4, 73–4.

Since King Antiochos (I)[1] has | written that when, having suffered a wound | in the neck during the battle,[2] | he was treated by Metrodoros,
5   the ‖ physician, and is out of danger,[3] [and] (since) a letter has been sent | concerning Metrodoros also by Meleagros, the stra|tegos[4] with a view toward the ci|ty's advantage, it has been resolved by the Boule |
10   and the People that they shall praise ‖ Metrodoros, son of Timokles, a citizen of Amphi|polis, for his excellence and | good will toward the Kings, | Antiochos (I) and Seleukos,[5] and (toward) the | People, and
15   that he shall be both proxe‖nos and benefactor of the city, | and that there shall be granted to him also citizenship | and the right to own (property) and the right of access to the | Boule and the People immediately | after the sacred business and that he shall also be allowed
20   ‖ [to be enrolled] in whatever tribe and phratry he may | wish . . .

1   Note the royal initiative in procuring civic honors for Metrodoros.
2   The occasion is unknown.
3   For this interpretation see *I. Ilion* p. 101, note on line 5.
4   The title of the governor of the Hellespontine satrapy. For Meleagros see also no. 21.
5   For Seleukos see no. 19 n. 1.

21   Dossier concerning a grant of royal land by Antiochos I to Aristodikides of Assos. Ilion 281–262. Marble stele.

OGIS 221; Welles, *RC* 10–13 with photograph; *I. Ilion* 33.

Rostovtzeff, *SEHHW* 1.493–5; Magie, *RRAM* 1.138–9; K. M. T. Atkinson, *Antichthon* 2 (1968) 32–57; Orth, *Machtanspruch* 55–61.

I

Meleagros[1] to the Boule and the people of the Ilians, gre|eting. Aristodikides, the Assian, has given to us let|ters from King Antiochos (I), of which cop|ies for you have been subjoined by us. He also met
5   with us and him‖self stated that, although many others with him have spo|ken and given (him) a wreath, as w|e are aware because some ambassadors fr|om the cities have also come to us, he wishes that the |
10   land given to him by King An‖tiochos, both because of the sanctuary[2]

and because of his good will toward you, | be attached to your city.[3]
What, | therefore, he expects to receive from the city for himself, he
him|self will reveal to you. You, however, would do well to vo|te all the
15   (usual) privileges[4] to him and ‖ to make a copy of the terms of his grant
and ins|cribe it on a stele and place it in the sanctuary in order that you
may retain | securely for all time what has been granted. | Farewell.

II

vv King Antiochos (I) to Melea|gros, greeting. We have given to
20   Aristodikides, the Assian, ‖ two thousand plethra[5] of arable land (with
permission) for it to be attached | to the city of the Ilians or that of the
Skepsians. You, therefore, arrange | that there be conveyed to
Aristodikides from the (land) bordering | Geritha[6] or Skepsis, wher-
ever you decide, the two thousand | plethra of land, and that it be added
25   to the boundaries of the (city) of the Ilians or that ‖ of the Skepsians.
Farewell.

III

King Antiochos (I) to Mele|agros, greeting. There has met with us
Aristodikides, the | Assian, and he requested that we give to him, in the
Helles|pontine satrapy, Petra,[7] which formerly | Meleagros[8] held, and
30   from the land belonging to Petra ‖ a thousand five hundred plethra of
arable land, and another | two thousand plethra of arable land from
that bor|dering on the portion previously given to him. | And we have
given to him both Petra, un|less it has been given to another pre-
35   viously,[9] and the land ‖ next to Petra and another two thousand plethra
of land | that is arable, because, being our friend,[10] he ren|dered his
services to us with all | good will and zeal. You, therefore, having deter-
mined | whether or not Petra has been given to another previously,
40   con‖vey it and the land next to it to Aris|todikides; and from the royal
land border|ing upon the land given previously to Aristodi|kides
arrange to have surveyed and conveyed | to him two thousand plethra
45   and allow him to at‖tach it to whichever city he wishes of those (cities)
in the land | and (in our) alliance.[11] As for the royal peasants from the
ar|ea in which Petra is (located), if they wish to dwell in | Petra for the
sake of security, we have instructed Aristo|dikides to allow them to
50   dwell (there). Farewell. ‖

IV

King Antiochos (I) to Meleagros, greeting. There has met with u|s

Aristodikides and he stated that the place Petra and the | land belonging to it, concerning which we previously wrote, | when we gave it to him, has not even now been taken over (by him) because to Athe|naios[12] it had been granted, the commander of the naval station.[13] He, there-

55   fore, re‖quested that, instead of the land of Petra, there be conveyed | to him an equal number of plethra and that he also be granted another | two thousand plethra to be attached to whichever he wishes | of the cities in our alliance, just | as we previously wrote. Seeing, therefore,

60   that he ‖ is well intentioned and zealous for our af|fairs, we wish to be attentive to the affairs of the man, and, regarding | these matters, have consented. He says that of the | land of Petra he had been granted | one thousand five hundred plethra. Arrange, therefore, that there be

65   sur‖veyed for Aristodikides and conveyed (to him) of land | that is arable the two thousand five hundred ple|thra and instead of the (land) near Petra another | thousand five hundred of arable land from the

70   royal la|nd bordering that originally given ‖ to him by us; and also allow attachment of | the land by Aristodikides to whichever city he wishes | of those (cities) in our alliance just | as we wrote in the previous letter. | Farewell.

The dossier consists of three letters from Antiochos I to Meleagros, governor of the Hellespontine satrapy, and a cover letter from Meleagros to the Boule and People of Ilion.

1   The governor of the Hellespontine satrapy; cf. no. 20.
2   The sanctuary of Athena Ilias.
3   In the three known examples of this practice, attachment to a city is at the discretion of the recipient of the grant and not mandatory.
4   Cf. no. 20.
5   A plethron is a square measuring 30 m (100 feet) on a side.
6   Probably a dependency of Ilion and not an independent city. For the site see J. Cook, *The Troad* (Oxford 1973) 347–51.
7   The description of Petra as a place (*chorion*) in line 51 indicates that it was a fort and not a village.
8   Obviously someone other than the governor.
9   The king's inability to ascertain from the royal archives the precise status of Petra is striking.
10   Aristodikides' position at Antiochos' court is unknown, but the size of his grant suggests that he was an important figure.
11   'Land and alliance' together are equivalent to the kingdom. E. J. Bickerman (*Institutions des Séleucides* (Paris 1938) 141) suggested that a distinction was implied between subjects without privileges ('land') and the privileged Greek cities ('alliance'), but this is unlikely. Rather 'alliance' is probably only a euphemism for allegiance intended to avoid too offensive an allusion to the cities' real lack of independence.
12   Probably the man attested at Erythrai about 274 (*SIG*³ 410, line 17) collecting money for the war against the Gauls.
13   Strabo (13.1.36,C 599) mentions a naval station near Ilion.

22   Treaty between Antiochos I or II and Lysimacheia. Ilion, 281 to early 260s. Rectangular fragment of a marble stele. Lettering characteristic of the first half of the third century.

Z. Tasliklioğlu and P. Frisch, *ZPE* 17 (1975) 101–6 with photograph; *I. Ilion* 45 with the corrections of J. L. Ferrary and P. Gauthier.

J. L. Ferrary and P. Gauthier, *Journal des Savants* (1981) 327–45 with photograph.

[I swear by Zeus, Ge,[1] Helios[2] --- | and all the other gods | and
goddesses] *to abide* by the | [friendship and] *alliance* which I have made
5 || [---] of the descendants | [---] just as *I have* | *agreed*, and *I shall preserve*
the city | [in autonomy and] in democracy | [---] and ungarrisoned
10 || [and exempt from tribute].[3] If anyone makes war | [either on the city]
of the Lysimacheians or their *for|ts* [or their] territory, I shall come to
their aid just as *I have* | *agreed*, employing the harbors of the
Lysima|[cheians] as *bases*, by means of those (forces) which I shall
15   designate || [and] just as *I specified* in the treaty,[4] | and I shall not abandon
the al|liance [which] *I have made* with the Lysima|cheians in any way or
20   on any pre|text, provided they *also* abide || by their alliance with me. |
May my affairs prosper if *I keep my oath,* | and the opposite if *I forswear.* |
Oath of the Lysimacheians. | *I swear* by [Z]eus, Ge, Helios, Poseidon,
25 || [Deme]ter, Apollo, Ares, Athena | [Ar]ei[a and] the Tauropolos[5] and
| all the [other] gods and goddesses[6] | *to abide* by the friendship and
30   alliance | [which] *I have made* with King Antiochos || [and] his
descendants. If anyone | [makes war on him], I shall fight as his ally,
and I shall not ab|andon the alliance which | *I have made* with King
35   Antiochos | in any way or on any pre<te>xt, || provided King Antiochos
also abides | by the alliance. If I keep my oath, | may my affairs prosper
and the reverse if I forswear.

I. Ilion 45 consists of two parts: 'a', a small fragment discovered in 1902 and referring to
the erection in the temple of Zeus at Lysimacheia and on Samothrace of steles bearing
copies of a treaty between King Antiochos, probably Antiochos III, and an unknown
city; and 'b', a fragment of a stele containing part of the oaths exchanged between a
King Antiochos and Lysimacheia at the time they concluded an alliance. Although
these two fragments were associated by the editor of 'b' and dated by him to the reign
of Antiochos III, Ferrary and Gauthier have shown on the basis of letter forms,
formulae and the historical situation presupposed by 'b' that this cannot be correct,
and that 'b' should instead be dated to the reign of Antiochos I or the early years of
Antiochos II who Polyaenus 4.16 shows campaigned in Thrace at some point in his
reign.
1   The goddess of earth.
2   God of the sun.
3   Compare the situation in the 190s when Antiochos III rebuilt Lysimacheia after its
   destruction by the Thracians to serve as the residence of his son Seleukos, the future

Seleukos IV (Polybius 18.51.8; Livy 33.41.4, 36.7.15). Until Seleukos' return to Asia
in 191/90 the city was garrisoned and served as the principal Seleucid military base
in Europe (Livy 36.33.6; Appian, *Syriaka* 21; cf. Ferrary and Gauthier, 331–3).
4   Contained in the lost portion of the inscription.
5   A goddess from Amphipolis.
6   The oath is restored from *OGIS* 266, line 23.

23   Letter of Antiochos I or II to Erythrai. Erythrai, 278/7–261 or 261–246. Stele lost, with only photograph and squeezes of its first twenty-six lines extant.

OGIS 223; *Welles, *RC* 15 with photograph; *I. Erythrae* 31.

Welles, *RC* pp. 78–85; Rostovtzeff, *SEHHW* 1.528–31; Magie, *RRAM* 1.95–6 and 2.928
n. 23; Habicht, *Gottmenschentum* 95–6; Orth, *Machtanspruch* 77–82, 85–97; R. Bernhardt,
Historia 29 (1980) 190–207.

King Antiochos[1] to the Boule and the people of the Erythraians, |
greeting. Tharsynon and Pythes and Bottas, your ambas|sadors, gave
to us the decree[2] in which you voted | us honors, and they brought the
5   wreath with which you crown‖ed us, and likewise also the gold for the
hospitality gifts; and, | having given an account both of the good will
which always | you have had for our house, and, in general, of the
grati|tude the People feels toward all its bene|factors, and in addition,
10   also of the honored position of the city in the time of the for‖mer kings,
they requested with all urgency and | zeal that we be disposed in a
friendly manner toward you and that likewise in all matters per|taining
to honor and repute we promote the interests of the city. Both the |
honors and the wreath we have accepted in a friendly manner, and
likewise | also the hospitality gifts, and we praise you as being grateful
15   people in all‖l matters. For you appear generally to act in that manner.
Wherefore, from the first | we continued to adopt an attitude of good
will toward you, observ|ing you behaving in all affairs honestly and
truly, and now | even much more are we persuaded (of this), perceiving
your nobility | also from many other things and not least from the
20   de‖cree given to us and from the statements made by | the embassy.
And since the men with Tharsynon and Pythes and Bot|tas declared
that both in the time of Alexander and of Antigonos[3] | your city was
autonomous and exempt from tribute and that our ances|tors always
25   exerted themselves on behalf of it,[4] and observing these men ‖ making
just decisions and ourselves not wishing to be inferior in *bene|factions*, we
shall assist in maintaining your autonomy[5] and | we shall grant that you
shall be *exempt* from all other levies as well as | [from those] being col-
lected [for] the Galatian fund.[6] Further, you shall also have the | [---

30   and] *whatever* other benefaction either we may think of or ‖ [you may
request]. We also urge you, being *mind|ful* [of us always] having made
the most strenuous effort | [---] good will as is just | [---] | you will
35   remember worthily those [by whom] you are benefited. ‖ [But more
about these things and] the other matters which we discus|sed [will be
reported to you by the] ambassadors who both for the *ot|her* [things
which they did we praise and] for the zeal which they display|ed [for
those matters which were advantageous to the city). Farewell.[7]

1   Often identified with Antiochos I although Welles argued strongly for Antiochos II.
2   Four fragments of a marble stele containing this decree have been discovered and
published as *I. Erythrae* 30.
3   The omission of Lysimachos implies that Erythrai did not enjoy these privileges
during his reign.
4   The vagueness of the allusion to Seleukos I is remarkable, suggesting that relations
between him and Erythrai were cool despite the establishment of a festival in his
honor, the Seleukeia (cf. *SIG*[3] 412, line 13).
5   The phraseology indicates that autonomy is not being granted but confirmed. The
separate references to autonomy and exemption from tribute suggests that 'free'
cities might pay tribute under Seleucid rule.
6   A fund to support Seleucid counter-measures against the Gauls. Its existence
provides the *terminus post quem* for dating the inscription, namely 278/7, the date of
the Gallic invasion of Asia.
7   The beginning of the decree honoring Antiochos follows.

24   Letter of Antiochos II concerning a sale of land to his wife Laodike. Didyma, 254/3. Marble stele.

OGIS 225; *Welles, *RC* 18; *I. Didyma* 492 with photograph.

Bevan, *Seleucus* 1.171–80; R. Clausing, *The Roman Colonate* (New York 1925) 206–19;
G. Macurdy, *Hellenistic Queens* (Baltimore 1932) 82–7; Magie, *RRAM* 2.735 n. 21;
K. M. T. Atkinson, *Antichthon* 2 (1968) 32–57; Will, *Histoire* 1[2].234–43.

King Antiochos (II) to Metrophanes,[1] greeting. We have | sold to
Laodike[2] the village of Pannos and the manor house[3] and the | territory
attached to the village, which is bounded by the territories of Zeleia and
of Kyzik|os and the old road which (used to run) above the village of
5   Pannos,[4] ‖ but which the nearby farmers have ploughed up in order to
ap|propriate the place – the existing [village] of Pan[nos] came | into
existence later – and (we have sold) whatever places[5] are in this terri-
tory, | the people who are in them, their | households and all their
10   possessions together with the fif‖ty-ninth year's revenue, for sil|ver
talents, thirty of them – in like manner also whatever persons fr|om this
village who have moved to oth|er places[6] – on condition that she (i.e.

31

Laodike) pay nothing to the crown and that she is entitled | to attach it
15   to whichever city she wishes.[7] In the same way ‖ also, whoever may
purchase or receive it from her will hav|e the full right and may attach
it to whichever city they wish, | unless Laodike previously happens to
have atta|ched it to a city. Thus, they will have possession wherever the
land has been at|tached by Laodike. As to the price, we have given
20   instructions that it ‖ is to be paid to the treasury at [---][8] | in three
installments, the first being made in the month Au|dnaios[9] in the
sixtieth year, the second in | the month Xandikos[10] and the third in the
next trimester. | Order that there be turned over to Arrhidaios, the
25   administrator of the property[11] of Laodi‖ke, the village, the manor
house and the attached territory | together with the people and their
households and all their possessions, | and record the purchase in the
royal records | at Sardis and on five stone stelae. Of the|se one shall be
30   set up at Ilion in the sanctuary of Athena ‖ and another in the sanctuary
on Samothrace and an|other at Ephesos in the sanctuary of Artemis
and the fo|urth at Didyma[12] in the sanctuary of Apollo, and the | fifth at
Sardis in the sanctuary of Artemis. Forth|with you shall survey the
35   territory and mark it with boundary stones, and [in‖scribe] the survey
on the stelae[13] [mentioned | above. Farewell. Year 59], Dios 5.[14]

1   Probably the governor of the Hellespontine satrapy. His cover letter to the official
      responsible for implementing the king's instructions is Welles, *RC* 19.
2   Wife of Antiochos II, divorced by him in 252 in order to marry Berenike, daughter
      of Ptolemaios II, a marriage that appears to have been one of the conditions for
      ending the Second Syrian War. This land sale was probably part of the divorce
      settlement.
3   Cf. Welles, *RC*, p. 320 *s.v.* Baris.
4   According to the survey (Welles, *RC* 20, lines 10–14) the course of the road was
      determined by questioning peasants long resident in the area.
5   Probably settlements smaller than villages.
6   While not serfs bound to the soil, royal peasants clearly were attached to their
      place of birth.
7   Cf. no. 21.
8   The text reads 'strateia', but it is not clear if this is to be interpreted as a corruption
      of the name of a city or a district or as a reference to a place controlled by the
      governor (the strategos).
9   The third month of the Seleucid calendar, approximately December 253.
10   Sixth month of the Seleucid calendar, approximately March 252.
11   Laodike is known to have owned property in Babylonia also.
12   Only the copy set up at Didyma has survived.
13   For the survey see Welles, *RC* 20.
14   First month of the Seleucid calendar, approximately October 253.

25   List of Milesian eponyms from 313 to 260 (selections). Didyma, 313/12–260/59. Late fourth- and third-century lettering with slight variations resulting from the annual addition of names to the list by different cutters.

I. Didyma 123 with photograph; *SIG*[3] 322 (selections).

Bagnall, *Administration* 173–4; Orth, *Machtanspruch* 17–32; S. Burstein, *The Ancient World* 3 (1980) 73–9, and *idem, Ancient Coins of the Graeco-Roman World*, edd. W. Heckel and R. Sullivan (Waterloo, Ontario) 61–2.

The following presided over the Molpoi:[1] |
Hippomachos, son of Theron. In his year the city |
became free and autonomous through | Antigonos

	and the democracy was restored.[2] ‖	(313/12)
5	Apollo the God[3]	(312/11)
11	Aristodemos, son of Parthenios[4]	(306/5)
18	Apollo the God	(299/8)
22	Demetrios, son of Antigonos[5]	(295/4)
35	Apollo the God[6] |	(282/1)
	Antiochos, son of Seleukos[7] |	(280/79)
	Antenor, son of Xenaros. In his year |	
	the territory was given to the People by |	
40	King ‖ Ptolemaios.[8]	(279/8)

1   The Molpoi, 'Singers', a guild of musicians attached to the cult of Apollo at Didyma whose president, the stephanephoros, was also the eponymous magistrate at Miletos. For their duties see *SIG*[3] 57.
2   Antigonos Monophthalmos' liberation of Miletos from the rule of Asander (Diodorus 19.75) was treated as the beginning of a new era at Miletos and hence the occasion for the beginning of a new list of eponyms.
3   The appearance of the god (i.e. Apollo) as stephanephoros is normally a sign of severe economic distress at Miletos. Apollo could also hold the office for more than one year as during the Galatian raids of the 270s when he was stephanephoros in 276/5 and 275/4 and during the period of warfare in the 260s alluded to in no. 95 when he held the office from 266/5 to 263/2 and again in 260/59.
4   Friend and general of Antigonos Monophthalmos (Diodorus 18.47.4, 19.57.5).
5   Demetrios Poliorketes. The reason for his holding the office of stephanephoros in 295/4 is unknown. Other rulers – Alexander, Asander and Antiochos I – seem to have held it at the beginning of their rule over Miletos.
6   A fiscal crisis at this time is indicated by *I. Didyma* 138, a decree honoring Knidos and her citizens for assisting Miletos with loans to enable her to pay the second installment of a large sum of money due Lysimachos.
7   Antiochos I (281–261). Miletos had become subject to the Seleucids as a result of the battle of Korupedion in 281.
8   Ptolemaios II (282–246) alludes to this gift in no. 95. Rehm suggested identifying the territory in question with Myos. Ptolemaios' ability to make this gift indicates

that he had taken advantage of the disturbances after the death of Seleukos mentioned in no. 15 to make gains in Anatolia.

26   Letter of Ziaelas, king of Bithynia, concerning the sanctuary of Asklepios on Kos. Kos, 242. Triangular marble prism.

R. Herzog, *Ath. Mitt.* 30 (1905) 174 with photograph; *SIG*[3] 456; *Welles, *RC* 25.

Welles, *RC* pp. 118–25; H. Seyrig, *Syria* 20 (1939) 35–9; G. Vitucci, *Il Regno di Bitinia* (Rome 1953) 29–35; S. M. Sherwin-White, *Ancient Cos* (Göttingen 1978) 92–9, 110–14, 340–4, 357–8; H. Heinen, *CAH*[2] 425.

King of the Bithynians, Ziaelas,[1] | to the Boule of the Koans and
Peo|ple, greeting. Diogeitos, Aristo|lochos, Theudotos,[2] who from you
5   ‖ have come and requested that the sanctuary | of Asklepios[3] estab-
lished a|mong you be recognized as inviolate,[4] and that | in other ways
10   we show favor to your ci|ty just as also Nikomedes (I), ‖ our father,[5] was
favorably inclin|ed toward the People. *vv* We for al|l Greeks coming also
15   to us happ|en to exercise care, ‖ being persuaded that our reputation is
not | a little enhanced in this | way. More especially do | our father's
20   friends conti|nue to be highly esteemed by us, including you ‖ because
of our father's acquaintance | with your | people, and because | King
25   Ptolemaios (III),[6] | who is suitably sympathetic to you,[7] ‖ is our friend
and al|ly. In addition, the men you | sent zealous|ly recounted the good
30   will | which you have for us; and in the fu|ture, just as you requested of
us, we shall attem|pt both to each of you individually and in com|mon
to all to show favor insofar as | we shall be able. As for those | who sail
35   the sea, ‖ as many as are | your (fellow citizens and) land at | places
which we rule, | we shall take care that security | be extended to them.
40   Likewise also ‖ in the case of those who, because of some misfortune |
which occurred during their voyage, | suffer shipwreck in our (land), |
every effort shall be made to see that | no one harms them.[8] Finally, we
45   recog‖nize also the sanctuary as inviolate just | [as] you thought it
ought to be, but to Diogeitos [and] | Aristolochos and Theudotos *con-*
cerning | these matters and the others [which] | we desired, I have given
50   instructions *to re‖port* to you. Farewell.

1   King of Bithynia from about 250 to 230/29.
2   The sacred envoys who traveled the circuit of the Aegean in 242 requesting recog-
    nition of the Asklepieion from various rulers and cities whose answers are also
    recorded on the prism.
3   The occasion was the completion of a major rebuilding of the sanctuary in 242 and
    the contemporary establishment of a penteteric festival, the Asklepieai, in honor of
    Asklepios.

4   Recognition of the privilege of inviolability (*asylia*), i.e. immunity from reprisal, was
     sought by coastal cities with important sanctuaries as protection from pirates.
5   Nikomedes I, king of Bithynia from about 280 to about 250.
6   As Ptolemaios II had been one of the executors of Nikomedes' will that had dis-
     inherited Ziaelas in favor of his son by a second wife (Memnon, *FGrHist* 434F14), a
     reconciliation between him and Egypt must have taken place after his overthrow of
     his brother. Heinen suggests that Ziaelas may have sought a Ptolemaic alliance as
     a counterweight to the threat posed by Antiochos II and his ally Pontos.
7   Kos, birthplace of Ptolemaios II, was an autonomous ally rather than a subject city
     with a governor and garrison.
8   For the Bithynians' reputation for hostility toward mariners see Xenophon (*Anabasis*
     6.4.2) and Nicolaeus of Damascus (*FGrHist* 90F113).

27   Decree of the Koan deme of the Aigelioi in honor of Anaxippos, a public physician. Kos. Marble stele, third- or second-century lettering.

J. B. Benedum, *ZPE* 25 (1977) 270–2;*SEG 27 (1977) 513.

L. Cohn-Haft, *The Public Physicians of Ancient Greece* (Northampton 1956) 61–5; S. M.
Sherwin-White, *Ancient Cos* (Göttingen 1978) 263–74.

In the magistracy of Eutychides, (month) Alseios, first day. Resolved |
by the people of the Aigelioi. Since Ana|xippos, son of Alexander, who
5   had been appointed doctor | by the assembly,[1] for many years, || with
regard to his craft and his | life, conducted himself in a praiseworthy
manner, | and (since) many citizens who had contracted severe |
10   illnesses and | were in great danger he saved, || sparing no effort; in
order, therefore, also | that [the] People may appear to be returning
proper rewards | to those who benefit it | willingly and that in the future
15 | it may become more zealous for persons work||ing for the advantage of
the People, it has been reso|lved by the people of the Aigelioi that it
praise | [Ana]xippos for the zeal and [con|cern] which [he continues] *to
display* [---].

1   There is no evidence that such public physicians provided free medical care.

28   Union of Teos and the fortress of Kyrbissos. Teos, third century. Blue marble stele, third-century lettering.

*L. and J. Robert, *Journal des Savants* (1976) 153–235 with photograph of squeeze.

[---] advantageously, the [citizens] in the city[1] shall swear[2] | [not] *to
destroy* Kyrbissos[3] nor to allow another so [far] | as they are able nor to

5   abandon any of the citizens [dwelling] in Kyrbissos; ‖ and the inhabi-
     tants of Kyrbissos shall swear [not | to abandon] the garrison com-
     mander sent by the People | [and] *to preserve* the fortress for the city. And
     if someone does not swear [--- | --- against][4] him the People as a
     wrongdoer. There shall be appointed as [garrison | commander] of
     Kyrbissos a person not younger than thirty years of age for a term of
10   four mon‖ths,[5] who possesses land and a house, free and unencum-
     bered, valued at four talents. | Any citizen wishing *to nominate* (someone)
     shall swear in the as|sembly. Let this be the oath. I shall nominate as
     garrison commander of Kyrbissos a person who [I | believe] will
     provide in the best and fairest way for the security of the *for|tress* and
15   who will preserve the fortress for the city, (I swear) by Apollo ‖ [---] and
     [may it go] well for me if I swear truly and ill if I forswear. The same
     person | shall not be reappointed garrison commander for five years. In
     order that we may know the garrison | commanders and [---], (their
     names) shall be recorded | by the timouchoi[6] on a whitened board [---]
     into the council building. The *garrison commander* shall have as gua|rds
20   not less than twenty citizens and ‖ three dogs.[7] The dogs shall be turned
     over to the garrison commander after being purchased | by the city, and
     the garrison commander shall maintain the dogs. Should anyone,
     having taken charge | of the fortress, not turn it over to the garrison
     commander sent by the city | regularly at the end of each four-month
     period, he shall be accursed and exiled | from Teos and from Abdera[8]
25   and from the territory both of the Teians and of the Abderi‖tes, and his
     property *shall be confiscated,* and whoever kills him, he shall not | be
     polluted. And if he [dies] fighting, his property shall be confiscated. |
     The one who has been appointed *garrison commander* shall [not] be absent
     (from his post). Payment | of his salary is to be made to him [--- for][9]
     four months by the *treasurers* | when he goes to the [fortress; and the]
30   *salary* of the ‖ garrison commander is to be four *Alexandrian* drachmas,
     and that of the guards | [one] *Alexandrian* drachma for each. [But if]
     someone is undisciplined or does not obey |the garrison commander,
     the garrison commander may place him in bonds and | discharge him.
     Let *each guard* have a shield and | a spear and a short sword and a helmet.
35   [The] garrison commander [and] ‖ the guards, before they are sent out,
     shall swear [in] the market place | that they will indeed turn over and
     preserve the fortress for the [city]. They shall also swear | the customary
     oath; and let the strategoi and the *timouchoi* administer the oath to them. |
     Further, let all who swear [---] | the guards present [---] and also let
40   those in *the* ‖ *city* swear. To be provided [---] in the fortress. The | *oath* of
     the inhabitants of the city is the following: I shall not destroy
     | Kyrbissos nor permit another (to do so) *in so far as* it is in my power nor
     shall I aban|don anyone of the citizens dwelling in K[yrbissos]. That

these | things are true (I swear) by Zeus and [Helios and Poseidon] and
45   Apollo and Athen[a ‖ and] all the *gods* and goddesses and [for me]
swearing truly, may all be well, and [for|swearing], ill. (The oath) of the
inhabitants of Kyrbissos.[10]

1   Of Teos.
2   The surviving portion of the decree contains the oaths to be sworn by the two
citizen-bodies and the regulations for the garrison of the fortress.
3   A previously unattested settlement, probably a fortress, that was presumably
contiguous to Teos. Its non-Greek name may be indicative of the character of the
population of Teos' hinterland.
4   A word meaning 'proceed against' is probably to be restored here.
5   Robert suggests that this and the other restrictions should be interpreted as
safeguards against the rebellion of a garrison commander.
6   'Office-holders' is the title of the magistrates at Teos.
7   Aeneas Tacticus (22.14) recommends that dogs be tethered to the outside of walls
to detect enemy spies or deserters (cf. Plutarch, *Aratos* 24.1).
8   A city on the north coast of the Aegean originally founded by Klazomenai in the
mid seventh century and refounded by Teos in the mid sixth century, and which,
as this passage indicates, still maintained close relations with Teos in the third
century.
9   Robert suggests restoration of 'his own and that of the guards'.
10   Omitted are lines 47 to 61 which contain: (1) the oath (47–54) in which the inhabitants of Kyrbissos swear loyalty and obedience to Teos and its garrison commander and to reveal and assist in the suppression of any plots against Teian rule;
and (2) the provisions (54–61) for administering the oath to the citizens of Teos
and Kyrbissos and its publication on two stelae.

29   Letter of Antiochos III concerning the foundation of a colony. About 212–205/4.

*Josephus, *Jewish Antiquities* 12.148–53.

Holleaux, *Études* 3.97; R. Marcus, *Josephus, Jewish Antiquities* 7 (Loeb ed., London 1943)
764– 6; A. Schalit, *Jewish Quarterly Review* 50 (1960) 289–318; G. M. Cohen, *The Seleucid
Colonies* (Wiesbaden 1978) 5–9.

(148) King Antiochos to Zeuxis,[1] his father, greeting. If you are well, it
is well. I myself am also well. (149) On learning that people in Lydia
and Phrygia are in revolt, I thought that this required great attention
on my part, and, after consulting with the friends about what ought to
be done,[2] I decided to transfer two thousand households of Jews from
Mesopotamia and Babylonia together with their possessions into the
forts and the most strategic places. (150) For I am persuaded that they
will be loyal guardians of our interests because of their piety toward the
divinity,[3] and I know that evidence of their trustworthiness and zeal for

what is requested of them has been given by my ancestors. I wish, therefore, although it is difficult, that they may be transferred with the promise that they shall use their own laws. (151) And when you bring them to the aforementioned places, you shall give to each of them a plot on which to build his house and land for farming and the growing of vines, and you shall grant them exemption from the taxes on the produce of the soil[4] for ten years. (152) In addition, until they harvest crops from the land, let there be measured out grain for the sustenance of their servants. Let there also be given a sufficiency to those perform-ing essential functions[5] in order that, meeting with kindness from us, they might be more zealous for our interests. (153) Take care also for the nation in so far as possible in order that it be disturbed by no one.

1   Zeuxis is probably to be identified with Zeuxis, son of Kynagos, governor of
    Babylonia in 220 (Polybius 5.45.4) and satrap of Lydia about 201 (Polybius 16.1.8).
    Josephus (12.147) dates the letter to the period of Antiochos' eastern campaign
    (212–205/4). For its authenticity see Marcus and Schalit.
2   The king's closest associates who functioned as his council of advisers (see
    Glossary).
3   The emendation of Holleaux. The manuscripts read 'God' or 'their god'.
4   Probably a tithe.
5   Meaning unclear. Cohen renders 'military service' and identifies the Jews as
    soldiers and the settlement as a military colony.

30   The founding of the festival of Artemis Leukophryene at Magnesia on the Maeander. Magnesia on the Maeander, about 207.
An excerpt from a sacred history of Magnesia inscribed on the wall of the south stoa in the market place at Magnesia as an introduction to the inscribed series of replies of kings and cities recognizing the festival.

I. Magnesia 16; *SIG[3] 557; *FGrHist* 482F2.

O. Kern, *Hermes* 36 (1901) 491–515; Holleaux, *Études* 1.313–43; L. Robert, *REA* 38
(1936) 12–15; Magie, *RRAM* 1.102 and 2.941 n. 38; *FGrHist* 3b, pp. 385–7.

[---] the god, by which (laws?) they will maintain as sacred the [city.[1]
5   And afterwards, her] ‖ *brother*, Artemis Le[ukophryene][2] having
     appeared to them [through the p|riestess] Aristo, *vv* gave the following
     answer in response to [their] *question,* | that affairs would be more
     [agreeable] and better for those who revere Ap[ollo Pythios] | and
     Artemis Leukophryene and recognise the [city and the] | *land* of
10   Magnesia on the Maeander [as sacred and invio‖late].
         The manifestation [of Artemis] having taken place | and they having

received it favorably – the oracle occurred in the year in which the
stephanephoros | was Zenodotos, and the archon at Athens was
Thrasyph[on (221/20) and in the Pythi|an games] the victor in the
previous year in the lyre (contest) was [---], | a Boiotian, and in the next
15 year which was the [one hundred] || fortieth Olympiad (220/19) the
victor [in the men's] | pankration was Agesidamos, a Messenian – for
the first time | [they attempted] to establish [wreathed] games[3] for the
inhabitants of Asia, | assuming this to be the intent of the oracle, [that] |
they would thus honor Artemis Leukophryene, being *otherwise*
20 || reverent toward the divinity, if, *coming* to Magnesia to the [holy] |
altar, [they would bring] gifts pleasing to the foundress;[4] | and since
other games were initially established with money prizes | and later, as
a result of oracles, *became wreathed.* | But when they made the attempt,
25 *they were disregarded.* [In || the year in which the] stephanephoros was
Moiragoras, which is the *fourteenth* | after that of Zenodotos,[5] when they
received the *oracle*, they, *re|calling* ancestral (?),[6] revealed also to others
this [event]. | In the year in which the stephanephoros was Moiragoras,
the son of Stephan[os], | in which they awarded a wreath equivalent to
30 that at the Pythian games and valued at *fifty gold staters*,[7] || the kings
having agreed and *all* the *other* [Greeks] | to whom they had sent
embassies, both nations and *cities*,[8] [having agre|ed] to honor Artemis
Leukophryene and to recognize as inviolate | the city of the Magnesians
and its territory because of the *recommendation* [of the | god][9] and the fact
35 that all of *them* were ancestral [friends || and] kin of the Magne[sians ---].

1 After three lines too fragmentary for translation, connected sense begins with the
   conclusion of the account of a consultation of Apollo at Delphi by the Magnesians
   following a manifestation of Artemis Leukophryene.
2 Like Artemis at Ephesos, she is probably a local form of an Anatolian nature goddess that was identified with Artemis. Cf. R. Fleischer, *Artemis von Ephesos und
   verwandte Kultstatuen aus Anatolien und Syrien* (Leiden 1973) 140–6.
3 Cf. Pollux, *Onomasticon* 3.153: 'As for the so-called sacred contests, those for which
   the prize is only a wreath they call crowned . . . thematikos those with money
   prizes.'
4 Artemis.
5 Either 208/7 or 207/6 depending on whether the years are counted inclusively or
   exclusively.
6 The reference is unclear.
7 Kern suggested that Magnesia's first appeal failed because the prizes were
   inadequate and that the successful second appeal coincided with both an upgrading
   of the prize and the construction of a splendid new temple to Artemis (Vitruvius 7,
   Preface 12; Strabo 14.1.40, C 647).
8 Response to the second Magnesian appeal was widespread. In addition to the
   Aitolian League (cf. no. 31) and Antioch in Persis and its neighbors (cf. no. 32),
   recognition was also obtained from the cities of the Akarnanian, Achaian and
   Ionian Leagues, the League of the Islanders, Epidamnos, Ithaka, and Chalkis

(*SIG*³ 558–62). In addition, of the contemporary kings favorable replies were received from Antiochos III and his son, Ptolemaios IV and Attalos I (*RC* 31–3), and, although a similar letter from Philippos V is not preserved, he probably also responded positively since Chalkis recognized the Leukophryenia at his request (*SIG*³ 561, lines 1–5).
9   Apollo.

31   Decree of the Aitolian League recognizing the inviolability of Magnesia on the Maeander. Thermos, about 207/6.

**SIG*³ 554.

Flacelière, *Aitoliens* 311–12, 323–5; F. W. Walbank, *CAH*² 234–5.

The strategos being Agelaos from Naupaktos for the | second time,[1] the hipparchos[2] being Polemarchos from Thy|riskaia, the secretary being Skopas[3] from Trichone, | it was resolved by the Aitolians. Since the
5   Magnesians, those f‖rom the Maeander, having sent as ambassador(s) | Mnasiptolemos and Hipponikos, both | renewed the friendship with the nation and | declared the good will which is held for the League | of the Aitolians by the Magnesians, it has been resolved that the
10   friend‖ship with them be preserved and that their city | and its territory be sacred and inviolable just as the | ambassadors request;[4] and that it not be permitted to anyone | of the Aitolians or of those residing in Aitolia to seize | anything from the land of the Magnesians, no matter
15   where they set out ‖ from, either by land or by sea; but if someone | seizes, the strategos then in office shall distrain upon his real property, | and from his personal property the synedroi[5] shall levy | a fine which they shall determine because the general interest | was harmed
20   by them. As for those exacting the penalties and effecting ‖ restitution to those who have been wronged, they shall have full power. And they (*sc.* the Magnesians) shall be given | also a hieromnemonic vote among the Amphiktiones.[6] This decree | shall be inscribed and set up in Thermos and in Delphi.

1   Chief magistrate of the Aitolian League and commander of the league army. Agelaos' first generalship was in 217/16 (Polybius 5.107.5).
2   'Cavalry commander', the second-ranking magistrate of the Aitolian League and commander of the league cavalry.
3   Strategos in 220/19 and 212/11.
4   Cf. nos. 30 and 32.
5   Members of the council of the Aitolian League, chosen to represent the member cities of the league in proportion to their population.
6   One of the twenty-four votes on the Amphictionic council that managed the Delphic sanctuary, see Glossary. Flacelière suggests that the vote was one of the two originally

belonging to Magnesia in Thessaly, the other of which the Aitolians had given about 225 to Kephallenia which claimed kinship with Magnesia on the Maeander.

32   Decree of Antioch in Persis recognizing the festival of the Leukophryenia established by Magnesia on the Maeander. Magnesia, about 205. Two columns of text inscribed on two wall blocks.

I. Magnesia 61; *OGIS* 233. Cf. Welles, *RC* 31–2.

Tscherikower, *Städtegründungen* 196–7; W. W. Tarn, *JEA* 15 (1929) 11; M. Holleaux, *CAH*[1] 8.142; Rostovtzeff, *SEHHW* 1.491; Magie, *RRAM* 2.941 n. 38; Orth, *Machtanspruch* 114–16.

(Decision) of the citizens of Antioch in P[ersis].[1] | In the year in which the priest of Seleukos Nikator and of Antiochos | Soter and of Antiochos Theos and of Seleukos Kallini|kos and of King Seleukos[2] and of King
5   Antiochos (III) ‖ and of the son of King Antiochos[3] was Herakleitos, | the son of Zoes, first six-month (period), decisions of the main assembly, | which were recorded by Asklepiades, the son of | Hekataios, the son of Demetrios, the secretary of the Bou|le and of the assembly,
10   month Pantheos, third day ‖ before the end of the month; resolved by the assembly, the prytaneis introduced the motion. | The citizens of Magnesia on the Maeander, being kinsmen | and friends of the People and having performed many conspicuous servic|es on behalf of the [Gre]eks [of the sort which] lead [to good repute], | both formerly when
15   Antiochos Soter, ‖ being zealous to strengthen our city, which was | named for him, wrote to them concerning | a colony,[4] they voted fine and notable decrees and, offering prayers and | sacrifices, sent an adequate number of men | who were distinguished for their excellence
20   because they were eager ‖ to assist in strengthening the people of Antioch; and (now) preserv|ing their good will toward all the Greeks | and wishing to make clear that to all their kinsmen | they give a share of the libations and sacrifices and of the ot|her honors, which relate to
25   the divinity, because a revelation has been granted to them, ‖ they have declared through all Gree|ce that they will celebrate in honor of the foundress of their city sacri|fices and a festival and a truce and wreathed games | every fifth year – musical and athletic | and equestrian – (thus)
30   returning just thanks to their benefact‖ress.[5] They have sent as ambassadors to the People | Demophon, son of Lykideus, Philiskos, son of Philos, Pheres, | son of Pheres, who, on appearing before the Boule and | the assembly, duly handed over the decree of the
35   Magnesi|ans; and, after renewing their kinship and fr‖iendship, they

41

recounted at length the goddess' m|anifestation and the services which
the Magnesians have furnished | to many Greek cities, and they urged |
that we recognize the wreathed games which they will cele|brate in
honor of Artemis Leukophryene in accordance with the oracle of the
40   god. ‖ (Since these things are so), the People, because it reveres the
gods common to it and | the Magnesians and desires to increase *its* |
goodwill toward its kinsmen and [many] other cities, | [which have
decreed these same things --- | ---] (and) especially because it thinks it
45   ought not to pass over [any] *suitable* occasion ‖ on which [both] to each
individually and to all in | common *it might demonstrate* the zeal [which] it
continues to have | [for the] *advantage* of the Magne[sians]; with good
fortune, | *it has been resolved* by the Boule and the People that *they praise*
the Ma|gnesians for their piety toward the divinity and for their
50   ‖ friendship and good will toward King Antiochos and | the people of
Antioch, and because, by using well their own advantages | and the
prosperity of their city, they will pres|erve their ancestral constitution.
Prayer shall be offered by the | priests to all the gods and goddesses that
55   the Magnesians maintain ‖ for all time in good fortune their *constitu|tion.*
Further, *recognition* shall be accorded to the sacrifice and the festival |
and the [sacred truce and the wreathed games as equivalent to the
Pythian] | – *the musical* [and the athletic and equestrian – which | the
Magnesians] will celebrate [(in honor) of Artemis Leukophryene]
60   ‖ because of the ancestral [---][6] | [--- | --- | --- | --- and the citizens of
65   Antioch shall also send sacred ambassadors] ‖ to Magnesia [to sacrifice
to Artemis Leuko]|phryene for the security [of the king and of both the]
| cities, and [they] shall receive [a travel allowance from the public
fund] | in the amount which the People shall determine by *vote* [(to be)
sufficient and proper | for the] city. The sacred ambassadors shall be
70   chosen on the [--- of the] ‖ month of [Hera]kleios, [when other
governmental offices] | are filled, and those [chosen shall be sent] |
from the [common] hearth [of the People. The] | sacred ambassadors,
who come [from Magnesia to us shall be giv|en] by the treasurers [from
75   the public fund gifts of hospitality such as are giv‖en] also to
[embassies] from *rulers* [and cities]. | The *sacred ambassadors* shall join in
sacrificing [--- Artem|is Leuk]o(ph)[rye]ne the [---]. | Those [citizens]
who shall be victorious in [the contests of the Leuko]|phryenia shall
80   receive the [same honors and benefits from] ‖ the city as [those who
have been victorious in the Pythian games] | receive according to the
law.[7]

Similar resolutions were also passed by | the Seleukeians | near the
105   Tigris, | the Apameians | near the Sellas, ‖ the Seleukeians | by the
110   Erythraean | Sea, | the Seleukeians | near the (Eu)laios, ‖ the

Seleuk[eians] | by the [---], | the An[ti](o)[chenes] by [---], | the
Al[exandrians ---].

1 Probably to be identified with the modern port of Bushire on the Persian Gulf.
2 Seleukos III Soter (225–223). The reference to him as king instead of by his cult title
   is probably an error. For titles, see Glossary.
3 The eldest son of Antiochos III who died in 193.
4 Orth rightly notes the implied royal command in this 'request'.
5 Artemis Leukophryene. Cf. nos. 30 and 31 for these events. The envoys from
   Magnesia, while at Antioch, met Antiochos III there on his return from his eastern
   campaign in 205. As did their sovereign, the citizens of Antioch recognized the
   festival but not the inviolability requested by Magnesia.
6 Four lines too fragmentary for translation follow.
7 Nineteen lines too fragmentary for translation follow.

33   Teos awards Antiochos III and his queen Laodike III divine honors for granting the city inviolability and relieving it of the tributes it had paid to Attalos I. Teos, about 204/3.

*P. Hermann, Anadolu 9 (1965) 29–159 with photograph.

J. and L. Robert, REG 78 (1965) 210–13; L. M. Gluskina, Vestnik Drevnej Istorii (1977
no. 1) 82–94; D. Musti, CAH[2] 209.

[Resolution of the] *timouchoi*[1] [and the strategoi. King] | Antioch[os
5 (III) ---] | [---] | [---] attitude *and preserving* [---] ‖ [--- the] *good will*
inherited by him from his *ancestors* and | [---] preferring increased [---]. |
He decided to become the common [benefactor] both of the other Greek
[cit|ies and] of our city; and he was previously, while | in the (territory)
10 on the other side of the Tauros, the cause of many good things ‖ for us;
and, having arrived in our vicinity, he re|stored affairs to a prosperous
condition. During | his stay in our city, he observed us weakened | in
both our public and private affairs by the continuous | wars[2] and the
15 greatness of the levies we were paying; and, wishing ‖ to be reverent to
the god to whom he consecrated our city | and land[3] <and> desiring to
show favor to both the People and the association of | Dionysiac artists,[4]
he himself came into the assembly | (and) granted that our city and
land be sacred and inviolate and exempt | from tribute. As for the other
20 levies we used to pay King Atta‖los (I),[5] he promised that we would be
relieved (of them) through him so that, | if an improvement in the city's
affairs occurred, he would receive not only | credit for a benefit (con-
ferred) on the People but also for its salvation. Further, he spent time |
in the city together with his friends and his military es|cort, giving a

25   most notable demonstration of his con‖fidence to all men; and after
these events, | he has continued to be the cause of many good things for
us, (thereby) furnishing an example to all the Greeks of the | way he
deals with his benefactors and those who are favorably inclined toward
him. Some | of the benefactions through which our city is becoming
prosperous he has completed, | and some he will complete *in the future*.
30   Having written to the People, he indicated that it ought to send ‖ [him]
an embassy which would discuss matters (which), he said, he believed
also *would be advantageous* to the People. | The People, having sent as
ambassadors Dionysios, son of Apollo|[---], Hermagoras, son of
Epimenes, Theodoros, son of Zopyros, he declared to them | [that] *he
had freed* the city forever, just as he had promised, from the | tribute we
paid to King Attalos. Having written also about these matters, he said
35   he had given instructions to the ‖ [ambassadors] to report to us, and the
ambassadors did report *the|se things to the People*. Likewise, his sister,
Queen Laodike,[6] also on | *every occasion* continues to have the same
opinion as the king, and | [---] and in her kindly feelings toward the
city | she shows herself to be fervent and in acts of good will zealous;
40   ‖ and the People has received the greatest *goods* from both. (Since these
things are so), in order, therefore, that we also on | *every occasion* shall
appear as returning appropriate thanks to both the ki|ng and the queen
and surpassing ourselves in the *honors* (given) to | them for their
benefactions and that the People appear to all as strong|ly inclined
toward the expression of gratitude, with good fortune, it shall set up
45   *beside* ‖ the statue of Dionysos marble statues of the finest (quality) and
most re|ligiously appropriate (character) of both King Antiochos and
his sister *Qu|een* Lao[di]ke, in order that, having granted that the city
and its land be sacred | and inviolate and freed us from tribute and
shown favor in th|ese ways to both the People and the association of
50   Dionysiac artists, ‖ they may receive from everyone honors to the extent
possible, and that, *sharing* the temple and | other things with Dionysos,[7]
they may be the *common saviors* of | our *city* and jointly confer *benefits on
us*. In order, further, that *what* | *has been voted be completed, two supervisors*
55   shall be appointed from all | [the] *citizens wh‖o* shall watch over [both]
the preparation of the *stat|ues* [and their] *erection*; and the (*sc*. officials of
some sort) shall give *money* for these things [---].

The first of three inscriptions from a dossier concerning relations between Teos and
Antiochos III that are preserved on four non-contiguous marble blocks from a pilaster
of the temple of Dionysos.
1   'Office-holders', the title of the chief magistrates at Teos. Cf. no. 28 n. 6.
2   Reference unclear. Hermann suggests the Cretan War that began in 205/4 or,
     otherwise, some unknown local war.
3   To Dionysos. For decrees of the Aitolian League, the Delphic Amphictiony and

Delphi recognizing the inviolability of Teos see *SIG*[3] 563–66. As to date, the *terminus post quem* is Antiochos III's return from his eastern campaign in 205 and the *terminus ante quem* is 204/3, the year the Aitolian League recognized Teos' inviolability. If this date is correct, this inscription would establish the important fact that the initiative in establishing a city's inviolability could come from its sovereign. It should be noted, however, that Gluskina has suggested that Antiochos merely confirmed a grant of *asylia* which Teos had obtained while still under Attalid rule.

4   See Glossary *s.v.* Dionysia.
5   Hermann argues that the loss of Teos to Antiochos III about 204 was an isolated event and not part of a Seleucid offensive against Attalid possessions in Karia.
6   Actually his cousin, being the daughter of Laodike, the sister of Seleukos II, and wife of Mithridates II of Pontos.
7   A springhouse named for Laodike was to be built in the marketplace from which the magistrates were to obtain water for religious uses (Hermann, inscr. II, lines 70–3).

34   Sidon honors Diotimos, son of Dionysios, for his victory in the chariot race at the Nemean games. Sidon, about 200. Statue base with inscribed official dedication, sculptor's signature and an elegiac epigram. Marble block now lost, the text known only from nineteenth-century transcriptions.

*L. Moretti, *Iscrizioni agonistiche greche* (Rome 1953) 41.

E. Bikerman, *Mélanges Syriens offerts à Monsieur René Dussaud* I (Paris 1939) 91–9.

The city of the Sidonians | (honors) Diotimos, son of Dionysios, judge,[1] | who was victorious in the chariot race at Nemea. | Timocha[ri] s[2] from Eleutherna made (this).

When all drove [their swift horses] from their chariots [in the] Argive [valley], / *rivals* in the competition, / to you, O Diotimos, [the people] of Phoronis[3] [gave] noble / fame, and you received the eternally
5   memorable *wreath*. // For, first of the citizens,[4] the *glory* of an equestrian (victory) from Greece / have you brought to the home of the noble sons of Agenor. / Thebes, sacred city of Kadmos, also boasts, / seeing her mother-city glorious with victories. / As for your
10   father Dionysios, fulfilled was [his vow concerning the] contest // when Greece shouted this clear [message]: / 'Not only for its ships [is Sidon] *extolled* [above others], / but now also for *prize-winning* [chariot teams].'

1   'Judge' renders Phoenician 'suffet', the title of the chief magistrate at Sidon.
2   A Cretan sculptor active during the last quarter of the third century.
3   Argos. According to the fifth-century historian Hellanicus (*FGrHist* 4F36a), Phoronis, king of Argos, was the father of Agenor, the first king of Sidon, and the father of Kadmos, the founder of Thebes. The web of mythical allusions in this epigram, therefore, is intended to establish Sidon's kinship with Argos and Thebes,

major Greek cities, just as the Jews attempted to do by claiming kinship with the Spartans (*I. Macc.* 12).

4   Permission to compete in major pan-Hellenic games implied recognition of Greek status (cf. Herodotus 5.22). This inscription, therefore, provides important evidence for the Hellenization of the Sidonian aristocracy in the late third century. At the same time, the presence of the office of suffet at Sidon indicates that Hellenization was a cultural process that did not involve the suppression of Sidon's traditional political institutions.

35   Letter of Antiochos III granting privileges to the Jews for their aid during the Fifth Syrian War. About 200.

*Josephus, *Jewish Antiquities* 12.138–44.

E. J. Bickermann, *REJ* 197/198 (1935) 4–35; Rostovtzeff, *SEHHW* 1.469–71; R. Marcus, *Josephus* 7 (Loeb ed.), pp. 751–64; V. Tcherikover, *Hellenistic Civilization and the Jews* (Philadelphia 1959) 76–84.

(138) King Antiochos (III)[1] to Ptolemaios,[2] greeting. As the Jews immediately upon our entering their land demonstrated their enthusiasm for us and received us splendidly upon our arrival at their city, meeting us with their Council of Elders and furnishing in abundance supplies to our soldiers and elephants and helping in expelling the Egyptian garrison in the citadel, (139) we thought it proper that they be rewarded for these actions and to restore their city (*sc.* Jerusalem), which had been devastated by the events during the war,[3] and to people it with those who had been dispersed abroad and had returned to it again. (140) First, we decided, because of their piety, to provide for the sacrifices a subvention of sacrificial animals, wine, olive oil and frankincense valued at twenty thousand pieces of silver and sacred artabae[4] of wheat flour in accordance with their native law, one thousand four hundred and sixty medimnoi of wheat and three hundred seventy-five medimnoi of salt. (141) And I wish these things to be made over to them just as I have written, and that the work on the temple be completed and the porticoes and whatever else must be built. Let the wood be brought from Judaea itself and from other nations and from the Lebanon without a tax being levied; and likewise also with regard to other things necessary for the more splendid equipping of the temple. (142) Let all members of the nation be governed according to their ancestral laws,[5] and let the Council of Elders and the priests and the scribes of the temple and the temple singers be exempt from the poll tax[6] and the crown tax[7] and the salt tax.[8] (143) In addition, in order that the city be settled more expeditiously, I grant to the present inhabitants and to those who shall return before the month of

Hyperberetaios[9] exemption from taxes for three years. (144) We also free them in the future from one third of the tribute so that the harm suffered by them may be corrected. And as for those carried off from the city and enslaved, they themselves and their children we set free and order that their property be returned to them.

1   For the authenticity of this letter see Bickermann.
2   Probably to be identified with Ptolemaios, son of Thraseas, a phalanx officer of Ptolemaios IV in 219 (Polybius 5.65.3) who later defected to Antiochos III and was rewarded with an appointment as general and high priest of Koile Syria (*OGIS* 230).
3   The Fifth Syrian War (202–200).
4   It is probable that an indication of the quantity has been lost. For artaba and medimnos see Glossary.
5   Specifically, the Laws of Moses, i.e. the Torah, but probably to be understood in the broader sense of the laws currently in force in the temple state of Jerusalem.
6   This is the only reference to a Seleucid poll tax, but such taxes were, however, regularly levied by the Persians (cf. Ps.-Aristotle, *Oikonomikos* 2.4, 1346a) and are likely to have been continued by the Seleucids.
7   Ostensibly a contribution toward the preparation of an honorary wreath but treated as a regular tax.
8   Salt sources were treated as royal monopolies, and taxes were levied on their use.
9   Last month of the Macedonian calendar, approximately equivalent to September.

36   Letter of Queen Laodike III, wife of Antiochos III, to Iasos. Iasos, about 197.

Marble stele containing part of a dossier of documents concerning relations between Antiochos III and Iasos that was inscribed on two columns. The lettering is essentially second century in character but with conservative features such as alpha without broken cross-bar.

*G. Pugliese Carratelli, *Annuario della R. Scuola Archeologica di Atene* 45–6 (1967–8) 445–53 with photograph.

J. and L. Robert, *REG* 84 (1971) 500–10; S. B. Pomeroy, *Mnemosyne* 35 (1982) 120–3.

In the year in which Kydios, the son of Hierokles, was stephanephoros, | letter *vv*[1] Elaphebolion. *v* | Queen Laodike to the Boule and the people of the Iasians, | greeting. Having heard often from my brother both
5   what ‖ concern he continues to show his friends and his allies | and how, on regaining your ci|ty which had met with unexpected mishaps,[2] | he returned freedom to you, | and how he introduced laws and other
10   measures ‖ to improve your government and bring it to a better con|dition, I, desiring also to | act in conformity with his earnestness and zeal, and for | this reason, to institute some benefaction for the |
15   poorer citizens but of general utility ‖ to the whole people, have written

to Strouthi|on, the dioiketes,[3] that yearly for ten years | he should have
brought into the city one thousand Attic medimnoi of wheat | and turn
them over to (representatives) of the People. You will, therefore, do

20   well | by instructing both the treasurers that, on rece||iving it, they
should sell a set amount, and the prosta|tai[4] and whoever else you may
designate, that they are to see that the | money realized from these
(sales) be assigned to dowries | for the daughters of the poorer citizens,

25   giv|ing not more than three hundred Antiochene drachmas to ea||ch of
those to be married; and as for you, should you act toward | my brother
and our house in general as is proper | and be mindful of all our benefac-
tions, | I shall *gladly* endeavour to arrange also other (benefits) which I

30   may think of, | intending in every way to act in accordance || with the
desire of my brother. For I perceive that | he is very zealous for the
restoration | [of the] city. *v* Farewell.[5]

1   At this point the editor read the numeral 84 which he interpreted as indicating the
     84th year of the Seleucid era or 228. Robert, however, noted that the photograph
     showed the space actually to be blank, and that, therefore, the inscription should be
     associated with the other texts on the columns which have identical lettering and
     refer to events connected with Antiochos III's occupation of Iasos in 197 (cf. Livy
     37.17.3). Confirmation of this date is provided by Laodike's reference to Antiochos'
     regaining and freeing of Iasos in lines 6–8, the latter of which is alluded to in the
     following Iasian decree which is also dated to the year of Kydios.
2   The phraseology and the later reference to the 'restoration [of the] city' suggests
     that it had been damaged in a recent earthquake.
3   'Administrator'. Either the financial minister of Antiochos III or the administrator
     of Laodike's estates from which, in the latter case, the grain would be drawn.
4   'Presidents'. It is not known if they were a committee of the Boule or an independent
     board of magistrates.
5   Fragments follow of an Iasian decree thanking Antiochos for his benefactions to
     Iasos and of regulations for the offering of cult to him and Laodike.

37   Treaty ending a war between Miletos and Magnesia on the Maeander. Didyma, about 196. Four fragments of blue marble, lettering characteristic of the late third or early second century.

I. Miletos 148 with photograph; *SIG*³ 588.

Rostovtzeff, *SEHHW* 2.634; Holleaux, *Études* 4.229–32, 331; Magie, *RRAM* 2.204, 2.944
n. 43, 2.945 n. 47; Schmitt, *Antiochos* 288; Mastrocinque, *Caria* 182–3; Walbank,
Commentary 3.169.

Treaty between the M[il]esians and the Mag[nesians]. | With good
fortune. On the following terms the Magnesians and the Mile[sians]
came to an agreement. | They were reconciled and when ambassadors

met and | restored them to their *original friendship*, the ambassadors
5   (having come) from the (following)cities: from Rh[o‖d]es.[1]
There shall be for all | *time* peace and friendship between the
Magnesians and the Milesians. *vv* As for the *area* | of the peraea[2] about
30   which the Magnesians and the Milesians disputed, the *b‖oundary*
between their territories shall be the Hybandos River, and from this |
river everything upstream shall belong to the Magnesians [and] | every-
thing *downstream* from it to the sea[3] shall belong to the Milesians. |
[And] each shall plant firmly (in the ground) stone (bases) and erect on
35   them stelae along the [chan‖nel] of the river in their portion just as ‖ the
ambassadors, who had been sent to the *negotiations*, designated the
spots, | and for all time their border shall be the *present* | *channel* of the
Hybandos River and the stone (bases) placed along it | and the stelae
(erected) on them. *vv* Further, in order that the [agreements] be secure
40 | and that peace and friendship continue forever between both ‖ cities,
the Magnesians shall not be allowed to gain possession of territory
belonging to the Milesians – (nei‖ther] their peraea nor any other
(territory) or fort – and the Milesians | shall not be allowed to occupy
territory belonging to the Magnesians – neither their peraea nor any
other (territory) or | *fort* – in any manner either as a result of their own
actions or those of others, neither by *purchase* | nor by gift nor by dedi-
45   cation or consecration nor in any other way ‖ nor on any pretext what-
ever. But if not, invalid shall be | the gift or dedication or consecration
or purchase or whatever other pretext [or] *de‖vice*, whether that of themselves or of another. *vv* And with regard to those possessing the right of
seizure either against the Mag[ne]‖sians or against the Milesians,
neither (city) is to serve as a base or *to rece‖ive* any of the property seized
50   in any way or on any *prete‖xt*. *vv* In addition, should, with regard to any
property carried off or removed | at the outbreak of the war, the
Magnesians desire to convey it through the | territory of the Milesians
or the Milesians through that of the Magnesians, they shall be exempt
from duties i|f they convey it within two months from the date of the
treaty. | *vv* As for those properties which were carried off or removed
55   during the war – either by Magnesians ‖ to Miletos or by Milesians to
Magnesia or by aliens resident in | or visiting *either* city – in order that
they may be restored to their homes, *they shall* | *be* exempt from taxes
and care for them shall be exercised by the magistrates in ei|ther city. *vv*
This peace shall be also (binding) on the Prieneans, *who were al‖lies* of
the Magnesians, and the Herakleotes,[4] who were allies of the Milesians.
60   *vv* As for those ‖ who are strategoi or have been strategoi or who led or
recruited (as mercenaries) for any| city of those listed[5] or allied in any
way, there shall be | for all these pardon and amnesty for all their
actions in the war and *they shall not be lia|ble* to suit, public or private, for

anything that happened pri|or to the date of the treaty. *vv* As for all
65   citizens taken prisoner ‖ in the war who are either in Magnesia or in
Miletos | or in Herakleia or in (Priene) in public (hands), each city shall
return an equal *number* through | the embassies sent for the nego-
tiations. As for the dignitar|ies of the Milesians who were captured, the
people of the Magnesians, as a gesture of good will, has turned them
over *with|out* ransom to the Rhodians. Prisoners in the possession of
70   individuals – Magne‖sians or Prieneans or Milesians or Herakleotes –
are to be redeemed, by the Magnesians, | all who are Milesians or
Herakleotes in Mag[ne]s[i]a or Priene; by the Milesians, | all who are
Magnesians or Prieneans in Miletos and in Herakleia. | [In addition,
gifts of hospitality] *are to be sent to the ambassadors who came* by the magis-
75   trates in | [each of the cities --- ‖ --- | ---]|. When the agreements [have
been ratified], [the ambassadors sent by the Magnesians shall | on their
arrival] at Miletos administer the [oath to the people of the Milesians
and those] | *sent* [by the Milesians] for the negotiation shall [on their
80   arrival at Magnesia administer ‖ the oath to the] people of the
Magnesians. [The Magnesians shall furnish the oath for the Milesi|ans
and the Milesians] for the Magnesians; and they shall swear, *while
burning* sacred victims, [the oath sub|scribed: Oath] of the Magnesians.
I swear by Artemis [Leukophryene and] | *all* [the other gods] and god-
desses to maintain the *treaty* [and to abide by its | terms and] not to bear
85   grudges for any previous [occurrences. For me swearing ‖ truly, may
things turn out well], and for me forswearing, the reverse. Oath of the
Milesians. *I swear* [by Apoll|o of Didyma and] all the other gods and
goddesses to maintain the | [treaty and] *to abide* by its terms and not to
bear grudges for any | *previous occurrences.* For me swearing truly, may
things turn out well, and for me forswearing, the reverse. | *vv The treaty*
[shall come into force], as the Milesians reckon, in the year in which the
90   stephanephoros is the god, which is the year af‖ter [that of Apollonios],
in the month of Pyanopsion,[6] on the sixteenth day; and as the
Magnesians | [reckon], *in the year in which the stephanephoros* is Aristeus, in
the month of Hagneon, on the fifteenth day. | A sealed copy *of the treaty*
[is to be given] to the Rhodian | [ambassadors] in order that it be pre-
served until *it is cop|ied onto the stelae.*

1 Omitted are lines 5 to 27 which contain a list of the delegates to the negotiations
from Miletos and Magnesia and the list of ambassadors from: Rhodes, Athens,
Knidos, Myndos, Samos, Halikarnassos, Mylasa, Teos, Kyzikos, and the Achaian
League. Precise dating of the treaty is based on the prominent role of Rhodes in
arranging the treaty implied by lines 67 to 69 and 92 to 93 which suggests that it
belongs to the period immediately following Rhodes' expulsion of Macedonian
forces from Karia in 197 (cf. Livy 33.18).

2 Literally 'the territory across the river'. The reference is probably to Myos which
   Philippos V transferred from Miletos to Magnesia in 201 (Polybius 16.15.5–6).
3 Upstream and downstream, that is, from the junction of the Hybandos and
   Maeander Rivers.
4 Citizens of Herakleia by Latmos.
5 I.e. Magnesia, Miletos, Priene and Herakleia by Latmos.
6 Eighth month of the Milesian calendar, approximately equivalent to October–
   November.

38   Athens honors Eumenes II and his brother Attalos for aiding Antiochos IV to become king. About 175/4. Two fragments of white marble. Copy of an Athenian decree found at Pergamon.

OGIS 248; cf. Appian, *Syriaka* 45.

M. Holleaux, *REG* 23 (1900) 258–80; Bevan, *Seleucus* 2.226–7; A. Aymard, *Historia* 2
(1953) 49–73; M. Zambelli, *RFIC* 88 (1960) 362–89; O. Mørkholm, *ANS-MN* 11 (1964)
63–76; Mørkholm, *Antiochus IV* 38–49; R. B. McShane, *The Foreign Policy of the Attalids of
Pergamum* (Urbana 1964) 163–4; Will, *Histoire* 2.254–7; Hansen, *Attalids*[2] 107–8.

[---] Seleukos (IV) *having died*[1] [and | the situation] inviting, observing |
that the moment offered [an occasion] for doing | a favor and a good
deed, considering all other things incidental, | they[2] both associated
15   themselves, and ‖ as far as the borders of their own kingdom they
advanced | together, | and they furnished (him with) money and | pro-
vided military forces and adorned (him) with the diadem | together
with the other regalia | as was his due; and, sacrificing oxen and
20   exchanging pledges ‖ with each other with all good will | and affection,
they worthily restored to his | ancestral realm King Antiochos (IV).[3] In
order, therefore, | that the People may appear foremost in the returning
of a favor | and be conspicuous in honoring those benefitting the People
25   and its friends ‖ voluntarily and in committing the goodness of their |
deeds to eternal memory, now, just as | also before, with good fortune,
it has been resolved by the Boule | that the proedroi selected by lot shall
in the next assembly | deliberate on these matters and convey the
30   decision ‖ of the Boule to the People,[4] that the Boule resolves that | it
praise King Eumenes (II), son of King Atta[los] (I) | and of Queen
Apollonis,[5] and crown him with a gold | wreath for valor in accordance
with the law for his excellence | and the good will and nobility of charac-
35   ter which he revealed ‖ to all men by exerting himself on behalf of King
Antiochos | and joining in restoring him to the *kingdom* of his ancestors; |
and in the same manner that it crown also Attalos,[6] because, together
with his | brother Eumenes, he accomplished everything without shirk-
40   ing | and boldly; and that it praise also the brothers ‖ of these men,

Philetairos and Athenaios, and crown with a gold | wreath each of them
for the good will and | zeal which they displayed in regard to the return
of | King Antiochos; and that it praise also the parents | of these men,
45   King Attalos and Queen ‖ Apollonis, and crown them with a gold
wreath | for valor for the excellence and nobility of character, | which
they stored up for their sons, having supervised the education | of them
well and prudently;[7] and that it proclaim these | wreaths both at the
50   games we hold at any time ‖ and likewise also in those which King
Eumenes together with his | brothers and the Pergamenean people
(shall hold), and in the same manner | also in those which King
Antiochos will hold at Daphne just as | was their custom. And in order
also that this memorial remain *manifest* | for all time, this decree shall
55   be inscribed on stelae ‖ of stone, and they are to be set up, one in the
Agora[8] beside the statues | of King Antiochos, and one in the sanctuary
of Victory-bringing | Athena, and one in the sanctuary of Apollo at
Daphne. | And, as for the transmission of it to the king and his | mother
60   and his brothers, the strategoi shall take care ‖ that it be done carefully
and as quickly as possible.

1   After ten lines that are too fragmentary for translation the intelligible portion of the
    text begins with a euphemistic allusion to the death of Seleukos IV (187–175), who
    was assassinated by his chief minister, Heliodoros, on 2 or 3 September 175 (cf.
    A. J. Sachs and D. J. Wiseman, *Iraq* 16 [1954] 208).
2   Eumenes II (197–160) and Attalos II (160–139).
3   Antiochos IV (175–164), the younger brother of Seleukos IV, who, after being a
    hostage at Rome from 189 to 176, was living at Athens at the time of his brother's
    murder (Polybius 26.1.10, Livy 41.20.8 and Pausanias 5.12.4).
4   The legislative procedure identifies the decree as probably Athenian.
5   From Kyzikos (cf. Polybius 22.20; and Walbank, *Commentary* 3.211).
6   The future Attalos II.
7   These virtues were emphasized in the epigrams concerning the temple dedicated to
    Apollonis that are preserved in the third book of the *Greek Anthology* and in a decree
    recognizing her divinity from Hierapolis (*OGIS* 308).
8   At Athens.

39   Antiochos IV as king of Egypt. 169 or 168.

A. *Daniel 11.21–4 (New English Bible version).* **B.** Porphyry, *FGrHist* 260F49a = St Jerome,
commentary on *Daniel* 11.21. **C.** *P. Tebt.* 698; *C. Ord. Ptol.*[2] 32. Papyrus from the carton-
age of a mummy. Fayum, Egypt. Precise provenance unknown but possibly from
Tebtunis. Cf. Polybius 18.18–21; Diodorus 30.15–18.

B. V. Head, *Historia Numorum*[2] (London 1911) 768; Bevan, *Ptolemy* 283–5; Rostovtzeff,
SEHHW 1.719, 3.1496 n. 14; H. I. Bell, *Egypt from Alexander to the Arab Conquest* (Oxford
1948) 60; Mørkholm, *Antiochus IV* 92; Will, *Histoire* 2.269; Fraser, *Ptolemaic Alexandria*
2.211 n. 213; J. D. Ray, *The Archive of Hor* (London 1976) 125–7.

A. *Daniel* 11.21–4

A contemptible creature will succeed but will not be given recognition
as king; yet he will sweep away all forces of opposition as he advances
. . . He will enter into fraudulent alliances and, although the people
behind him are but few, he will rise to power and establish himself in
time of peace. He will overrun the richest districts of the province and
succeed in doing what his fathers and forefathers failed to do, dis-
tributing spoil, booty and property to his followers. He will lay his
plans against fortresses, but only for a time.

B. Porphyry, *FGrHist* 260F49a

Up to this point (i.e. *Daniel* 11.21) historical order has been followed
and between Porphyry and us (i.e. Jewish and Christian commentators)
there is no dispute. What follows to the end of the book (i.e. of *Daniel*)
he interprets as referring to Antiochus, whose cognomen is Epiphanes,
the brother of Seleucus (IV), the son of Antiochus (III) the Great, who
ruled after Seleucus for 11 years in Syria and seized Judaea . . . They say
that Antiochus Epiphanes, his brother, stood in the place of Seleucus.[1]
At first, those in Syria who favored Ptolemaeus did not give him royal
honors. Afterwards, however, by the pretense of clemency he gained
the kingdom of Syria . . . Not only, he (i.e. Porphyry) says, did he (i.e.
Antiochus) conquer Ptolemaeus (VI) by guile, he also overcame Judas
Maccabaeus by stratagems. By Ptolemaeus, however, he does not
mean Epiphanes, who was the fifth to reign in Egypt, but Ptolemaeus
Philometor, the son of Cleopatra,[2] the sister of Antiochus (IV), who
was his uncle. When after the death of Cleopatra, Eulaius, the eunuch
(and) tutor of Philometor and Leneus, governed Egypt and sought to
regain Syria[3] which Antiochus had occupied by fraud, a war broke out
between the uncle and the boy Ptolemaeus; and when they joined
battle between Pelusium and Mount Casius, the generals of
Ptolemaeus were defeated. Antiochus, sparing the boy[4] and feigning
friendship, went up to Memphis, and, there, taking possession of the
kingdom according to Egyptian tradition and declaring that he would
watch out for the boy's affairs, he subjugated with a small force all
Egypt to himself. He entered rich and prosperous cities and did what
neither his fathers nor his father's fathers had done, for no king of Syria
had thus ravaged Egypt. And all their riches he dispersed . . .

C. *Ord. Ptol.*[3] 32

By order of King Antiochos,[5] | to the *kleruchs* of the Krokodilopolite
(nome)[6] [---]

1 Cf. no. 38.
2 Married to Ptolemaios V in 195/4 and died in the spring of 176.
3 The reference is to Koile Syria, that is, that portion of southern Syria and Palestine that had been occupied by Ptolemaios I in 301 and claimed by the Seleucids until its re-conquest by Antiochos III following his victory at Panion in 200. The reference to fraud probably refers to the Ptolemaic claim (cf. Polybius 28.20.9; Appian, *Syriaka* 5) that Koile Syria was included in Kleopatra I's dowry when she married Ptolemaios V. Josephus (*Jewish Antiquities* 12.154–5), however, says that she received only the *revenues* of the region.
4 Ptolemaios VI was captured by Antiochos IV while trying to escape to Samothrace.
5 Until recently this prostagma and coins struck by Antiochos IV in Egypt provided the only support for Porphyry's claim that Antiochos IV had himself crowned king of Egypt at Memphis in 169 or, perhaps, 168. The publication of the prophecies of the Egyptian prophet Ḥor, discovered at Saqqara near Memphis in 1965, have greatly strengthened the case for Porphyry's reliability since they reveal (2, line 92; 3, lines 11–12) that while in Egypt Antiochos appointed a Greek named, it would seem, Kleon as governor of Memphis.
6 The Arsinoite nome.

40   Miletos honors Eirenias, son of Eirenias. Miletos, about 167–160. The sections translated are on two of three non-contiguous marble blocks from a round monument, second-century lettering.

P. Hermann, *Istanbuler Mitteilungen* 15 (1965) 71–117 with photograph; **Nouveau Choix* 7.

Welles, *RC* p. 215; Mørkholm, *Antiochus IV* 56.

I

Resolved by the People. The prytaneis[1] and the security officials[2] intro-
duced the motion. | Eirenias, son of Eirenias,[3] demonstrating always on
behalf of what is advantageous to the | city his zeal and always joining
in promoting anything conducive to fame and repute | for his father-
land, and also meeting with King Eumenes (II)[4] in accordance with the
5 ‖ instructions given to him by the People and through his own recom-
mendation | having induced him to give to the city a gift of | 160,000
medimnoi of wheat for the construction of the gymnasium and wood
sufficient for the works specified,[5] | and the People having voted for the
aforementioned actions appropriate | honors to the king and having
10 sent as ambassador Eirenias, ‖ he, having spoken with all zeal and
having inspired him to increa|se what had been promised and to
assume the costs of the com|pletion of the honors himself so that the
Peop|le's gratitude toward its benefactors might be made manifest to
all | and that the supplies for what has been specified be from the
15 resources of the king ‖ [---].[6]

II

Of Antiochos (IV) and having induced her[7] to obtain from her brother, |
King Antiochos, exemption from taxes for the People for everything
from Miletos im|ported into the kingdom so that through this | grant
5   his gift might become famous for all time || and tend to increase the
revenues both of the city and of each of its | individual (citizens)[8] and
in all things both by word and deed he, striving on behalf of the | city
just as is proper for a good citizen. *v* | (Since these things are so), in
order, therefore, that the People might appear as awarding appropriate
honors to fine | and good men who make the greatest demonstration of
10   their zeal and good will toward the People || often through their own
deeds, | being champions of the most distinguished (causes), it has
been resolved by the Milesians | that Eirenias be praised for these
things and that he be in the care of the | Boule and the People and that
a gold statue of him be set up in whatever | spot the People indicates,
15   and the honors having been confirmed in the court || [---].[9]

1   Board of magistrates at Miletos with close connections with the Boule and which
    represented the city in relations with other cities.
2   Cf. no. 88, line 3.
3   A member of a distinguished Milesian family and a councillor during the years 167
    to 160.
4   For this embassy see no. 88.
5   Probably with monies realized from its sale.
6   An untranslatable phrase follows. There is a gap of about seven lines between
    blocks I and II.
7   Identification uncertain since 'sister' was used as an honorific title for female
    members of the Seleucid royal family. The editors of *Nouveau Choix* suggest Laodike,
    daughter of Antiochos III and wife of Seleukos IV and, perhaps, of Antiochos IV.
8   A unique example of a city taking official action to promote its own exports.
9   Block III is too fragmentary for translation but clearly dealt with the proclamation
    of Eirenias' honors, the erection of his statue and the inscribing of this decree.

**41   A dedication to Antiochos IV as founder of Babylon. Babylon,
166.** Two contiguous blocks of white limestone, second-century lettering. Provenance unknown but said to have been found at Babylon.

OGIS 253; M. Zambelli, *RFIC* 88 (1960) 378; **SEG* 26 (1979) 1624.

V. Tscherikower, *Städtegründungen* 92; Tarn, *Bactria* 194–5; Mørkholm, *Antiochus IV*
117–18; Will, *Histoire* 2.261, 295; J. F. Bunge, *Chiron* 6 (1976) 53–71; S. M. Sherwin-
White, *ZPE* 47 (1982) 64–70.

In the reign of Antiochos, g[od Manifest], | savior of Asia[1] and *founder*
[and benefactor] | of the city,[2] year [1]46,[3] | [at the sacrifices(?)[4] and]

contest of thanksgiving [which were held at Daphne][5] on [the twenty-
5   fifth day] ‖ of Hyperberetaios,[6] [to King Antiochos], god Manife[st, an
altar] *was dedicated* [in the agora by] | Philippos, son of Dia[---][7] | in [year
1]44[8] [---].

1   Numerous explanations of this title have been proposed. Tarn suggested that
    it referred to an otherwise unattested victory over Demetrios II of Baktria, while
    Will argued that it was an anticipatory allusion to Antiochos' proposed Iranian
    campaign. More recently, Bunge has seen in it a reference to Antiochos' recent
    victories in the Sixth Syrian War.
2   In the sense that Antiochos established at Babylon a core of Greek citizens as he did
    at Jerusalem.
3   167/6. Restored by Dittenberger on the assumption that the document is dated
    according to the Seleucid era.
4   Restored by Zambelli.
5   A suburb of Antioch sacred to Apollo where Seleukos I built a famous temple for the
    god. Bunge suggests that the reference is to the great festival celebrated at Daphne
    by Antiochos in 166 (cf. Polybius 30.25–7).
6   Restored by Bunge who, following Zambelli, argues that the festival commemorated
    the accession of Antiochos as king, which took place in Elulu, the Babylonian
    month corresponding to Hyperberetaios, the twelfth month of the Seleucid calendar
    (= approximately September).
7   Possibly Antiochos' friend and the regent for Antiochos V (cf. Josephus, *Jewish
    Antiquities* 12.360).
8   169/8.

42   Dossier concerning the exemption of the Samaritans from the persecution of the Jews by Antiochos IV. 166.

*Josephus, *Jewish Antiquities* 12.258–63.

E. Bickerman, *RHR* 115 (1937) 188–223; Mørkholm, *Antiochus IV* 147–8; J. A. Goldstein,
I Maccabees (New York 1976) 136–7; E. Bickerman, *The God of the Maccabees*, trans. H.
R. Moehring (Leiden 1979) 80–3.

(258) To Antiochos, god Manifest,[1] a petition from the Sidonians in
Shechem.
(259) Our ancestors, because of a drought in our land, having followed
a certain old superstition, made it customary to observe the day called
among the Jews the Sabbath, and, having built a temple without a
name on the mountain called Garizein, they performed at it the appropriate sacrifices. (260) And while you are dealing properly with the
Jews because of their evil, your royal agents, thinking that because of
kinship we do the same things as they, are fastening (on us) similar
charges, although we are originally Sidonians.[2] And this is clear from
official documents. (261) We, therefore, ask you, our benefactor and
savior, to instruct Apollonios, the district governor,[3] and Nikanor, the

royal agent,[4] not to trouble us by fastening (on us) the charges made against the Jews as we are distinct both in origin and custom, and that the temple without a name be called that of Zeus Hellenios. For, if this happens, we shall cease being troubled, and, by devoting ourselves to our occupations with security from fear, we shall increase your revenue. (262) To the Samaritans' request the king sent the following reply: King Antiochos to Nikanor.[5] The Sidonians in Shechem have delivered a petition which has been recorded. (263) Since those sent by them proved to us in council with the friends that they have nothing to do with the complaints against the Jews, but that they choose to live using Greek customs, we both free them of the charges and, as for their temple, just as they requested, let it be called that of Zeus Hellenios.[6]

1 Antiochos IV (175–164).
2 The Samaritans identified themselves as Sidonians, that is, Phoenicians, from Shechem, which had been their metropolis since Alexander established a Macedonian colony at Samareia in 331 following a revolt by the Samaritans (Curtius Rufus 4.8; Eusebius, *Chronicle* 2.115 (Schoene)).
3 R. Marcus (in the Loeb ed. of *Josephus* 8, p. 134, note (a)) identifies him with the Mysarch sent by Antiochos IV to Jerusalem in 168 (cf. *II Macc.* 5.24).
4 R. Marcus (in the Loeb ed. of *Josephus* 8, p. 134, note (b)) suggests an identification with Nikanor, son of Patroklos, described in *II Macc.* 8.9 as one of Antiochos IV's first friends.
5 For the authenticity of these documents see Bickerman. Josephus (*Jewish Antiquities* 12.264) writes that Antiochos 'wrote to Apollonios, the district governor, in the one hundred forty-sixth year [166], on the eighteenth of Hekatombaion Hyrkanios (?)'. Bickerman explains the dating by reference to Apollonios on the assumption that Josephus cited these documents from Antiochos' letter to Apollonios to which Antiochos had attached them for Apollonios' information.
6 This indicates that Antiochos IV's persecution of Mosaic religion and practices was restricted to Judaea.

43 Letter of Antiochos V announcing the end of the persecution of the Jews begun by Antiochos IV. 163.

II Macc. 11. 22–6.

Bevan, *Seleucus* 2.162–87, 299; Mørkholm, *Antiochus IV* 135–9; V. Tcherikover, *Hellenistic Civilization and the Jews* (Philadelphia 1959) 224–6; Will, *Histoire* 2.286–9; C. Habicht, *HSCP* 80 (1976) 1–18; J. A. Goldstein, *I Maccabees* (New York 1976) 81–2, 252–5; E. Bickerman, *The God of the Maccabees* (Leiden 1979) 55–8, 113.

(22) King Antiochos[1] to his brother Lysias,[2] greeting. (23) As our father has gone over to the gods,[3] and since we desire that the peoples of the kingdom be undisturbed in the management of their own affairs, (24) we, having heard that the Jews do not agree with the change to Greek

ways (sought) by my father,[4] but prefer their own way of life, grant, as they request, their customs to them. (25) We, therefore, in order that this people also be free from disturbance, have decided to restore their temple to them and to allow them to be governed in accordance with the customs of their ancestors.[5] (26) You will do well, therefore, to send to them and give pledges so that they, knowing our policy, will be encouraged and gladly take up their own affairs.

1   Antiochos V Eupator (the Nobly-fathered god; 163–162).
2   Chief minister of Antiochos IV, regent for the western provinces of the Seleucid kingdom during Antiochos IV's eastern campaign in 164 and guardian for the child-king Antiochos V (cf. *I Macc.* 3.32–4). He, therefore, was the real author of this letter and of the policy announced in it.
3   Antiochos IV died in Iran sometime between mid November and mid December 164 (cf. *I Macc.* 6.1–16).
4   A paraphrase of Antiochos IV's edict of 167 ordering the Jews of Judaea to cease living according to Mosaic Law, that is, withdrawing the privileges granted them by Antiochos III (cf. no. 35), is preserved in *I Macc.* 2.41–54.
5   The present document extends to all Jews the provisions of an amnesty declared by Antiochos IV in 164 (*II Macc.* 11.27–33) for those Jews who had ceased fighting and returned to their homes by March 164. As Habicht has shown, this letter was issued at the beginning of Antiochos V's reign and is a programatic statement of a type commonly made by Hellenistic kings at the time of their accessions. These usually contain amnesties or declarations of privilege. In the present instance, its effect was to restore Seleucid policy toward the Jews of Judaea to the *status quo ante* the outbreak of persecution in 167.

44   Treaty of alliance between Rome and the Jews. 161.

I Macc. 8. 22–32.

E. Taubler, *Imperium Romanum* I (Leipzig 1913) 239–54; M. Sordi, *Acme* 5 (1952) 502–19; Sherk, *RDGE* 97–9; H. Müller, *Museum Helveticum* 28 (1971) 156–71; E. Schürer, *The History of the Jewish People in the Age of Jesus Christ* I, new ed. by G. Vermes and F. Millar (Edinburgh 1972) 171 n. 33; D. Timpe, *Chiron* 4 (1974) 133–52; E. Gruen, *Chiron* 6 (1976) 86–7; J. A. Goldstein, *I Maccabees* (New York 1976) 344–69.

(22) And this is the copy of the letter,[1] which they recorded on bronze tablets[2] and sent to Jerusalem to be among those there as a memorial of peace and alliance:
(23) May it be well for the Romans and the nation of the Jews on the sea and on land forever, and may the sword and the enemy be far from them. (24) But if war befalls Rome first or any of their allies in their whole empire, (25) the nation of the Jews shall fight beside them, as the occasion may dictate to them, wholeheartedly. (26) To their enemies they shall neither give nor supply grain, weapons, money, ships, as was

decided at Rome; and they shall observe these terms without reservation. (27) And in the same way, if war befalls the nation of the Jews first, the Romans shall fight beside them faithfully, (28) as the occasion may dictate to them; and to those fighting against them the Romans shall not give grain, weapons, money, ships, as was decided at Rome. They shall observe these terms without deceit. (29) On these terms the Romans, thus, have made an alliance with the Jewish people. (30) But if later either party wishes to add or delete (something), they shall do it according to their own decision, and whatever they add or delete shall be valid.

(31) Further, with regard to the wrongs which King Demetrios[3] is committing against you, we wrote to him to this effect: 'Why are you making heavier your yoke on our friends (and) allies, the Jews? If, therefore, they again appeal to us against you, we shall decide in their favor and make war against you on sea and land.'

1 The authenticity of this document is generally accepted. Its form, however, is puzzling, particularly its description as a letter. Greek copies of treaties with Rome normally consisted of two parts, a Senatus Consultum and the treaty proper. Timpe has pointed out that a paraphrase of the relevant SC appears to be preserved in *I Macc.* 8.19–22 (cf. the standard formula 'to be enrolled as your allies and friends' in line 20) so the normal dossier would have been sent. Goldstein's explanation, therefore, is probable, namely, that in addition to the bronze copy the dossier was communicated to the Jews in the form of a letter together with a copy of the note to Demetrios, and that it was this copy that the author of *I Maccabees* used.
2 Normal Roman procedure required that such copies of treaties be set up, one in the temple of Jupiter Capitolinus at Rome and the other in the city of the ally.
3 Demetrios I (162–150). The dating of the treaty to 161 is assured by Josephus' quoting of a letter (*Jewish Antiquities* 14.233) from G. Fannius, Consul in 161, to Kos requesting that the city provide assistance to the Jewish envoys on their return from Rome. For the controversy concerning the authenticity of the note to Demetrios see Timpe (against) and Goldstein (for).

45 Monument in honor of Phile, daughter of Apollonios. Priene, first century BC (?). Blue marble pier, lettering not earlier than the first century BC.

I. Priene 208; *Epigraphica* 2.5

P. Veyne, *BCH* 90 (1966) 150 n. 1; Pomeroy, *Goddesses* 126.

[Phil]e, daughter of Apollonios | and *wife* of Thessalos, | the son of
5   Polydektes, | having held the office of stephanephoros,[1] ‖ the *first*
woman (to do so), con|structed at her own expense the | reservoir for
water and the city | aqueduct.

1 The eponymous magistrate at Priene, probably conferred on Phile because of her
willingness to use her wealth for public purposes.

46   The Lindos Chronicle. Lindos, Rhodes, 99. Marble stele, late second- or early first-century lettering.

C. Blinkenberg, *Bull. de l'Acad. Royale des Sc. et Let. de Danemark* (1912) 317–457 with
photograph; *SIG*³ 725; *FGrHist* 532; *C. Blinkenberg, *Lindos*, vol. II, *Inscriptions* (Berlin
1941) 2.

F. Susemihl, *Geschichte der griechischen Literatur in der Alexandrinerzeit* (Leipzig 1892) 2.188–
9; M. Guarducci, *Epigrafia greca* 2.302–8 with photograph; *FGrHist* 3b, pp. 443–51.

A

In the year[1] in which the priest was Teisyl[os, the son of Sosikrates],
twelfth day of [Arta]mitios,[2] resolved by the mastroi[3] and the
Lindia[ns; | A]gesitimos, son of Timachidas, [a citizen of] L[indos,
introduced the motion. Since the sanctuary] of Athena Lindia, being
very ancient and distinguished, | has been adorned with many [fine
dedications from] *the most ancient* times because of the manifestation of
the goddess; | but since it happens that [the most ancient] *dedications*
[together with their] inscriptions have been destroyed because of time,[4]
5   with good fortune, it has been resolved ‖ by the mastroi and the
Lindians that, *following the approval* [of this decree], two men *shall be
chosen*, and after they have been chosen, they shall prepare a stele | of
Lartian stone, in accordance with the *architect's* [specifications, and they
shall record] on it this decree, and they shall also record in accordance
with the | *letters*[5] and *public records* [and other sources] whatever may be
appropriate concerning the dedications and the manifestations | of the
goddess; and they shall prepare the [account in the presence of the]
secretary of the mastroi, (the secretary) who is now in office. Further, the
sacred tr|easurers shall pay to those selected [to prepare the] stele|
10   and the record not more than the amount specified by Pyrgo‖teles, the
architect, (that is), two hundred drachmas; [and they shall designate a
spot] in the sanctuary of Athena Lindia in which the overseers shall
erect the stele | in the next Agrianios.[6] But if anyone does not carry out
the provisions [of this] decree, the priest of Athena Lindia shall levy a
fine of five hundred drachmas. | Those chosen were Tharsagoras, son
of Stratos, from Lada[rma and] Timachidas, son of Agasitimos, a
citizen of Lindos.[7] |
The following were dedicated to Athena.

C

(37) [The] People (dedicated) a shield in accordance with [an oracle], that foretold that, | having dedicated it to Athena, there would be an
100 end to the then exi|sting war with Ptolemaios Philadelphos.[8] || And this happened as is declared | [by Tim]okritos [in] the fourth book | of his *Chronicle*.[9] There is inscribed on the shield: | 'The people of the Rhodians to Athena Lin[dia] in accordance with the oracle.'
(38) King Alexander (III) (dedicated) [ox heads] on which is
105 inscribed: | 'King Alexander, having defeated in battle Da||reios (III) and become lord of Asia,[10] sacrific|ed to Athena Lindia in accordance with an oracle | in the year in which the priest was Theugnis, the son of Pistokrates.' Con|cerning these matters the public records of Lindos contain information. | He also dedicated weapons on which there are
110 inscriptions. || (39) King Ptolemaios (I)[11] (dedicated) twenty ox skulls[12] | on which is inscribed: 'King Ptolemaios | sacrificed to Athena Lindia in the year in which the priest of Athena was Athana|goras', as *is documented* by the public records of Lindos. | (40) King Pyrrhos[13] dedi-
115 cated ox heads and weapons which || he used in battles in accor|dance with an oracle from Dodona, as is shown | by the public records of Lindos. This is recorded also by Zenon[14] | in the second book of his
120 *Chronicle*, Agelochos[15] | in the second book of his *Chronicle*, Agestra||tos[16] in the second book of his *Chronicle*. There are also in|scriptions on the weapons. | *v*
(41) King [Hi]ero[n][17] (dedicated) weapons which he used, as *is do|cumented* by the public records of Lindos. This also *is recorded* | by
125 Age[st]ratos in the second book of his *Chronicle*, || [---] in his *Chronicle*. There is inscribed on the | *weapons*: '*King* Hieron, son of Hierokles, to Athena Lindia.' |
(42) *King* Philippos (V) (dedicated) ten peltas, ten sarissas,[18] | ten *helmets*, on which is inscribed: '*King* | of the [Maced]o[n]ian[s],
130 Philippo[s], son of King De[metri]os (II), having de||feated the Da[r]d[ani]an[s and Maidoi,[19] to Athena L]india.' *The public records* of [Lin]dos [document this].

D

95 (3) Another (manifestation of Athena Lindia). || When Demetrios was besieging the c|ity, [Ka]llikles, who had retired from the | priesthood of Athena Lindia but was still | residing in Lindos, thought that there
100 appeared to him | in a dream the goddess who ordered him to decl||are to Anaxipolis, one of the prytaneis,[20] | that he should write to King Ptolemaios | and urge him to aid the city since | she would lead and

105   arrange victory and domination. | But if he himself did not re‖port to
the prytanis and the latter did not | write to Ptolemaios, it would be a
source of regret | to them. At first the individual who had the vision, |
Kallikles, kept silent, but when oft|en the same thing happened – for
110   continuously for six ‖ nights she appeared (to him) and gave her | order
– Kalli[kles] came | to the city and to|ld the councillors | these things
115   and informed Anaxipolis. And the *councillors* [sent] A[naxip]oli[s] ‖ to
Ptolemaios [---].

1   99 BC.
2   The seventh month of the Rhodian calendar, approximately equivalent to April.
3   The members of the common council of the three constituent cities of Rhodes –
Lindos, Kamiros and Ialysos.
4   Most were destroyed in a fire that ravaged the sanctuary sometime in the fourth
century prior to 330 (cf. **D**, lines 38–42). The sections of the inventory translated
below describe dedications – all of Hellenistic date and illustrative of the prestige
of Rhodes and the sanctuary of Athena Lindia prior to Rhodes' unfortunate
confrontation with Rome in 167 BC – still extant in 99. Those not translated
(sections B 1 to C 36) concern dedications allegedly made during the mythical and
archaic periods.
5   The reference is to two probably fourth-century documents, the letter of the priest
Hieroboulos to the mastroi (*FGrHist* 529) and that of the priest Gorgosthenes to the
Boule (*FGrHist* 530) which are cited in sections B 1 to B 14 as authorities for
dedications made prior to the Trojan War.
6   The eighth month of the Rhodian calendar, approximately equivalent to May.
The whole document, therefore, was compiled in less than two months.
7   The son of the proposer of the decree who is probably to be identified with a
similarly named Rhodian poet and grammarian and was most likely responsible
for the compilation of the inventory and record of the manifestations of Athena
Lindia.
8   A war between Rhodes and Ptolemaios II (282–246) is otherwise unattested.
9   Otherwise unknown.
10   The dedication was probably made in 330 following Alexander's victory at
Gaugemala in October 331 and his subsequent acclamation by his army as king of
Asia (Plutarch, *Alexander* 34.1).
11   The dedication is probably to be dated to about 304 and to be connected with the
siege of Rhodes by Demetrios Poliorketes and the manifestation of Athena
recounted in **D** section 3.
12   The term used indicates that the dedication did not consist of the whole skulls but
only of part of the faces together with the horns.
13   King of Epiros from 296 to 272.
14   Second-century author of a history of Rhodes that was used but vigorously
criticized by Polybius. For fragments see *FGrHist* 523.
15   Otherwise unknown.
16   Otherwise unknown.
17   Ruler of Syracuse in Sicily from 265 to 215.
18   The light shield (pelta) carried by light-armed troops or peltasts and the long
lance – up to 18 feet – employed by the soldiers that made up a Macedonian
phalanx.

19   About 211; cf. Livy 26.25.
20   A college of magistrates closely connected with the Boule of Rhodes, perhaps presiding over it, but not forming a subcommittee of it.

47   Mytilene honors Theophanes, son of Hiroitas. Second quarter of the first century, probably about 62. Round marble statue base, first-century lettering. Discovered at Istanbul whither it was transported in late antiquity from Mytilene.

*L. Robert, *CRAI* (1969) 42–64 with photograph.

G. W. Bowersock, *Augustus and the Greek World* (Oxford 1965) 4–5.

[The People has honored][1] | Gna[e]us Po[mp]aeus, son of Hiroitas, | Theophanes,[2] who recovered | from the common benefactors,[3] the
5   Rom[a]ns, ‖ the city and its territory and | its ancestral freedom[4] and restored | the ancestral sanctuaries and the honors | of the gods, for his excellence and reverence | toward the divine.

1   Restoration suggested by Robert.
2   Close confidant of Pompey who obtained Roman citizenship for him. He was the historian of Pompey's campaigns in Asia from 67 to 62; cf. *FGrHist* 188 for fragments.
3   Cf. no. 87, lines 17–18, for this common epithet of the Romans.
4   Mytilene posthumously deified him as Zeus of Freedom (*SIG*[3] 753; *FGrHist* 188T10).

48   A syncretistic ruler cult: the self-deification of Antiochos I of Kommagene (about 69–about 36). Nemrud Dağ, about 40. The text translated is that inscribed on the backs of the thrones of the seated colossi set up on the east terrace of his burial monument at Nemrud Dağ, Turkey, first-century lettering.

OGIS 383; *H. Waldmann, *Die kommagenischen Kultreformen under König Mithridates I. Kallinikos und seinem Sohne Antiochos I.* (Leiden 1973) 61–6.

A. D. Nock, *HSCP* 41 (1930) 26–7; *idem, HTR* 27 (1934) 79–82; Magie, *RRAM* 2.1239 n. 50; H. Dorrie, *Der Königskult des Antiochos von Kommagene im Lichte neuer Inschriften-Funde*, Abh. Akad. Wiss. Gött., Phil.-hist. Kl.[13], 60 (1964); R. D. Sullivan, *ANRW* 2.8 (1977) 732–98.

Great [King] Antiochos Theos[1] | Dikaios, [Epiph]an[es], Philoromaios[2] and | Philhe[ll]ene, son of King Mithrida|tes Kallinikos[3] and of Queen
5   Lao‖[di]ke Thea Philadelphos, daughter of Ki|ng Antiochos Epiphanes Philo|metor Kallinikos,[4] recorded on conse|crated bases in inviolate |
10   letters the works of his own benevolence for ‖ all eternity. |

I thought that of all good things not only the se|curest to possess but
also the sweetest to enjoy | for men is | piety. I considered this deter-
15   mination also ‖ to be the source of (my) army's good fortune and its
most happy employment. | Throughout my who|le life I was seen by all
to be of my kingdom | the most trustworthy guardian, and | one (who)
20   considered holiness to be an inimitable joy. ‖ Because of this, great
dangers did I unexpect|edly escape,[5] and unhoped-for deeds | did I
skillfully accomplish, and a life of many | years did I fill out in blessed
fashion.[6] |
25   When I *took over* my ancestral realm, ‖ that the kingdom subject to my
thr|one would be all the gods' common abode was the pious decision |
I proclaimed. | Images of their form, (which were prepared) with every
30   kind of art, just | as the ancient lore of the Persians and ‖ Greeks – my
family's most fortu|nate roots[7] – required, I honored | with sacrifices
and festivals as is the an|cient law and the universal | custom of men.
35   Further, my just thought ‖ devised additional honors of august |
majesty. Therefore, for this monument a foun|dation secure from the
ravages of time | near their heavenly thrones[8] | I planned to prepare. In
40   it ‖ my body, as it had existed blessedly until *old* age, | after to the
heavenly | throne of Zeus Oromasdes[9] my divinely loved soul | has been
sent forth, will sleep for endless eternity. | Then also this sacred place
45   ‖ I decided to designate as the common seat | of all the gods in order
that | not only this which you see, my ancestors' | heroic company,
50   established by my efforts, might | exist, but also ‖ that the divine images
of these visible daimones,[10] | which have been consecrated on this holy
ridge; | and that this very spot, which is not forsaken, | might be a
witness to my piety. Wherefore, | as you see, of Zeus Oromasdes and of
55   Apol‖lo Mithras Helios Hermes[11] and of Arta|gnes Herakles Ares[12] and
of my fa|therland, all nurturing Kommagene,[13] | I have prepared these
wondrous images. | From a single stone, together with these daimones
60   who listen to prayer, ‖ a figure of my own form have I enthroned | and
a New Fortune,[14] a comrade in | the ancient worship of the great gods
have I | made. Thus, I preserved a just representation | of that immortal
65   thought which of‖ten was seen as my visible and friendly helper | in my
royal struggles. | Sufficient land and the rev|enues from it in per-
70   petuity | were assigned by me for lavish sacrifices ‖ and uninterrupted
cult. | Having appointed priests, with suitable | raiment of Persian
character[15] I outfitted them, | and I established a ritual and complete
75   service | worthy of my fortune and of the daimones' ‖ pre-eminence.
With regard to | the permanence of the religious rites, suitable arrange-
ments | I made in order that together with the sacrifices which the
80   ancient | and common law required | also new festivals for ‖ the worship
of the gods and our | honors will be celebrated by all the inhabitants of

my kingdom. | For my body's | birthday, Audnaios the sixte|enth,[16] and
85   for my coronation, Loos the ten||th,[17] these days have I dedicated to the
great daimones' manifes|tations who guided me | during my fortunate
reign and were my entire kingdom's | sources of common advantages. |
90   For the sake of numerous sacrifices || and great | feasts I have addition-
ally consecrated two days | annually for each | festival. The population
of my kingdom | I have divided for these assemblies and celebrations
95 || and sacrifices by | villages and cities, (and) I have ordered (them) in
the nearest | sanctuaries, which are convenient to each, | to celebrate
100   these festivals in their vicinity. | In the future, || I have ordered that each
month one (day) equivalent to the afore|mentioned – for my birthday
the | sixteenth and for my assumption | of the diadem the tenth – shall
105   always be | honored by the priests. || For the sake of perpetuating these
things, | which, for prudent men it would be pious | always to observe –
not only for our own honor | but also for the dearest hopes | for the
personal fortune of each individual – I, who consecrated them, have
110   had on inviolate || stelae engraved, with the guidance of the gods, | a
sacred law, which it would be right | for the generations of all men,
whom time | without end appoints to inherit | this land as their lives'
115   particular portion, || to maintain inviolate, in the knowledge that a
harsh ven|geance from the royal daimones[18] punishes similarly | negli-
gence and arrogance (and) pursues impiety; | and that also the law of
the deified heroes, should it be dishonored, | possesses pitiless punish-
120   ment. All holiness || is a light task, but behind impiety punishment
follows | necessarily. My voice proclaimed this law, | and the will of the
gods ratified it.

1   'The god who is Just, Visible, a Friend of the Romans and a Friend of the Greeks.'
His titles indicate that Antiochos had been deified while still alive.

2   Pompey confirmed Antiochos as king of Kommagene in his final settlement of the
east in 63, and Antiochos and his successors remained allies of Rome until
Vespasian suppressed the dynasty in 72 AD.

3   Mithridates the Gloriously Victorious (about 96–69).

4   Laodike, the Brother-loving goddess, daughter of the Seleucid king Antiochos
VIII Grypos (125–96) and Kleopatra Tryphaina, the daughter of Ptolemaios VIII.

5   A reference, perhaps, to Antiochos' success in retaining his throne despite having
supported Tigranes I of Armenia (95–about 55) in the Third Mithridatic War
(74–67) and Pompey in 49.

6   This and the reference in line 40 to Antiochos having reached old age date the
inscription to the latter part of his reign, about 40.

7   Through his mother he claimed descent from Alexander the Great and through
his father from Dareios I of Persia.

8   The planets.

9   Zeus identified with the Persian god Ahura Mazda.

10   Contrary to normal Hellenistic usage, daimones, except for line 116, refers to the

great gods and not lesser divinities and heroes. Dorrie, p. 56, explains their characterization as 'visible' by reference to their connection with the planets.

11   Apollo identified with the Persian god Mithras and Helios and Hermes.
12   Herakles identified with the Kommagenian god Artagnes and Ares.
13   The personified Tyche or Fortune of Kommagene.
14   Antiochos himself, who is ranked with the great gods rather than with the heroes as his ancestors are.
15   A reflection of the prominence of the Persian aspects of the cult.
16   The third month of the Seleucid calendar, approximately equivalent to December.
17   The tenth month of the Seleucid calendar, approximately equivalent to July.
18   Antiochos' heroized ancestors rather than the great gods.

Chapter 3
THE GREEKS IN BAKTRIA AND INDIA

49   Pillar base containing an elegiac dedication and five Delphic maxims. Ai Khanum, Afghanistan. Limestone base, epigram in elegiac pentameters. On the basis of the lettering dated to the first half of the third century.

*L. Robert, *CRAI* (1968) 421–39 with photograph.

MacDowell and Taddei, *Afghanistan* 197–8 with photograph, 225.

A

These wise (words)[1] of ancient men *are set up*, / utterances of famous men, in holy Pytho.[2] / Whence Klearchos,[3] having copied them carefully, / set them up, shining from afar, in the sanctuary of Kineas.[4]

B

As a child, be orderly. | As a youth, be self-controlled. | As an adult, be
5   just. | As an old man, be of good counsel. ‖ When dying, be without sorrow.

1   The five preserved sayings form the conclusion of a collection of 147 'Sayings of the Seven Wise Men' attributed to an otherwise unknown Sotiades which are preserved by Stobaeus (3.125 Wachsmuth-Hense) and in an inscription from Miletopolis in Mysia (*SIG*³ 1268).
2   This proves that the series of maxims was displayed at Delphi.
3   Robert identifies him with Klearchos of Soli, a Peripatetic active in the first half of the third century.
4   Probably the founder of the Greek city at Ai Khanum. The base was found in the pronaos of his heroon – the shrine in which he received cult as a hero – which archaeological evidence suggests may have been built in the last third of the fourth century.

50   Bilingual inscription of Aśoka. Kandahar, Afghanistan, 258.
Greek inscription of fourteen lines accompanied by an Aramaic text of eight lines carved on living rock and containing material similar to the Major Rock Edicts of the Buddhist Maurya ruler Aśoka.

Choix 53.

D. Schlumberger *et al.*, *Journal Asiatique* 246 (1958) 1–48; N. A. Nikam and R. McKeon, *The Edicts of Aśoka* (Chicago 1959) 1–22, 25 n. 2; R. Thapar, *Aśoka and the Decline of the Mauryas* (Oxford 1961) 137–81; M. Wheeler, *Flames over Persepolis* (New York 1968) 65–9 with photograph; Will, *Histoire* 1².265–6; P. M. Fraser, *Afghan Studies* 2 (1979) 12–13; MacDowell and Taddei, *Afghanistan* 192–8.

Ten years *having been completed,*[1] King | Piodasses[2] made piety known to m|en,[3] and afterwards more pious | he caused men[4] to be and all things
5 || to flourish throughout the whole land; and abstinence | the king practised from animate (things), and also other | men and all who were hunters or fishermen | of the king have ceased hunting, and | if there
10   were some incontinent men, they have ceased from their incon||tinence to the extent possible, and they are obedient to their father | and mother and the elders in contrast | to before, and in the future more profitably | and better in every way | will they live by doing these things.

1   Inscribed, therefore, in year 11 or 258.
2   Aśoka (268–232), third king of the Maurya dynasty who converted to Buddhism about 260. Piodasses is a Greek rendering of his Sanskrit title Priyadarśi, 'One who sees to the good of others'.
3   In Rock Edicts 3 and 5, Aśoka refers to his efforts to establish Buddhism in the frontier regions of his empire including those inhabited by Greeks, while in Rock Edict 13 he says that he sent missionaries to the Greek kings: Antiochos II, Ptolemaios III, Magas of Cyrene, Antigonos Gonatas, and Alexander of Epiros (?). This inscription confirms the reality of Aśoka's missionary efforts at least in the frontier zones, as well as pointing to the existence in those areas of a nucleus of educated Greeks willing to co-operate with him.
4   Piety ('eusebeia') = Sanskrit Dharma, a term with religious, ethical and social connotations (cf. Nikam and McKeon, ix: ' "Dharma" means the insights and precepts of religion and piety; it also means the principles and prescriptions of ethics and morality').

51   The Greeks in Baktria.

A. Justin 41.4.5–9. **B.** Justin 41.6.1–5. **C.** (a) Apollodorus of Artemita, *FGrHist* 779F7a = *Strabo 11.11.1, C 516–17; (b) Apollodorus of Artemita, *FGrHist* 779F7b = *Strabo 15.1.3, C 686. **D.** Strabo 11.8.2, C 511; cf. Polybius 10.49, 11.39; Trogus, *Prolog* 41.

Tarn, *Bactria passim*; Narain, *Indo-Greeks passim*; A. Simonetta, *East and West* 9 (1958) 154–83; J. Wolski, *Der Hellenismus im Mittelasien*, ed. F. Altheim and J. Rehork (Darmstadt 1969) 188–280; Will, *Histoire* 1².281–90, 2.301–13, 336–8, 348–9; F. Holt, *Revue Numismatique* 23 (1981) 7–44; D. Musti, *CAH*² 214–15, 219–20.

A. Justin 41.4.5–9

(5) At the same time[1] also Theodotus (I),[2] the governor of the thousand

cities of Bactria, revolted and gave orders that he be called king. The peoples of the whole east followed his example and revolted from the Macedonians. (6) There lived at this time a man, Arsaces (I),[3] of uncertain origin but proven valor.(7) He had been accustomed to live from theft and rapine, but on learning that Seleucus (II) had been defeated by the Gauls[4] (and being thus) freed from fear of the king, he invaded Parthia with his band of marauders and killed Andragoras,[5] the governor of Parthia. With Andragoras removed, he assumed rule over Parthia. (8) Not long afterwards, he occupied also Hyrcania and thus having become ruler of two kingdoms, he readied a great army because of his fear of Seleucus and Theodotus, the king of Bactria. (9) The sudden death of Theodotus, (however), freed him from fear and soon after he contracted an alliance and made peace with his son, likewise (named) Theodotus (II),[6] and not much later he was victorious in a confrontation with King Seleucus who had come to punish the rebels.

B. Justin 41.6.1–5

(1) Almost at the same time, both Mithridates (I)[7] in Parthia and Eucratides[8] in Bactria, both great men, established kingdoms. (2) But the fortune of the Parthians was happier under this leader who led them to the peak of power. (3) The Bactrians, however, ruined by various wars, lost not only their kingdom but also their freedom. Thus, exhausted by wars against the Sogdians, Arachosians, Drangianians, Arians and Indians, finally, as if bled dry, they were overcome by the Parthians,[9] hitherto their inferiors. (4) Nevertheless, Eucratides waged many wars with great vigor. Although worn down by these wars, he endured being besieged by Demetrius,[10] the king of the Indians; and with three hundred soldiers he defeated by repeated sallies sixty thousand enemy troops. Thus freed in the fifth month (of the siege), he brought India under his control. (5) But when he was returning (from India), he was killed during his journey by his son[11] whom he had made his co-regent. The latter did not keep secret his parricide but killed him as though he were an enemy and not his father and drove his chariot through his blood and cast out his body unburied.

C. (a) Strabo 11.11.1, C 516–17

The Greeks, who had revolted, grew in strength to such a degree because of the excellence of the country (*sc.* Baktria) that they conquered both Ariana and the Indians, as Apollodorus of Artemita[12] records, and they subdued more nations than Alexandros. Especially is this true of Menandros[13] – if, indeed, he crossed the Hypanis toward the east and advanced as far as the Isamos.[14] Some were subdued by Menandros and some by Demetrios (I), the son of Euthydemos,[15] the king of Baktria. Not only did they gain control of Patalene, but also of the whole coastal region which is called the kingdom of Saraostos and Sigerdis.[16] And in general, he (*sc.* Apollodorus) says, Baktria is the jewel of all Ariana. And they even extended their realm as far as the Seres and the Phryni.[17]

C. (b) Strabo 15.1.3, C 686

Apollodorus, who wrote the *Parthika*, having mentioned the Greeks who caused Baktria to revolt from the Syrian kings, the descendants of Seleukos (I) Nikator, says that, having grown in power, they attacked India. He reveals nothing that was not known previously but even contradicts (earlier knowledge), asserting that they subdued more of India than the Macedonians.[18] Indeed, Eukratides had a thousand cities under his rule.

D. Strabo 11.8.2, C 511

Especially notable (*sc.* among the nomads) are those who took away Baktria from the Greeks – the Asioi, Pasiani, Tochari and the Sakarauli who set out from the territory beyond the Jaxartes, that of the Sakai and Sogdians which the Sakai used to possess.[19]

1 About 256. The apparent precision of Justin's synchronism of the revolt of Baktria and Regulus' invasion of Africa during the First Punic War is probably spurious since Justin 41.4.4–9 as a whole suggests a date in the 230s.
2 Theodotus = Diodotos I (cf. Trogus, *Prolog* 41).
3 Arsaces I of Parthia (about 238–215).
4 The reference is to the battle of Ankyra about 240 or 239 which suggests a date about 238 for Diodotos' revolt.
5 Probably a satrap of Parthia who would have revolted about 245 during the Third Syrian War.
6 Theodotus = Diodotos II. For the campaign of Seleukos II Will suggests a date of ±230–±227. His reign, therefore, must fall somewhere in the period between ±230–±227 and 208 when Polybius (10.49) attests Euthydemos I as king of Baktria.
7 Mithridates I (about 170–139).
8 Probably a relative of Demetrios I who revolted and overthrew the Euthydemid dynasty some time between 180 and 160.
9 The reference is probably to the western portion of the area ruled by the kings of Baktria.
10 Narain (57–8) suggests Demetrios II (about 180–165), a descendant of Demetrios I; Holt (41–2) suggests Demetrios I.

11   Identity unknown. Narain (70) rightly notes that Tarn's identification (220) of the assassin as a son of Demetrios I cannot be reconciled with the explicit evidence of Justin 41.6.5.
12   Author of a history of Parthia (cf. 3(b)). Jacoby suggests a date in the early first century BC.
13   About 155–130. According to Buddhist tradition reflected in the *Questions of King Milinda* which is supported by Plutarch's account (*Moralia* 821D) of his funeral, he converted to Buddhism. For a speculative reconstruction of his Indian campaign based on the discovery of a purported Prakrit inscription of his in the Ganges Valley see G. R. Sharma, *Reh Inscription of Menander and the Indo-Greek Invasion of the Gangā Valley* (Allahabad 1980).
14   The name of the river is corrupt. The most likely emendation, Imaos or Iomanos = Jumna River (cf. Jacoby, *FGrH* 3C, p. 775 apparatus *ad FGrH* 779F7a), would mean that Menandros penetrated the Ganges Valley.
15   Euthydemos I from Magnesia – whether Magnesia on the Maeander or ad Sipylum is not indicated – overthrew Diodotos II (cf. n. 6). For his war with Antiochos III between 208 and 206 and the subsequent peace and marriage alliance between them see Polybius 10.49 and 11.39.
16   The area around the Ran of Kutch in north-west India.
17   For the Seres and Phryni see Narain (170–1) who locates them near Kashgar instead of in the vicinity of China as the name Seres might suggest.
18   The insistence on the *Greekness* of the rulers of Baktria should be noted.
19   Will (2.348–9) dates the conquest of Baktria by nomadic Skythian tribes about 135. Further information is provided by the Chinese historian Ssu-Ma Ch'ien (*Records of the Grand Historian*, trans. Burton Watson (New York 1961) 2.268–9) who records that a nomadic confederation, the Yueh-chih, conquered Ta-hsia = Baktria after retreating westward as a result of a defeat inflicted on them by another nomadic confederation, the Hsiung-nu.

52   A dedication to the god of the Oxos River. Takht-i Sanguin in the valley of the Amu-Darya River, Soviet Tadjikistan. Miniature stone altar surmounted by a bronze statue of Marsyas playing a double flute. Compared with material from Ai Khanum the lettering suggests a mid second-century date.

*B. A. Likvinkij and I. P. Pitchikjan, *RA* (1981.2) 202–5 with photograph.

An ex-voto[1] | that was dedicated | by Atrosokes | to Oxos.[2]

1   A dedication made in fulfilment of a vow.
2   An interesting example of Greco-Iranian cultural syncretism in Baktria is provided by this miniature Greek-style altar with its Greek inscription dedicated to the god of the Oxos River (Oxos = Iranian Wakhsk) by an Iranian fire priest (Atrosokes = 'He who shines with a sacred fire' or 'is useful to the god of fire').

53   Dedication to the Hindu god Vishnu by Heliodoros, son of Dion. Besnegar, India. Prakrit inscription in Brahmī script of the late second century. Stone pillar topped by an Achaemenid-style capital.

*D. C. Sircar, *Select Inscriptions bearing on Indian History and Civilization* (Calcutta 1965) 1².2. The translation is based on versions prepared by Professors K. Bolle and J. Puhvel.

Tarn, *Bactria* 313–14, 380–1, 388; Narain, *Indo-Greeks* 42, 118–20 with photograph.

This Garuda[1] pillar of the god of gods, Vasudeva,[2] | was caused to be made by Heliodoros, the devotee,[3] | the son of Dion, from Taxila, | who came as Greek ambassador from the court of the Great King
5   ‖ Antialkidas to Bhagabhadra, the son of Kasi,[4] the Savior,[5] | who was then in the fourteenth year of his prosperous reign.[6]

1   The sacred bird of the solar god Vishnu.
2   A form of Vishnu.
3   Heliodoros used the technical term for a worshipper of Vishnu.
4   He has usually been identified with one of the kings of the Sunga dynasty, but Narain, noting that no other Sunga ruler used a matronymic, suggested that Bhagabhadra may instead have been a local ruler near Besnegar.
5   The title *Trātāra* appears to be a translation of the Greek title Soter, Savior.
6   A two-line catechism follows: 'Three immortal precepts when practised lead to heaven – self-restraint, charity, conscientiousness' (translated by Narain).

Chapter 4
MACEDON AND THE GREEKS OF EUROPE

54 Manumission of slaves with paramone restriction. Beroia, Macedonia, either about 280 or 235. Marble stele, late third- or second-century lettering suggesting reinscription of an older document.

M. Andronikos, *Ancient Inscriptions of Beroia* (Thessaloniki 1950) 1 with photograph; *SEG* 12 (1955) 314; *Choix* 30; **ISE* 109.

W. L. Westermann, *The Slave Systems of Greek and Roman Antiquity* (Philadelphia 1955) 35; R. M. Errington, *Ancient Macedonia* (Thessaloniki 1977) 2.115–22.

vv With good fortune. *vv* | In the reign of King Demetrios,[1] seventh and twenti|eth year, month Peritios,[2] in the priesthood of Apolloni|des, the son of Glaukios.[3] *v* Payment for their freedom was made by Kosmas,
5 ‖ Marsyas, Ortyx to Attinas, daughter of Alketas, for themselves *v* | and their wives, Arnion, Glauka, *v* Chlidane, | and for their children, both those now alive and any that may later | be born, and for all their
10 possessions, ea|ch fifty gold (staters);[4] *v* and Spazatis for her‖self and her possessions paid gold (staters), twenty-five of them. | And for them if they remain *vvv* | with Attinas while Attinas lives and do whatever At|tinas orders, and Attinas dies, they may depart | to wherever they
15 wish.[5] And it shall not be possible for Alketas nor Al‖ketas' wife nor the descendants of Alketas nor Lare|ta to seize them or their wives or | their children or {a} Spazatis or to reduce (them) to slav|ery or to take away anything of their possessions | on any *pretext* nor by another on their
20 behalf. But *if* not, ‖ they shall be free and the one attempting to reduce (them) to slavery shall *pay* | for each person one hundred gold (staters)[6] and to the *king v* | another hundred for each person. And if anyone *from their* | possessions takes (something), he shall pay | double the value of
25 that which *he took* from them. [But if] *they do not remain* ‖ and do not do *whatever* Attinas *orders*, they and [their] | wives and their [children], *while* Attinas [lives, for the] one not doing (thus), | his *freedom* shall be invalid [---].[7]

---

1 A date of about 235 was originally proposed on the assumption that the king is Demetrios II and that his twenty-seven years of rule included a long co-regency with his father, Antigonos Gonatas. Errington, however, has argued that this cannot be correct and that, therefore, the king must be Demetrios Poliorketes by whose regnal years Beroia continued to date even after his death.
2 January.

3 Presumably the eponymous magistrate at Beroia.
4 If Alexander staters are meant, the amount is equal to about 600 drachmas (see Glossary).
5 The manumission is of the paramone type in which the slave's freedom is conditional on his continuing to serve his master for a specified period of time, in this case the remainder of Attinas' life.
6 Apparently to the city of Beroia. The absence of any deity in the manumission process is notable.
7 Five fragmentary lines follow that contain allusions to the king and the remains of a list of witnesses.

55 Athens honors Kallias, son of Thymochares, from Sphettos, Ptolemaic governor of Halikarnassos. Athens, 270/69. Marble stele, third-century lettering.

*T. Leslie Shear, Jr, *Hesperia* Supp. 17 (1978) 2–4 with photograph; cf. Plutarch, *Demetrios* 46, *Pyrrhos* 12; Pausanias 1.26.1–3, 29.13; *IG* II² 666–7, 682.

F. Frost, *Anatolian Studies* 21 (1971) 167–72; Habicht, *Untersuchungen* 45–67; M. J. Osborne, *ZPE* 35 (1979) 181–94; H. Heinen, *GGA* 233 (1981) 189–95.

The People (praises) | Kallias, | son of Thymochares, | from Sphettos.¹
5 ‖ In the archonship of Sosistratos (270/69), in the prytany of Pandionis (which is the) sixth, | in which Athenodoros, son of Gorgippos, from Acharnai, was secre|tary, on the eighteenth day of Poseideon, twenty-first day of t|he prytany; main assembly; of the proedroi the motion was put to the vot|e by the chairman, Epichares, son of Pheidostratos, from
10 Erchia, and by his fellow proedroi. ‖ *vv* Resolved by the Boule and the People; *vv* | Euchares, son of Euchares, from Konthyle, introduced the motion. Kallias, | when the People rose against tho|se occupying the city, and it expelled the soldiers from the city,² | but the fort on the
15 ‖ Museion hill was still occupied and the countryside was engaged in war | by the (soldiers) from Piraeus and Demetrios was | marching from the Peloponnesos with an arm|y against the city, Kallias, learning of the danger f|acing the city and having selected a thousand soldiers
20 ‖ from those stationed with him on Andros and having dis|tributed their salary to them and furnished their provisions, came | quickly to the city to help the People, acting in accordance with the | benevolent attitude of King Ptolemaios (I) toward the People. Marching | out the
25 soldiers who were with him ‖ into the countryside, he provided protection for the harvesting of the wheat, making every | effort that as much wheat as possible into the city might be brou|ght.³ And when Demetrios arrived, in|vested the city and laid siege to it, | Kallias, fighting on
30 behalf of the People and making sallies with his sold‖iers and being

wounded, | shrank from no risk on any occasion for the sake of | saving
the People. And King Ptolemai|os, having sent Sostratos[4] to
accomplish what was advantageous | for the city, and Sostratos inviting
35   an embass||y to (meet) him at Piraeus with which he would arrange
terms of | peace on behalf of the city with Demetrios, Kallias yielded i|n
this to the strategoi and the Boule, un|dertook the embassy on behalf
of the city and did everything that was advan|tageous for the city; and
40   he remained in the city with t||he soldiers until the peace was com-
pleted.[5] Then, having sail|ed to King Ptolemaios with the embassies |
sent by the People, he co-operated | in every way and worked for the
advantage of the city. | After the succession to the throne of Ptolemaios
45   (II),[6] the younger || king, Kallias, having visited the city and th|e
strategoi having summoned him and informed him of the | state in
which the city's affairs were and urged him to hast|en on behalf of the
city to King Ptolemaios in or|der that as soon as possible there might
50   be some help for the city (in the form) of gr||ain and money, at his own
expense Kallias sailed | to Kypros and, by there making a strong appeal
to *the king* on | behalf of the city, he obtained for the people fifty talents
of silver[7] | and a gift of twenty thousand medimnoi of wheat, | which
55   was measured out at Delos to those sent by th||e People. When the king
held for the first time the Ptolemaia, th|e sacrifice and the games in
honor of his father,[8] the *People, having voted* | to send a sacred embassy
and having requested [Kall]ias *to agree* | to be the chief envoy and to lead
on behalf of the People the [sacred embassy], | K[al]lias agreed to this
60   request with enthusiasm; and, || having refused the *fifty* minas that *had
been voted* to him by the People for the (expenses) of the office of chief
envoy | and having contributed them to the *People*, he led [the sacred
embassy] | at his own expense well and (in a manner) [worthy] of the
People, [and] | he took care of the sacrifice on behalf of the city and all
the other things, | which were appropriate, in association with the
65   sacred ambassadors. At the time the People was [firs||t][9] about *to hold*
the Panathenaia in honor of the *Foundress*[10] afte|r the city had been
recovered, K[allias], having spoken with the king [abou|t] the tackle
that had to be prepared for the peplos[11] [and] | the king having donated
it to the city, took care *that* | it be prepared [as] well as possible for the
70   goddess; and the sacred ambassadors who with [him] *had been* || *elected*
immediately brought [the tackle] *back here*. And | now, having been
stationed in Halikarnassos by [King Ptol]|emaios, Kallias continues
zealously (aiding) [both the] e|mbassies and the sacred embassies sent
75   by the *People to Ki*|*ng* Ptolemaios,[12] and he *privately on behalf of each* || citizen
coming to him | exerts *every effort* as well as for the *soldiers* [*there*] stat|ioned
with him, considering as most important [the advantage] | and, in
general, the well-being of the city; [---] | with regard to the fatherland

80 Kallias not ever having endured [---] ‖ when the people had been suppressed, but [his own property] | he allowed to be given as a contribution[13] during the oligarchy[14] so that | he did [nothing] against either the laws or the *democrac|y*, which is that of all the Athenians. (Since these things are so), in order, therefore, that all may know *who*
85 *wi|sh* to exert themselves for the city that the people [alway‖s] remembers those conferring benefits on it and returns thanks to each; | with good fortune, it has been resolved by the Boule that the p|roedroi, who shall be chosen by lot to preside at the Assemb|ly according to the law, shall deliberate and refer the resolution | of the Boule to the People
90 that the Boule resolves to ‖ praise Kallias, son of Thymochares, from Sphettos, for his excellence and the g|ood will which he continues to have for the Athenian People, and t|o crown him with a gold wreath in accordance with the law, and to p|roclaim the wreath at the contest for new tragedies at the Greater Dionysia.[15]

1 An honorary decree dating to the 250s for his brother Phaidros (*IG* II² 682) is also extant.
2 The reference is to the battle in spring 286 in which the Athenians led by Olympiodoros defeated the Macedonian garrison in Athens and forced it to take refuge in the fort on the Museion hill.
3 Kallias was aided in this by his brother Phaidros (*IG* II² 682, lines 35–6). Shear dates these events to 286, but Habicht and Osborne have made strong cases for dating them to 287. Ptolemaic military involvement was hitherto unattested.
4 Probably to be identified with Sostratos of Knidos, the architect of the Pharos at Alexandria, who is also attested as a diplomat during the reign of Ptolemaios II (Sextus Empiricus, *Adv. Gramm.* 276).
5 Shear assumes that a general peace involving Ptolemaios I, Pyrrhos, Seleukos I, Lysimachos, Athens and Demetrios is meant. More probable is Habicht's view that the peace was limited to Demetrios, Ptolemaios I and Athens.
6 282.
7 For this embassy which was authorized by a motion introduced by Demochares see Ps.-Plutarch, *Moralia* 851E.
8 Cf. no. 92.
9 The reference is apparently to the Panathenaia of 278 and not that of 282 as would be expected.
10 Athena.
11 Cf. no. 11, lines 14–16.
12 Cf. Frost for a Halikarnassian decree in honor of an Athenian in the service of Ptolemaios II.
13 A euphemism for confiscation.
14 The reference is to the government that ruled Athens during the domination of Demetrios Poliorketes from 294 to 287. Unlike his brother Phaidros, Kallias was in exile during this period.
15 See Glossary *s.v.* Dionysia. Omitted are lines 94 to the end which provide for: (1) the preparation of the wreath, (2) a bronze statue in the Agora, (3) a front seat at all Athenian contests, (4) the required judicial scrutiny of these gifts and (5) the publication of this decree.

56   The Chremonides decree. Athens, first half of the 260s. Four
fragments of a marble stele, partially stoichedon, third-century
lettering.

IG II² 687 plus 686; *SIG*³ 434/5; *Schmitt, *Staatsverträge* 3.476. For photograph see
J. Kirchner, *Imagines Inscriptionum Atticarum*² (Berlin 1948) pl. XXXIV. Cf. Pausanias
3.6.4–8.

Ferguson, *Athens* 175–8; Tarn, *Gonatas* 293–7; Heinen, *Untersuchungen* 95–141; R. Étienne
and M. Pierart, *BCH* 99 (1975) 51–75; B. D. Meritt, *Historia* 26 (1977) 174; Habicht,
Untersuchungen 108–12; Will, *Histoire* 1².219–24; Burstein, 'Arsinoe II' 207–10;
N. Robertson, *Phoenix* 36 (1982) 1–44; F. Walbank, *CAH*² 236–40.

Gods. | In the archonship of Peithodemos,[1] in the (prytany) of
Erechtheis (which is) the second p|rytany; *v* | ninth (day) of Meta-
5   geitnion, ninth (day) of the prytany; ‖ main assembly; the motion was
put to the vote by (the chairman) of the proedroi, Sostratos, son of
K|allistratos, from Erchia, and by his fellow proedroi; *vv* resolved by
the Pe|ople; *vv* Chremonides,[2] son of Eteokles, from Aithalidai, intro-
duced the motion. | Previously the Athenians and Lakedaimonians and
the allies | of each, having established friendship and alliance in com-
10 mon ‖ with each other, struggled often and nobly to|gether against
those attempting to enslave the cities; | (and), thus, they both gained
fame for themselves, and for the other | Greeks they established free-
dom.[3] Now again, crises | of a similar kind having overtaken all Greece
15 because of those ‖ attempting to abolish the laws and the ancestral |
constitutions of each (city), and King Ptolemaios (II), in accordance
with | his ancestors' and his sister's[4] policy, is openly | concerned for
the common freedom of the Greeks;[5] and | the Athenian People, having
20 made an alliance with him, also ‖ voted to urge the other Greeks to
(adopt) this same | policy. Likewise also the Lakedaimonians, being
friends and al|lies of King Ptolemaios, | have voted to be allies with the
Athenian people together with the Eleians | and the Achaians and the
25 Tegeians and the Mantineians an‖d the Orchomenians and the
Phig[alians] and the Kaphyans and the Kretans,[6] as many as are in the
alli|ance of the Lakedaimonians and of Areus[7] and of the other allies, |
[and] they have sent ambassadors (chosen) from the synedroi[8] to the
Peo|ple; and their ambassadors, who are (now) present, have made
known both the zeal, which the L|akedaimonians and Areus and
30 the other allies ‖ have for the People, and (also) the agreement | con-
cerning the alliance which they have brought. (Since these things are
so and) as there is a unity of purpose common | to the Greeks, in order,
therefore, that they shall be vigorous fighters against those who have
now wronged and broken | faith with the cities[9] – they and King

Ptolemaios | and the others – and that in the future, with unity of pur-
35   pose, || they shall save the cities; *vv* with good fortune, it has been
resolved by the P|eople that the friendship and the alliance between the
Athenians and | the Lakedaimonians and the kings of the
Lakedaimonians | and the Eleians and the Achaians and the Tegeians
and the Mantineians an|d the Orchomenians and the Phigalians and
40   the Kaphyans and the Kretans, || as many as are in the alliance of the
Lakedaimonians and [of Areus], | and of the other allies shall be valid
for all [time, (namely, the friendship and alliance) which] | the
ambassadors have brought, and [it] shall be inscribed by the se|cretary
for the prytany on a bronze stele[10] and [set up] on | the Akropolis next
45   to the temple of Athena Po[lias. And there shall be administered || by
the] magistrates to [their] ambassadors, who are present, | [the oath]
concerning the alliance in accordance with [ancestral custom (?); and
those] *who have been selected* | *by vote* by the People to be *ambassadors* [shall
be sent] *to* | *receive* the oaths [from] the [rest of the Greeks; *vvv*] *and there
shall be selected* | *by vote* also [two][11] synedroi [by the People immediately
50   from] || all [Athenians] who, together with Areus [and those the allies] |
send as synedroi, shall consult [about matters of common] ad|vantage;
and there shall be allocated to those appointed (ambassadors) *by the
financial* | *administrators* expense money for the period of the absence *in
the amount which shall be decided* | *by a vote* of the People; and they shall
55   praise [the ephors of the Lakedai]||monians and Areus and the allies
[and they shall crown them] | with a gold wreath in accordance with the
law; and *they shall praise* [also the] *am*|*bassadors*, who came from them, *v*
Theom[---, Lakeda]|imonian, *vv* Argeios, son of Kleinios, Eleia[n *v*,
and they shall crown] *ea*|*ch* of them with a gold wreath in accordance
60   with [the law for the zeal] || and good will which they have both for [the
other allies an|d] for the Athenian People; and [each of them may also
receive another] *bene*|*fit* from the Boule [and the People if they seem] |
worthy of it. And they shall invite them [also to dine as guests at the]
prytanei|*on* tomorrow. And [also this decree] shall be inscribed [by the
65   secretar||y] for the prytany on a [stone] stele [together with the treaty
and] | set up on the Akropolis, and for [the inscribing and erection of] |
the stele the [financial administrators shall allocate (money) equal to
the costs] *incur*|*red. vv* As synedroi the following [were selected by vote;
70   *vacat*] | *vv* Kallippos from Eleusis [---] || *vacat* | Treaty and alliance
[between the Lakedaimonians and the allies of the] Lakedaimonians
with [the Athenians and the allies of the Athen]|ians for all [time.
Each], *being free* | and *autonomous*, shall possess [his own constitution
and be governed in accordance with] | their ancestral customs; and if
75   *anyone* [invades the territory of the Athen]||ians or [tries to abolish] their
laws [or attacks] *the al*|*lies* of the Athenians, the Lakedaimonians shall

come to their aid together with the] *al|lies* of the L[akedaimonians in full force so far as they are able; and if] *any|one invades* [the territory of the Lakedaimonians or] | tries to [abolish] their laws [or attacks the
80   allies of the L]||akedaim[onians, the Athenians shall come to their aid together with the allies of the Athen|ians in full force so far as they are able ---] | [---] | [--- Lakedaimonians] and the allies to the Atheni|[ans and the allies; *vv*] and *the oath shall be sworn* on behalf of the Athenians to
85   the Lakedai||[monians and the (representatives) from each] city by the strategoi and *t|he* [Boule of 500[12] and the] archons and the phylarchs[13] and the *taxi|archs*[14] [and the hipparchs;[15] *vv*] *I swear* by Zeus, Ge, Helios, Ares, Athena and the Are|[ia, Poseidon, Demeter; *vv*] *I shall remain* in the present alliance; | [to those swearing truly], let there be an *abundance*
90   *of good things* and to those falsely, *the op||posite*; [*vv* and on behalf of the Lakedaimonians] the same oath shall be sworn to the Athe[ni]ans by the | [kings and the] *ephors* [and] the members of the Gerousia;[16] and in the same way | [the oath shall be sworn also in the other] cities by their magistrates. *vv* And if | [it shall be decided by the Lakedaimonians and] the allies and the Athenians | [that it would be better to add] or delete
95   [something] with regard to the *alli||ance*, [whatever may be approved by both parties], *it shall be in accordance* with the oath; and the treaty shall be inscribed | [by the cities on stelae] and set up in whichever temple *they w|ish. vv*

1   The date of his archonship is uncertain, 269/8 or 268/7 being possible (cf. Habicht, *Untersuchungen* 116 n. 11 and 120).
2   A friend of the philosopher Zeno (Diogenes Laertius 7.17; cf. *ISE* 21 for the base of a statue in his honor from Athens), he and his brother Glaukon fled to Egypt after the end of the war (Teles 23H; cf. Étienne and Pierart) where Chremonides is later attested as an admiral (Polyaenus 5.18). The war was named after him already in antiquity (Athenaeus 6.250F).
3   The reference is to the Persian Wars; cf. the so-called Themistokles Decree which was inscribed about this time (Fornara, *TDGR* 1.55).
4   Arsinoe II, sister-wife of Ptolemaios II who died in 270.
5   For this aspect of Ptolemaic policy see Étienne and Pierart.
6   The reference is unclear. Schmitt suggests Gortyna, Itanos, Olous, Aptera, Polyrrhenia and Phalasarna.
7   Areus I (309–265). Cf. *SIG*[3] 433 (a statue base from Olympia): '[King P]tolemaios, son of King [Ptolemaios. | Areus, son of Akro]tatos, *king* of the Lakedaimonians, | for [goodwill] toward him [and toward | all the] *Greeks*, to Zeus [O]lym[pi]o[s].'
8   Members of the council of the alliance.
9   The reference is to Antigonos Gonatas (283–239).
10   Only fragments of the stone stele authorized in line 65 have survived.
11   There seems to be space in line 69 for only two names.
12   See Glossary.
13   Commanders of the tribal cavalry units. In the third century their number varied between ten and twelve depending on the number of tribes.
14   Commanders of the tribal infantry units, parallel to the Phylarchs and like them

varying in the third century between ten and twelve depending on the number of
the tribes.
15   Three in number. One commanded the cavalry on Lemnos and each of the other
two was overall commander of one half of the tribal cavalry units.
16   The Council at Sparta. It consisted of 30 members (the two kings and 28 others
elected from Spartan citizens over the age of 60) who served for life and, as in other
Greek cities, its chief duty was to prepare the agenda for the Spartan assembly.

57   An Athenian patriot: the life of Philochoros.

FGrHist 328T1 = *Suda s.v. Philochoros.*

L. Pearson, *The Local Historians of Attica* (Philadelphia 1942) 105–36; F. Jacoby, *FGrHist*,
Supplement 1.221–55.

Philochoros.[1] Son of Kyknos, an Athenian, diviner and inspector of
victims. His wife was Archestrate. Philochoros flourished at the same
time as Eratosthenes,[2] so that while young, Eratosthenes overlapped
the elder.[3] He was executed, having been arrested by Antigonos (II)
because he was accused of having favored the kingdom of Ptolemaios
(II).[4] He wrote *Atthis* in 17 books. It contained the deeds of the
Athenians and their kings and archons until Antiochos the
+ TELEYTAIOS surnamed the god+.[5]

1   About 340–about 261.
2   About 275–194.
3   Reading the accusative as proposed by Siebelis (cf. *FGrHist* apparatus *ad loc.*).
Jacoby brackets the name.
4   Presumably Philochoros was executed for his role in the Chremonidean War. If his
Atthis reached the accession of Antiochos II, his death would have to be dated after
the end of the war.
5   Antiochos II Theos (the God; 261–246) if the *Suda*'s inclusion of his epithet is
correct, and an allusion to his predecessor is not concealed in the corrupt form
TELEYTAIOS. A list of Philochoros' other lost works follows.

58   The end of the Chremonidean War: Athens under Macedonian rule. 262/1.

*Apollodorus, *FGrHist* 244F44; cf. Pausanias 3.6.6.

Bengtson, *Strategie* 2.372–7; Heinen, *Untersuchungen* 180–9; F. Walbank *CAH*[2] 240–1.

And Apollo[do]rus [places] the *subjugation* of the city [in the archonship
of Antip]ater (262/1), the (archon) before Arrhenid[es] (261/0). A
garrison [then] *was introduced*, (he says), [into] the Museion [by]

Antigonos (II) [and the] magistracies *were suppressed*[1] and everything *was entrusted* to one person *to counsel*[2] [---].

1 The appointment of Demetrios, the grandson of Demetrios of Phaleron, by Antigonos to the office of thesmothetes (see Glossary) is attested by Athenaeus (4.167F).
2 The reference is to the appointment of an epistates (see Glossary), possibly the Demetrios mentioned in n. 1 if his office of thesmothetes was an extraordinary post and not one of the regular six thesmothetai. Direct rule of Athens lasted until 256/5 or 255/4 when 'Antigonos gave freedom back to the Athenians' (Eusebius, *Chronicle* 2.120 (Schoene)), that is, he removed the garrison from the Museion.

59 Athens honors Zeno, the founder of Stoicism. Athens, 261/0.

Diogenes Laertius, *Lives of the Philosophers* 7.10–12.

Tarn, *Gonatas* 31–6, 309–10; Will, *Histoire* 1².343.

(10) In the archonship of Arrhenides, in the fifth prytany (which is that) of Akamantis, twenty-first day of Maimakterion, twenty-third day of the prytany, main assembly, the motion was put to the vote (by the chairman) of the proedroi, Hippon, son of Kratistoteles, from Xupetaion, and his fellow proedroi. Thrason,[1] son of Thrason, from Anakaia, introduced the motion. Since Zeno,[2] son of Mnaseas, from Kition, having been involved with philosophy for many years in the city, both in other ways continued to be a good man and, by urging those young men who entered into association with him toward excellence and self-control, he stimulated them toward the very best things, having offered to all as an example his own life which was in agreement with the theories he professed; (11) with good fortune, it has been resolved by the People that it praise Zeno, son of Mnaseas, from Kition, and crown him with a gold wreath[3] in accordance with the law for his excellence and self-control, and that it build for him a tomb in the Kerameikos at public expense. For the manufacture of the wreath and the construction of the tomb the People shall immediately select by vote five men from the Athenians who shall be responsible. The secretary of the People shall inscribe <this> decree on two <stone> stelae, and he shall be allowed to place one of them in the Academy and one in the Lyceum. The financial administrator shall allocate the expense incurred for these stelae in order that all may know that the Athenian people honors good men both in their lifetimes and after their deaths. (12) For the construction (of the tomb) there were selected by vote Thrason from Anakaia, Philokles from Piraeus, Medon from Acharnai, Smikythos from Sypalettos, [Dion from Paiania].

1 According to Diogenes Laertius (7.15), Thrason acted on the instructions of
   Antigonos Gonatas, who had been a student of Zeno's, when he introduced this
   decree.
2 About 333/2–261/0.
3 Because of the oddity of a wreath being awarded to a dead man, Tarn suggested that
   this text represents a conflation of two decrees, one honoring Zeno during his
   lifetime and a second providing for his public funeral.

60 Honors for Herakleitos, son of Asklepiades, from Athmonea. Athens, 258 or 254 or 250. Marble stele, stoichedon.

*IG II² 677; *SIG*³ 401.

Tarn, *Gonatas* 327–8; Bengtson, *Strategie* 2.349–50, 379–81; N. M. Kontoleon, *Akte des IV
Internationalen Kongresses für griechische und lateinische Epigraphik* (Vienna 1964) 196–7;
Habicht, *Untersuchungen* 71; Will, *Histoire* 1².316–18.

[--- and] the People, [having revived | the] sacrifice and [the contests of
the Pa]nathenai|a,¹ he both *arranged excellently* the stadion race and
5   dedi|cated to Athena [Nike]² *stelae*³ containing m‖emorials of the deeds
done [by the king] against th|e barbarians for the salvation of the
Greeks.⁴ | *vv* In order, therefore, that the Boule and the People may
appear to main|tain gratitude [for their benefactors], *v* with good
10   for|tune, it has been resolved by the Boule that they praise Herakl‖eitos,
son of Asklepiades, from Athmonea,⁵ and crown (him) with a g|old
wreath for his reverence toward the g|ods and the good will and zeal
which *he continues* to have | [for] both [King Antigonos (II) and] the
Boul|e [and the] Athenian people.⁶

1 The first Panathenaia after the end of the Chremonidean War, therefore, that of
   either 258, 254 or 250.
2 'Victory'.
3 Dittenberger and Kirchner: '[pictur]es'. Kontoleon: '[stel]ai'.
4 The reference is to Antigonos Gonatas' victory over the Kelts at Lysimacheia in 277
   (Justin 25.2.1–7; Diogenes Laertius 2.141).
5 Also extant is an inscription in his honor from the Athenian kleruchs on Salamis
   dating to the end of the revolt of Alexander of Corinth (253/2) referring to his
   recent appointment by Antigonos Gonatas as 'strategos for the Piraeus and the
   other places administered with the Piraeus' (*SIG*³ 454, lines 8–9), that is, the remaining Antigonid possessions in Greece. Previously he may have been governor of
   Salamis.
6 Omitted are lines 15 to the end which provide for: (1) the proclamation and manufacture of the wreath and (2) the inscription of this decree.

61   Decree of the isoteleis stationed at Rhamnous in honor of the strategos, Apollodoros, son of Apollodoros. Rhamnous, Attika, 256/5 (?). Marble stele.

*ISE 22.

Bengtson, *Strategie* 2.374–81; L. Robert, *RPhil.* 70 (1944) 17–18; J. Pouilloux, *La forteresse de Rhamnonte* (Paris 1954) 118–20; Habicht, *Untersuchungen* 123; D. Whitehead, *The Ideology of the Athenian Metic* (Cambridge 1977) 11–13.

[Resolved] by the *isoteleis* stationed at Rhamnous,[1] Teisandros introduced the motion. *Sin|ce* [Apollodoros], both having been appointed strategos by King Antigonos (II) and | having been elected [by the People] for the coastal district[2] for the year | [in which Euboul]o[s] was

5   archon,[3] has taken care well and beneficially both of the *re||st* [of the whole garrison] and of the isoteleis in order that each as fairly as possible and equally | [performed his public duties], and *he took care* also for the scrutiny of the right of isoteleia in order that | [as quickly as possible] the gift to those (stationed) in Rhamnous might be confirmed in accordance with the | *intention* of the [king], and he also continues furnishing services in other matters *pub|licly* [and privately] *to each*; in

10   order, therefore, that all may know that also the isoteleis || honor those *who are zealous* both for King Antigonos and for themselves, with good | fortune, it has been resolved by those isoteleis stationed at Rhamnous that they praise the | *strategos* Apollodoros, son of Apollodoros, from Otrynys, and crown him with a gold | wreath in accordance with the law for his excellence and justice toward King | Antigonos and themselves

15   and the Athenian people, and that they inscribe || [this] decree on a stone stele and set it up in the shrine of Dionysos.[4]

1   Isoteleis were privileged metics, i.e. legally authorized resident aliens, exempted from paying the metic tax (the metoikon) and other similar levies. The status was conferred during Apollodoros' generalship at the instance of Antigonos Gonatas on the mercenaries who composed part of the garrison of the fort at Rhamnous, one of the forts occupied by the Macedonians after the end of the Chremonidean War.

2   One of several Athenian generalships with specialized functions attested during the Hellenistic period. This particular one is first documented in the third century and probably was in charge of the coastal district from Sounion to Rhamnous. In this context election by the People clearly involved only ratification of Antigonos' appointment.

3   Usually dated to 256/5 although Habicht notes that only its belonging to the period 260–245 is certain. Moretti records as possible alternate restorations for the archon [Kydenor] = 244/3 and [Antiphon] = 259/8.

4   Dionysos Lenaios. Omitted are lines 16 to the end which provide for: (1) the preparation of the stele and (2) praise for Apollodoros' assistants at Rhamnous.

62   Chios recognizes the Delphic Soteria as reorganized by the Aitolian League. Delphi, 246/5. Marble stele.

SIG[3] 402; **I. Delphi* 3.3.215.

Tarn, *Gonatas* 158–9; L. Robert, *BCH* 57 (1933) 536–7; Flacelière, *Aitoliens* 133–77; B. D. Meritt, *Studies in Honor of Harry Caplan* (Ithaca 1966) 26–31; Georges Nachtergael, *Les Galates en Grèce et les Sôteria de Delphes* (Brussels 1977) 209–380; Habicht, *Untersuchungen* 133–41; F. Walbank, *CAH*[2] 248.

[Resolved by the People], *the polemarch*[1] for the month Melesippos, son of Philo[---, and the exetastes[2] | for the month Apo]llonides, son of Aggeliskos, introduced the motion. The Aitolians, *who are kinsmen* [and ancestral friends] | of the People, making known their [reverence] toward the *gods* [and] | having sent [a decree and] *the sacred envoys,*[3]

5   Kleon and Herakon and [Sotion, have announ‖ced the] festival of the Soteria,[4] which they are celebrating as a memorial [of the deliverance of the Greeks] | and of the victory which was achieved over the barbarians [who marched again|st] the sanctuary of Apollo, which is common to the Greeks, and [against the Greeks].[5] | A letter concerning these matters has also been sent by the League of the Aitolians [and the strategos, Charix]enos,[6] to the People | that we should recognize the

10   contests, that in music *as equivalent to the Pythian* [and] *that in ath‖letics* and the equestrian as equivalent to the Nemean both as regards the ages and the honors [just as they also] | have voted. (Since these things are so), in order, therefore, that the People may appear [as increasing the] honors of the gods and *being mind|ful* both of the kinship and the friendship existing between it and the [Aitolians, with good] *for|tune*, it has been resolved by the People that it accept the proclamation and (recognize) the *festival* [of the Soteria which] | the Aitolians have established in honor of the sanctuary of Apollo at Delphi [and of the Greeks']

15   ‖ deliverance as wreathed[7] just as the League of Aitolians has voted, [the (contest) in music] *as equivalent* | *to the Pythian*, and that in athletics and the equestrian as equivalent to the Nemean both as regards the ages and [the honors; and that there shall be] | also (the same honors) for those citizens competing and being victorious in the contests of the S[oteria as also] | have been specified in the law for those who have been victorious in those of the Pythia and Nemea; and that it praise [also the League of the Aito]|lians and crown it with a gold wreath for

20   its excellence and its *reverence* [toward the gods] ‖ and its bravery against the barbarians. Further, in order that all may know [the honors which have been granted], | the sacred herald shall make in the theatre when the *boys'* [choruses are about] *to com|pete* this proclamation: 'The People of the Chians crowns the League of the Aito[lians with a gold wreath] |

for its excellence and its reverence toward the gods; and it has voted
[also to recognize the contests] | which the Aitolians are holding, that
in music as equivalent to the Pythian and that in *athletics* [and the
25   equestrian] *as equival‖ent to the Nemean* both as regards the ages and the
honors'. The *agonothetes shall be responsible* for the proclamation; | and this
decree shall be inscribed on a stone stele and *erected* [in the sanctuary of
Apol]‖lo at Delphi by the first sacred envoys to sail; and *there shall be
elected* [immediately] three *sacred | envoys* from all the Chians, when this
decree has been voted. [In the future] | the appointment of the sacred
envoys shall take place every fifth year, when also [the Aitolians] *make
30   the proclama‖tion;*[8] and there shall be given to those appointed for the
sacrifice [four (?) hundred drachmas, and for] | travel expenses what-
ever amount the People decides; and the costs for [the inscribing of the
decree and] | the stele shall be paid by those [administering] the
accounts [just as they are instructed by the polemarchs] | and the
exetastai;[9] and they shall also give for [the wreath --- and send with the
35   sacred envoys] | friendship gifts --- ‖ --- | --- | --- |[10] [And this decree]
concerns defense.[11] *Expense money* was assigned *to each* [sacred envoy] *in
the amount of thirty* [drachmas]. | As sacred envoys there were selected
40   Mikkos, son of Hermias, Oineus, son of Phesinos, [---], ‖ son of
Aristophon.

1   'War archon'.
2   'Auditor', an official charged with examining the financial transactions of magis-
    trates. Restored by Robert.
3   Restored by M. Holleaux in Robert.
4   The Aitolian League reorganized what had probably been an annual Delphic
    Soteria as a penteteric festival modeled after the Nemea most likely in 246/5. The
    date is based on the Athenian decree (*IG* II[2] 680) recognizing the festival which
    was passed during the archonship of Polyeuktos (246/5).
5   The reference is to the Keltic invasion of Greece in the winter of 279/8.
6   The chief magistrate of the Aitolian League. Charixenos is probably to be
    identified with the strategos who campaigned in Lakonia about 240 (cf. Walbank,
    Commentary 1.483).
7   Cf. no. 30 n. 3.
8   Restored by Nachtergael. *SIG*[3] 402 and *I. Delphi* 3.3.213 both restore: 'When [those
    for the Olympia] *are chosen*'.
9   Restored by Robert.
10 Three lines (35–7) too fragmentary for translation follow.
11 This clause allows the decree to be treated as an urgent measure.

63   Dedication by Antigonos Doson to Apollo in commemoration of the battle of Sellasia. Delos, about 222. Marble plaque from a statue base, Hellenistic lettering.

M. Holleaux, *BCH* 31 (1907) 94–100 with photograph; **SIG*³ 518; cf. Polybius 2.65–70; Plutarch, *Agis and Cleomenes* 27–30.

Walbank, *Philip V* 4–15; M. T. Piraino, *Antigono Dosone Re di Macedonia* (Palermo 1953) 326–44; W. G. Forrest, *A History of Sparta 950–192 B.C.* (London 1968) 146–8; B. Shirmon, *Late Sparta, Arethusa* Monograph 3 (1972) 45–52; Will, *Histoire* 1².371–401; F. Walbank, *CAH*² 467–73.

King Antigo[nos,[1] son of King] | Demetrios,[2] and [the Macedonians][3] | and the allies [from the] | *battle* [near] Sellasia,[4] to Apollo.

1 Antigonos III Doson (229–221).
2 Demetrios II (239–229).
3 The Macedonians organized as a league (*koinon*).
4 July 222. The allies were the members of Antigonos' new Hellenic League: the Achaian League, Thessaly, Epiros, Akarnania, Boiotia and Phokis. Walbank notes that the separate mention of the Macedonians indicates that, as in the earlier and similar leagues of Philippos II and Demetrios Poliorketes, a clear distinction was maintained between the allies and the Macedonians, who were represented by their king.

64   Lamia honors the poetess Aristodama of Smyrna. Lamia, 218/17.

**SIG*³ 532.

G. Daux, *BCH* 46 (1922) 445–8; S. B. Pomeroy, *AJAH* 2 (1977) 54–5.

Of the Aitolians | the strategos is Hagetas, a citizen of Kallion.[1] With good fortune. Resolved [by the city] | of the Lamians. Since Aristo[d]ama, daughter of Amyntas,[2] a citizen of Smyrna in Io[nia], | epic poetess, *while she was in* our city, gave several [public recitations]
5 || of her poems in which the nation | of the Aitolians [and] the People's ancestors were worthily commemorated | and since the performance was done with great enthusiasm, *she shall be a proxenos*[3] | of the city and a benefactress, and she shall be given citizenship and the right to possess land and [a house] | and the right of pasture and inviolability and
10   security on land and *sea* || in war and *peace* for herself and her descendants and their property for *all* | time together with all other privileges that are given to other proxenoi and benefactors. | And Diony[sios], her brother,[‡] and his descendants shall have the rights of

a proxenos, | citizenship, [inviolability]. The archons are [Py]thon,
Neon, Antigenes, the *strateg|os* is Epi[gen]es, the Hipparch is Kylon.
15   The guarantor for the *proxeny* ‖ is Py[tho]n, son of [Ath]anios.

1   218/17 (cf. Polybius 5.91.1).
2   *SEG* 2 (1925) 263 reveals that she was also awarded a proxeny and a fee of 100
    drachmas by the city of Chalaios.
3   See Glossary.
4   Her brother probably traveled with her as her guardian (*kyrios*).

65   A letter of King Philippos V of Macedonia to Larisa. Larisa 215 or 214. Marble stele.

IG IX 2.577 with photograph; **SIG*³ 543, lines 26–39.

Walbank, *Philip V* 35, 69 n. 6 and 296–9; E. T. Salmon, *Roman Colonization under the Republic* (London 1969) 69; E. Gruen, *Ancient Macedonian Studies in Honor of Charles F. Edson* (Thessaloniki 1981) 170–1.

King Philippos (V) to the tagoi[1] and the city of the Larisaians, greeting.
I have learned that those who had been enrolled as citizens in accord-
ance | with my letter and your decree[2] and listed on the stelae[3] have
been removed. If, | indeed, this has happened, those who advised you
have mistaken both the advantage of their fatherland | and my judge-
ment. That it would be the best of all things if, as many as possible
30   being members of the citizen-body, ‖ the city were strong and the land
not, as now, disgracefully left barren, I think not one of you would
dis|agree. It is also possible to observe others employing similar
enfranchisements, among whom are also the Rom|ans, who receiving
into their citizen-body even their slaves when they free them, *giv|ing
them even a share* in the offices,[4] have by such means not only
strengthened their country but also sent out colonies (a)lmost | [to]
35   *seventy* places.[5] But now, however, I urge you impartially to consider ‖
[the] matter, and to restore those who were chosen by the citizens to
the citizenship; and if | [some] have done something detrimental to the
kingdom or the city or for some other reason are not worthy | *to share* the
stele, concerning these persons, arrange a postponement until I, when
I have returned from the (present) | *campaign*, shall hold a hearing.
Make a public declaration, however, to those who are intending to
accuse these persons in order that they may not appear | to be doing
this from *prejudice*. Year 7, Gorpaios 13.[6]

1   Not the chief magistrates of the Thessalian League but rather the five executive
    officials of Larisa.

2   This letter is preceded on the stele by a letter of King Philippos (about late summer
     220 or 219) recommending that Larisa make good losses to its citizen-body caused
     by war by a policy of liberal enfranchisement of new citizens and a decree of Larisa
     implementing the king's 'suggestion'.
3   A decree of Larisa follows ordering their restoration and the erection of the stelae,
     one in the sanctuary of Apollo and another on the akropolis of Larisa.
4   This is incorrect. A freedman could vote, but only his son could hold office.
5   A considerable exaggeration. In 214 only thirty Latin and ten citizen colonies are
     known to have been founded.
6   August 215 or 214 depending on whether the accession of Philippos V is dated to
     221 or 220. If the letter dates from 215, the campaign cannot be identified; if 214,
     then Philippos' Aous campaign (Livy 24.40) is possible.

66   Regulations for the Macedonian army on campaign.

Amphipolis, 221–179. Two large marble blocks with remains of an
inscription that originally contained at least three columns of text,
lettering of the last quarter of the third or early second century.

P. Roussel, *RA*⁶ 3 (1934) 39–47 with photograph; M. Feyel, *RA*⁶ 6 (1935) 29–68 with
photograph; **ISE* 114.

Walbank, *Philip V* 289–94; Rostovtzeff, *SEHHW* 3.1470 n. 37; Will, *Histoire* 2.209;
J. Hornblower, *Hieronymus of Cardia* (Oxford 1981) 143–4.

Block A, col. 1

[---] (the sentinels ?) are to give no answer to those making the rounds
but silently | to reveal themselves (and) to remain on their feet. |
5   Making Rounds. | In each strategia[1] rounds are to be made in turn ‖ by
the tetrarchs[2] without lights. Anyone sitting down or *sl|eeping* on guard
duty is to be fined by the tetrarchs for each | infraction one drachma,
and the secretaries are to exact the *fi|ne* [---]

Block B, col. 1

[---] those not *bearing* the weapons appropriate to them | are to be fined
according to the regulations: for the kotthybos,[3] | two obols; for the
helmet, the same; for the sarissa, three obols; for the sw|ord, the same;
5   for the greaves, two obols; for the shield, a dra‖chma. | In the case of
officers, for the aforementioned weapons | (the fine is) double and for
the corselet, two drachmas and for the breastplate, a drachma. | The
fines are to be collected by the secretaries and the *chief adju|tants* after
10   they inform the king of those guilty of breaches of discipline. ‖
Regulation Concerning Booty. | [If] anyone brings booty to the camp,
they | are to be met by [the] strategoi accompanied by the speirarchs,[4]

tetrarchs | [and] the other officers, and with them | a *sufficient number of*
15 *adjutants* three stades before the camp. ‖ *These are not to yield* (the booty)
to those who seized it, but if there should *oc|cur such* a breach of disci-
pline, the determined value (of the booty) is to be paid by the | [com-
manders], speirarchs, tetrarchs and the chief adjutants | [for what
each] *owes* [---].[5]

Block A, col. 2

[--- If they do not indicate to the] *ki|ng* those guilty of breaches of disci-
pline, they are to be fined three twelfths of a drachma[6] | which are to be
paid to the hypaspists[7] if these anti|cipate them in turning in the list of
5   those guilty of breaches of discipline. ‖ Concerning the Construction of
Quarters. | When they have completed the palisade for the king | and
the other tents have been pitched and a space has been made,[8] | they
are immediately to prepare the bivouac for the hypaspists | [---].

Block B, col. 2

[---][9] Concerning Foraging. | If someone [conducts a foraging
expedition in enemy territory, a reward for information (?) (against
him)] | is to be promised and paid. [--- If someone] | burns grain or [cuts
5   down] vines [or] ‖ commits [some other] *disorderly act*, a reward for
information [is to be promised by the strategoi (?) ---].

Block A, col. 3

[---] *Strategia* [---] | *one who has recei|ved* a wreath is to receive a double
share of the [b|ooty], but nothing is to be given to the cheiristes.[10] The
5   *decision is to be made* | by the king's friends. ‖ *Passwords.* | They are also to
receive the [password . . . whenever] | they close the passages through
the *palisade* [---].

Although the lettering indicates that these regulations were in force during the reign
of Philippos V (221–179), it cannot be determined if he or an earlier king was their
author.
1   The largest Macedonian tactical military unit.
2   The officer in charge of a unit consisting of four phalanx files, sixty-four men.
3   This term is otherwise unattested. A connection has been suggested with the
    kossymbos, an apron-like protector for the lower ventral region.
4   The officers in charge of a speira, a military unit of unknown size intermediate
    between a strategia and a tetrarchia. The officers, therefore, are listed in rank
    order.
5   Five lines too fragmentary to translate follow.

6   The exact amount is uncertain. Moretti suggested three twelfths of a drachma,
     Roussel two drachmas.
7   The context suggests that these are not the soldiers of the phalanx but the mem-
     bers of the royal bodyguard who also function as camp police.
8   The reference is to the preparation of the royal compound in the center of the
     camp and of an open space separating it from the quarters of the rest of the troops.
9   Thirteen lines too fragmentary for translation precede the heading for the regu-
     lations governing foraging.
10 The cheiristes' duties are unknown but are probably connected with the distri-
     bution of booty.

67   Biographical inscription honoring Eurykleides, son of Mikion, from Kephisia, for a career of distinguished service to Athens. Piraeus, about 215. Marble stele, non-stoichedon, late third-century lettering.

IG II² 834; *SIG³ 497 with corrections by Habicht, Studien 82–9. For photograph see
S. Dow, AJA 40 (1936) 58; cf. Polybius 5.106.6–8.

Ferguson, Athens 205–7, 237–77; P. MacKendrick, The Athenian Aristocracy 399 to 31 B.C.
(Cambridge, Mass. 1969) 39–43; C. Mossé, Athens in Decline (London 1973) 132–7; Will,
Histoire 1².363.

[--- having become strategos] | of the *hoplites*[1] [---] | (the) duty [and] the
[office of treasurer of] the *military fund he ad|ministered* through his son,[2]
and he himself advanced also *no|t* a little money; and as agonothetes,[3]
5   having heeded (the appeal of the People ?), *he spe||nt* seven talents; and
again having entrusted his son [with this] | responsibility and [having
performed] his agonothesia well, | he advanced not a little money; and
[as the land during] | the wars[4] had lain fallow and been unsown, *he was*
10   *the* [cause] | of its being worked and sown, *having provided* [money]; || and
he restored freedom [to the city] *together wi|th* his brother Mikion after
those *who returned the* [Pi]|raeus, and for the wreath for the *soldiers,* [who]
| had restored with Diogenes [the forts],[5] | he provided *money,* and he
15   dredged the harbors, [and the walls of the] || city and of the Piraeus *he
repaired* [with Mikion, his] | brother, *and he attached* Greek cities [and
kings[6] (to Athens)]; | and with regard to all who [owed] money to the
People, | *he devised* how [their] obligations might be settled [---], *having
20   pro|vided* money and the Ath[en(?) --- || ---]; *he prepared* [--- for the] | People
useful things; *he attached* [---] | and he introduced also *laws* [advan-
tageous to the People]; and *he ma|de* both the spectacles [for the gods as
fine as possible and an additional] | contest [in arms] he introduced [as
25   a memorial of freedom]; || and in addition *he exalted the People* [by estab-
lishing for the gods temples and *pre|cincts*[7] and *by erecting* a stoa, [(thus)
demonstrating in every way] | his [zeal] for all A[thenians ---].

1   Restoration proposed by Habicht. This office and those following post-date
     Eurykleides' archonship in 240/39, which along with the rest of his early career was
     probably dealt with in the lost beginning of the inscription.
2   Eurykleides himself had held this office (*SIG*³ 491, lines 1–3) in the archonship of
     Diomedon (244/3). This reference, however, is most likely to be dated about 220
     since his son, Mikion, who is known to have been politically active in the 190s, is
     unlikely to have been eligible for it earlier than the late 220s.
3   See Glossary.
4   Probably the Demetrian War of the 230s (cf. Plutarch, *Aratus* 34).
5   In 229, Diogenes, commander of the Macedonian garrison in Piraeus, surrendered
     Piraeus, Salamis and Sounion for 150 talents, twenty of which were contributed by
     Aratos in an unsuccessful attempt to induce Athens to join the Achaian League
     (Plutarch, *Aratus* 34.4, Pausanias 2.8.5). Because of the reference to the liberation of
     Athens in 229, this inscription used to be dated about 229, but the mention of offices
     held and buildings dedicated after that date points to a date between 229 and the
     murder of Eurykleides and Mikion in 197, supposedly on the orders of Philippos V
     (Polybius 5.106.6–8, Pausanias 2.9.4). A date about 215 is likely since the cutter
     responsible for the inscription appears to have been most active between 221 and
     210.
6   Restored by Habicht. Ptolemaios III and Ptolemaios IV may be meant. Polybius is
     critical of the brothers' policy of neutrality in Greek affairs.
7   Wilamowitz suggested the shrine of the People and Charites (*IG* II² 4676), but
     Eurykleides' name has to be restored. Whatever is intended, the structures clearly
     were completed after 229.

68   Istria honors Agathokles, son of Antiphilos. Istria. Stele. Lettering suggests a late third- or early second-century date.

S. Lambrino, *Revue des Études Romaines* 5–6 (1960) 180–217; **Nouveau Choix* 6.

H. Bengtson, *Historia* 11 (1962) 21–7; D. M. Pippidi, *Scythia Minora* (Bucharest 1975)
31–55.

Resolved by the Boule and the People. The epimenios[1] is Di|[on]ysios,
son of Bianor. Apollonios, the son of Kleombrotos, intro|duced the
motion. Since Agathokles, the son of Antiphilos, being the son of a
father who was a bene|factor, continues to be a good and noble man

5   with regard to the ci||ty and its citizens, serving enthusiastically | in all
the city's crises both in magistracies and | on special commissions; and
in meetings he continues to say and to do | always what is best for the
People. When the [city] | was in turmoil, and many Thracians[2] were

10   raiding || both the countryside and the *city*, and the harvest was |
imminent, and the citizens were in distress, he, *after having been elec|ted*
commander of the archers, took with him mercenary soldiers and *stood
gu|ard* in the countryside (and thus) made it possible for the citizens to
gather in the harvest | safely. And when the Thracians of Z[oltes[3]

15 || with] a large force *arrived* [in] | *Skythia[4] (and) attacked the Greek cities subject*

to[5] *Ki|ng* Rhemaxos,[6] he, having been elected ambassador, *traveled*
[through] | enemy territory, passing through (the lands of) many
peoples, *shirking no risk,* | and persuaded the barbarians *not only not to*
20   *har‖ass* our city but also, (with regard to) [the flocks which] *previously* |
had been carried off by raiders subject to King Zoltes, | to seek them
out and [to return] all of them; *and with* | them he urged that [---] | that
the city would pay five [talents] for them to make an agreement with
25   the *ci‖ty* about its livelihood. Later, when they *entered* the *country|side* and
were besieging Bizone and ravaging | the countryside and our harvest
was imminent, he, having been elected | ambassador and traveled to
30   their camp | with instructions from the citizens ‖ to ransom by any
means the countryside and the crops, persuaded | Zoltes and his
Thracians, for the sum of six hundred gold (staters), not to | enter the
countryside or approach the city. In this way [the] | citizens obtained
possession of all the crops in the countryside. *Ag|ain* having been
35   elected *ambassador* to Thrace *and* [to] ‖ its ruler Z[ol]te[s], *he renewed* the
ex|isting agreements and *treaties* [with] them, and, *observ|ing* a large
raiding party being organized, *he in|formed* Zoltes [and], when *he returned,*
40   he also revealed to the *citi|zens* how their plot *was foiled.* ‖ But when the
Thracians *violated their oaths* and *agreements* | [and] *made repeated raids,* he,
having been elected by the [Peo|ple] *strategos with full power* for the
countryside, took | *volunteer* soldiers from [both] the citizens and | the
barbarians[7] *who had fled* for refuge [to the] city (and) protected the
45   countryside ‖ and the flocks [and] crops until the crossing (of the river)
by | *King* Rhe[maxos]. But the king, having crossed to the [other | side
(of the river)][8] and not left behind a guard *because of fear* but having sent |
messengers to demand tribute although the countryside | was under
50   attack, he, *having been elected* ambassador and having traveled ‖ *by* boat,
persuaded *King* Rhemaxos to give for *protec|tion* one hundred cavalry-
men. But when a strong Thracian attack *fell* | on the guards and they
withdrew | [to the] other side because of *fear* and left the countryside
unprotected, he, *having been elec|ted* ambassador to the king's *son,*
55   Phrad[mon,[9] ‖ persuaded] him to give a *guard* of six hundred *cavalrymen;*
[and] *these,* | *having gained control* of the camp, *defeated* | [their king, Zo]ltes,
and [---] of Thracians [---].

1   Presiding officer of the assembly for a month.
2   Apparently an independent band of raiders and not the subjects of Zoltes.
3   Described as king in line 21 and chief in line 35, he appears to have been the chief
    of a group of Thracians from somewhere south of the Dobrudja since there is no
    indication that he had to cross the Danube to enter the area.
4   The Dobrudja, known as Skythia Minor.
5   Pippidi notes that the restoration, although too large for the space, is probably
    correct as to sense.

6 A Getic or Skythian ruler whose territories lay across the Danube (cf. lines 45–6) in Wallachia or Bessarabia, but whose authority was recognized by an unknown number of Greek cities of the west coast of the Black Sea that paid him tribute in return for, as the inscription reveals, his not always effective protection against the raids and demands of other native chieftains. For the similar problems of Byzantion see Polybius 4.45.2.

7 Pippidi identifies these with dependent native peasants resident in Istria's territory similar to the *laoi* of Asia Minor.

8 The Danube.

9 The restoration of the name is speculative.

69   Honors for Satyros, son of Polemarchos, overseer of the sanctuary and city of Delphi for the Aitolian League. Delphi, 200/ 199. Two fragments of a limestone base, late third- or early second-century lettering.

P. Roussel, *BCH* 50 (1926) 124–34; *I. Delphi* 451.

Daux, *Delphes* 182; Flacelière, *Aitoliens* 333–5; Sherk, *RDGE* 210–21.

Gods. | The archon is Mant[ias (200/199), the councillors are ---], Aristarchos, Kleon. Resolved | by the city of the De[lphians in full assembly] with lawful votes. Since | Satyros, son of Pole[marchos, from Agrinion, both in] former times continued to be favorably inclined
5   ‖ toward the *city* [and now, having been appointed] by the Aitolians overseer | of both the sanctuary and [the city,¹ he piously and] honorably maintained the sanctuary and the city; | and [he dealt with] the [citizens] fairly and reasonably; and in addition, the | [concord] existing [between] *themselves* and the Aitolians | he helped to strengthen further; [and in dealing with those] *disputes* that both the Delphians and those
10   dwelling in Delphi ‖ [entrusted to him in accordance with the] agreement,² he resolved them all | fairly and [reasonably; it has been resolved that (the city)] *praise* Satyros, son of Polemarchos, from Agrinion, |*for* his piety [and his beneficence] *toward* [the] sanctuary and the city; and that he [be] | proxenos³ [of the city together with his descendants]; and that he and his descendants *have* the right of consultation (of the oracle), | *inviolability, exemption from levies,* [a front seat at]
15   *all* contests which the city holds and such other things ‖ *also* (as have been given) *to the other* [proxenoi and] *benefactors* of the sanctuary and the city. There has also been granted | *to him and* [his descendants the right of pasture in the territory] of Delphi for all time.

1 Five such overseers are known, all dating to the period *c.* 205–199.
2 The reference is to Aitolians and their allies, primarily Ozolian Lokrians, who were

settled in Delphi with special privileges. A letter to the Delphians from M' Acilius
Glabrio (*RDGE* 37) confirms their eviction from Delphi after the end of Aitolian
domination in 191. The mention of an agreement between Delphi and the Aitolian
League and the fact that Satyros was an overseer and not a strategos suggests that
officially Delphi was an autonomous ally and not a member of the Aitolian League
during the period of Aitolian domination.

3   See Glossary.

70   Delphic proxeny list. Delphi, first half of the second century.

*SIG*³ 585.

Daux, *Delphes* 17–47, 586–95 with photograph.

1   The following are proxenoi of the Delphians: |
     The archon being Kallikrates (190/89),¹ the councillors | for the first
     six-month period being Mnason, Thrasy|kles, Menon: Demetrios, son
80   of Mnaseas, | a citizen of Thera. ‖ The archon being Kallikrates, the
     councillors | for the first six-month period being Mnason, | Menon,
     Thrasykles: Orthon, son of Zopyros, | a citizen of Rhegium. | The
85   archon being Kallikrates, the councillors ‖ for the first six-month
     period being Mnason, | Menon, Thrasykles: Marcus Valerius |
     Muttines² and his sons, Publius, | Gaius, Marcus, Quintus, citizens
90   of Rome. | The archon being Kallikrates, the councillors ‖ for the first
     six-month period being Mnason, | Menon, Thrasykles: Leontis, | son of
     Sokrates, a citizen of Akragas. | The archon being Kallikrates, the
95   councillors | for the first six-month period being Mnason, Me‖non,
     Thrasykles: Strombichos, | son of Dionysodotos, a citizen of
     Apollonia. | The archon being Kallikrates, the councillors | for the
     second six-month period being Glaukos, Dexi|krates, Kallias: Eraton,
100 son of Amphitimos, ‖ a citizen of Leukas. | The archon being
     Kallikrates, the councillors for the| second six-month period being
     Glaukos, Dexikrate|s, Kallias: Onasimos, son of Epikratides, a citizen
     of Pella. |
105 The archon being Xenon (189/8), son of Ateisidas, the counci‖llors for
     the first six-month period being Agathon, Xeno|stratos, Kleodamos:
     Habron, son of Kallias, a citizen of Athens. | The archon being Xenon,
     son of Ateisidas, the councillors | for the second six-month period
110 being Kleodamos, Xeno|n, Torteas, son of Phaeinos: Tetagenes, ‖ son
     of Charias, Kallikrates, son of Theophanes, citizens of Thespiai. | The
     archon being Xenon, son of Ateisidas, the councillors | for the second
     six-month period being Kleodamos, Xeno|n, Dexikrates: Praulos, son
     of Phoxinos, a citizen of Skotussa. | The archon being Xenon, son of
115 Ateisidas, the councillors for the ‖ second six-month period being

Kleodamos, Xenon, Dexikrates: | Titus Quinctius, son of Titus,[3] a
citizen of Rome. | The archon being Xenon, son of Ateisidas, the coun-
cillors for the se|cond six-month period being Kleodamos, Xenon,
120   Dexikrates: | Lucius Acilius, son of Caeso,[4] a citizen of Rome. || The
archon being Xenon, the son of Ateisidas, the councillors for the
se|cond six-month period being Kleodamos, Xenon, Dexikrates: |
Marcus Aemilius Lepidus, son of Marcus,[5] a citizen of Rome. | The
archon being Xenon, son of Ateisidas, the councillors for the | second
125   six-month period being Kleodamos, Xenon, Dexi||krates: Lykos, son of
Phileas, a citizen of Taras.

The list of individuals designated Proxenos by Delphi between 197/6 and 165/4 with
an addition for the year 149/8 was inscribed at intervals during the first half of the
second century on blocks of the polygonal wall of the sanctuary of Apollo at Delphi.
The entries translated cover the years 190/89 and 189/8.

1   Comparison with complete proxeny decrees such as no. 84 indicates that the list
    was compiled by extracting from such decrees the date formula (i.e. the names of
    the archon and councillors in office at the time of passage) and the name and ethnic
    of the proxenos.
2   A Carthaginian general who betrayed Agrigentum to the Romans in 210. As a
    reward he received Roman citizenship on the recommendation of M. Valerius
    Laevinus (consul 210) (Livy 26.40.3–8, 27.5.5–7); cf. *RE* 8A1 (1955) 171 no. 272.
3   T. Quinctius Flamininus, consul in 198 and commander of Roman forces during the
    decisive phase of the Second Macedonian War. Delphi had previously honored him
    with a statue for which the base and dedication survives (cf. *SIG*[3] 616).
4   Probably the father of M' Acilius Balbus, consul in 150.
5   M. Aemilius Lepidus, consul in 187. The full decree in his honor survives (*SEG* 1
    [1923] 147) and suggests that his proxeny was prompted by the aid afforded by him
    in Rome to two Delphian ambassadors.

71   Decree of Elateia in Phokis honoring Stymphalos in Arkadia for giving refuge to the Elateians during their exile. Stymphalos, about 189.

Limestone stele. Dating based on content since the lettering, reflecting the provincial character of Stymphalos, is more typical
of the late third than the early second century.

M. Mitsos, *REG* 59 (1946–1947) 150–74 with photograph; **ISE* 55 as corrected by
G. Klaffenbach (= Sherk, *TDGR* 4, no. 17).

A. Passerini, *Athenaeum* n.s. 26 (1948) 83–95; S. Accame, *RFIC* 77 (1949) 217–48; J. and
L. Robert, *REG* 64 (1951) 162–4; Will, *Histoire* 2.134; G. Klaffenbach, *BCH* 92 (1968)
257–9; Errington, *Philopoemen* 132 n. 1; Y. Garlan, *BCH* 93 (1969) 159–60; J. Briscoe, *A
Commentary on Livy Books XXXI–XXXIII* (Oxford 1973) 214; Walbank, *Commentary* 2.608,
3.93; S. Accame, *RFIC* 110 (1982) 286–92.

[---]| [---] *zealousness and humanity appropriate* to the [kinship][1] *and* | *each*

received into his *own* home with all *en|thusiasm*, [and from] *the* public
stock they allocated provisions to everyone for a considerable period,
5 and everything ‖ [of which there was need they shared]. They also
shared their sacred rites and sacrifices, treating them as their own |
[citizens. And] they separated off some of their land [and] gave it to the
Elateians together with *ex|emption* [from all taxes] for ten [years].
Having recorded an account of these matters on a bronze stele, | [they
set it up in the sanctuary] of Artemis [Braur]onia, omitting none of
their *kind|nesses* [toward them; and later], when again after an interval of
10 several years the Romans arrived in Greece ‖ [with an army], and
Manius[2] *had gained control* of the area near [E]lateia, the Stymphalians
sent an embassy *t|o* [the Achaians in order that] an embassy be sent to
Manius concerning the return of the Elateians to *their | own home.*[3] [The
Achaians (then)] *sent* as ambassadors Diophanes and Atha[no]kles,
and Manius *grant|ed* that [there be returned] to the Elateians their *city*,
their *land*, and their slaves. As the Elateians [had l|ived in St]ymphalos
for a long time *without causing complaint* and in a manner worthy of their
15 *ancestors* ‖ [before returning to] their own home, and as the export of
grain was not allowed by the Achaians because of the *current* | [crisis and]
famine, the Stymphalians sent an embassy to the Achaians so that, when
they returned, | the Elateians freely carried away[4] their own grain also
[from] the land of the Stymphalaians [---] | [---] to reorganize and to settle
their (land); and after [their] | return to] their home, the Elateians, who
were disputing *among themselves* concerning the reconstruction and repopu-
20 lation (of the city), ‖ [sent concerning] *this matter* to the Stymphalians,
(and) the Stymph[alians] *dispatched* fine and *noble men*, | [---]os, Euremon,
Thearidas, son of I[s]agoras, who, *after arriving* [in El]ateia, | *rendered* the
[decision] about the walling of the place in a proper and just manner.
In order, therefore, that [our city] may appear | [also] *to be mindful* of the
kindnesses of the Stymphalians and *to return* [thanks | to its benefactors],
it has been resolved by the Elateians, that the *men* who have been desig-
25 nated, Daphnaios, ‖ [son of ---]krates, Theondas, son of Python, Agon,
Krito|[n, son of ---], *take care* that the *kindnesses of the* [El]ateians and
Stymphalians *are recorded* | [on a stone stele and] set up in Elateia in the
agora by the altar of Zeus the Savior, | [and in Stymphalos in the]
sanctuary of Artemis Brauronia. The Stymphalians shall possess in
E|[lateia security], *freedom from reprisal*, the right of admission to the
Boule and assembly immediately after the sacred business and ‖ [they
30 shall share in Elat]eia the public sacrifices and the other honors and *all*
benefactions. | [Finally, the city shall crown the people] of the
Stymphalians with a gold wreath, and every *year* it shall be proclaimed
| [by the sacred heralds during the] competition in *gymnastics* during the
Boadromia,[5] making it clear that [the | city of the Elateians crowns the

city of the Stymphalians with a] *gold* [wreath] of valor [for its excellence
and kindness toward it ---].

1 According to Pausanias (8.4.1–4), Elatos, the eponymous founder of Elateia, was
   the son of Arkas and the father of Stymphalos, the eponymous founder of
   Stymphalos.
2 Manius Acilius Glabrio (consul in 191) who gained control of central Greece after
   defeating Antiochos III in spring 191.
3 Who was responsible for the exile of the Elateians is disputed. Pausanias (10.34)
   and Livy (32.24.7) imply that they were exiled by T. Quinctius Flamininus in 198
   because of their alliance with Philippos V. Passerini, followed by Errington, however, argued that the Aitolians did so after receiving Phokis in the final Roman
   settlement of the Second Macedonian War in 196.
4 Reading established by Y. Garlan.
5 A festival of Apollo.

72   Ordinance of King Philippos V concerning the property of Sarapis at Thessalonike. Thessalonike, 187. Marble stele.

IG 2.1.3 with photograph; *ISE 111.

S. Pelekides, *BCH* 45 (1932) 540–1; C. B. Welles, *AJA* 42 (1938) 249–51; E. Bikerman,
RPhil. 64 (1938) 295–312; Walbank, *Philip V* 267; C. Edson, *HTR* 41 (1948) 181–2; P. M.
Fraser, *Opuscula Atheniensia* 3 (1960) 38–40; F. Walbank, *CAH*² 227–8.

From Andronikos.[1] The dia|gramma,[2] which I have sent | to you (and
5   which) the king sent to me, | concerning Sarapis' ‖ property, have it
inscribed | on a stone stele and set <up> | in the sanctuary[3] in order
that they may know, they | who are responsible for these matters, his
10 dec|ision. Year 35. Daisios 15.[4] ‖
Ordinance issued by King | Philippos (V). And[5] from Sarapis' | *property*
let no one alienate | anything in any manner nor | pledge any of the
15 other dedi‖cations nor introduce concerning the|se a decree. But if
someone do|es any of the things which have been forbidden, [he shall
be] subject | to the punishment for theft; | and, after exaction of the
20 (amount) *alienated* from ‖ his *property*, it shall be *restored* to the sanctuary. |
And similarly, | the *treasuries* of the god shall not be opened | [without]
the (presence of the) epistates[6] and the *jud*|*ges* nor the money from them
25 ‖ *be expended* carelessly but | [with] their knowledge. And if not, | let *the*
person who did any of these things be subject | [to the same] penalties.

1 A royal official, perhaps the epistates of Thessalonike.
2 Cf. Bickerman's definition: 'A diagramma was an ordinance promulgated in the
   residence of its author and dealing, generally, with several subjects. It was officially
   transmitted to the competent authorities who published the relevant provisions.'

3 Royal patronage of Sarapis at Thessalonike dates from the third century when a Sarapieion was established in the city. For its remains see Pelekides and Edson.
4 May 187.
5 Bikerman noted that 'And' in line 11 indicates that this text is an excerpt from a more comprehensive document.
6 The royal representative in Thessalonike.

73   Megalopolis honors Philopoimen with heroic honors. Megalopolis, about 183/2. Marble stele.

*SIG³ 624.

Errington, *Philopoemen passim.*

[In order] | that also in the *fatherland* [--- | ---] it be increased in *every way*, [it has been resolved by the] | *city* that it honor Philo[p]o[imen, son of
5 Kraugis],[1] ‖ with honors equal to a god[2] [for] his *excellence* [and] *n|oble deeds*; and *it shall build* [in his honor] | *in* the agora a *tomb* [and it shall bring back from Messa]|nia his bones[3] to [our city], | and *it shall construct* an altar [of white marble] as beautiful as possible, and [it shall sacrifice
10 an ox on the day of ‖ Ze]us the Savior,[4] and *it shall honor* [him] *with stat|ues*[5] of bronze, [four in number, and set up] | one in [the] *theatre* [---]
15 | a standing (statue), and *another* [in ---], | and *another* [in ---] ‖ and *another* [in ---, and] *it shall procl|aim* at the [festival of the Soteria both the]
25 *wreath*[6] [and the other honors --- | --- ‖ --- | --- | --- | --- | ---] *to conduct* [a
30 procession] ‖ around Akerseko[m[7] ---] | *precincts* for the [--- | ---] *to this honor* [---] | worthy of the Arkadians, and *it shall establish* also [contests] *in*
35 *ath|letics* and *horsemanship* [---], ‖ and the treasurer *shall disburse* [for the sacrifice] | to [each of] the city's *sacrificial priests* [two] | minas, and [they shall burn completely] the *edible* meat, | and they shall distribute the
40 skins *to the priests* [in office], | and for the Soteria [--- ‖ ---] *to those possessing* [---] | Zeus the Savior [---] | to the precinct of Philo[poimen, and] *there shall be sup|plied* for them *wine* from the sacrifices [and] *there shall be*
45 *an|nounced* at the sacrifices [yearly and] ‖ *there shall be crowned* by the [priest] of Hestia [and] he shall take the [perquisites ---].

1 Philopoimen (about 252–182) died in prison, allegedly by poison, after being captured by the Messenians during an Achaian campaign intended to prevent the secession of Messenia (cf. Polybius 23.12; Plutarch, *Philopoimen* 18–20; Pausanias 8.51.5–7).
2 The restorations in the following lines are based in part on the description of Philopoimen's honors in Diodorus 29.18 and Livy 39.50.
3 The bones were carried by the historian Polybius (Plutarch, *Philopoimen* 21.3).
4 For this sanctuary see Pausanias 8.30.10.
5 Pausanias (8.52.6) quotes the inscription on the statue set up at Tegea. For

Polybius' role in preserving these statues after the Achaian War see Plutarch,
Philopoimen 21.6.
6   Presumably the awarding of the wreath was authorized in the lost beginning of the
inscription.
7   Dittenberger suggested that the reference is to a small sanctuary of Apollo.

74   The Spartan exiles honor Kallikrates for restoring them to Sparta. Olympia, 179/8. Gray limestone statue base.

I. Olympia 300 with drawing; **SIG*³ 634; cf. Polybius 24.8–10.

Errington, *Philopoemen* 195–205; J. Briscoe, *Studies in Ancient Society*, ed. M. I. Finley
(London 1974) 63–6.

Those Lakedaimonians exiled by the *tyrants*[1] | (honor) Kallikrates, son
of Theoxenos,[2] from Leontion who restored them[3] | to their fatherland
and reconciled them with the citizens | and *re-established* them in the
friendship that *existed* originally.

1   The Spartans who had been exiled by Kleomenes III, Lykourgos, Machanidas and
Nabis and who had not yet returned to Sparta in 182.
2   A leading Achaian politician from about 180 to 149/8 who was identified with a
policy of co-operation with Rome.
3   During Kallikrates' generalship in 179/8.

75   Decree of the Roman senate concerning the Sarapieion at Delos. Delos, 164. Stele of white marble with small projections at the top in the form of acroteria, second-century lettering.

*SIG*³ 664; *Sherk, *RDGE* 5 = Sherk, *TDGR* 28.

W. M. Laidlaw, *A History of Delos* (Oxford 1933) 178–9; Sherk, *RDGE* pp. 37–9; S. V.
Tracy, *HSCP* 83 (1979) 214.

The strategoi[1] to Charmides the gover|nor of Delos, greetings. There
was | lengthy discussion in the Boule[2] | concerning the decree which
5   was brought ‖ from Rome by Demetrios the Rhenai|an concerning
events at the Sarapi|eion. It was decreed not to prevent hi|m from
10   opening and administering | the sanctuary as be‖fore, and to write to
you too, | in order that you might know about these matters. We have,
below, atta|ched for you, in addition, | a copy of the decree brought | by
15   him. *vv* ‖ Quintus Minucius, son of Quintus, | praetor,[3] consulted the
senate | in the Co|mitium on the intercalary Ides.[4] | (Witnesses) present
20   at the writing were: ‖ Publius Porcius, (son) of Publius; Ti|berius

Claudius, (son) of Tiberius, | (of the tribe) Crustumina; Manius
Fonte|ius, (son) of Gaius. Whereas Demetrios | the Rhenaian said
25   ‖ that on Delos the sanctuary of Sara|pis was his to administer, | but
that he was prevented by the Delians and | by the governor, who from
30   Athens | had come there, fr‖om administering it, about this | matter it
was as follows de|creed: just as formerly he used to ad|minister it, as far
35   as we are concerned | he is to be permitted to administer it, ‖ so that
nothing contrary to the | decree of the senate is to be done. | Decreed.[5] *vv*

1 These were Athenian 'generals', officials elected annually to administer the government. In 167/6 BC Rome made Delos a free port and placed it under the general
   supervision of Athens.
2 I.e. the one in Athens. On the Boule see Glossary.
3 The year of his praetorship is unknown, but the events took place not very long after
   167/6. See Sherk, *RDGE* p. 39.
4 The word 'intercalary' is transliterated in this document from Latin into Greek.
   Since the Roman calendar in this period was lunar, i.e. based on the phases of the
   moon, and thus had only 354 days in its year – eleven days less than a solar year –
   the months that were supposed to come in the spring gradually slipped backward
   into the winter. To avoid this the Romans at irregular intervals inserted an extra
   month into their lunar year. This was called an intercalary month, and the special
   days that were used to divide each month into three parts were then called the
   intercalary Kalends, Nones and Ides. This intercalary month was inserted in the
   month of February. Thus, 'the intercalary Ides' means the thirteenth (or fifteenth)
   day of this month that was inserted in the calendar. Further details in A. K. Michels,
   The Calendar of the Roman Republic (Princeton 1967) 9–15 and 160ff.
5 For the background see no. 102.

76   Base for a statue of the philosopher Karneades. Athens, before about 163. Square marble base, second-century lettering.

*SIG*³ 666; *IG II² 3781.

Ferguson, *Athens* 300–1; B. D. Merritt, *The Athenian Year* (Berkeley 1959) 229–30; H. B.
Mattingly, *Historia* 20 (1971) 28–32; B. Frischer, *The Sculpted Word* (Berkeley 1982) 194–6.

Karneades,[1] from Azenia.[2] | Attalos and Ariarathes, (both) from
Sypallettos,[3] | dedicated (the statue).

1 Philosopher, principal representative of Middle Platonism, head of the Academy
   from about 164/160 to 137/6, and member of the Athenian embassy to Rome in
   156/5.
2 The demotic indicates that Karneades, originally from Kyrene, had become an
   Athenian citizen.
3 Frischer has answered Mattingly's objections to the identification of the donors as
   Attalos II (160–139) of Pergamon and Ariarathes V (about 163–about 130) of
   Kappadokia who would have honored their teacher prior to their accessions.

Diogenes Laertius (4.654) refers to a collection of letters from Karneades to
Ariarathes, a king noted for his interest in philosophy (Diodorus 31.19.7–8).

77   Treaty between King Pharnakes I of Pontos and the city of Chersonesos. Chersonesos in the Crimea, 155. Marble stele broken at the top.

Inscriptiones Antiquae Orae Septentrionalis Ponti Euxini Graecae et Latinae I² 402 = Sherk,
TDGR 30; cf. Polybius 25.2 for background to the treaty.

Magie, *RRAM* 1.192–4; 2.1090 n. 45; V. P. Gajdukevič, *Das Bosporanische Reich* (Berlin
1971) 312; Walbank, *Commentary* 3.20 and 274; S. Burstein, *AJAH* 5 (1980) 21–30.

[--- we will assist in guarding his] *kingdom* | [with all our power, as long
as he remains] with *us* [in | friendship and] maintains his friendship
5   [with the Rom]ans | [and does nothing] in opposition to them; ‖ and
may it be good for us swearing a true oath and for us swearing a false
oa|th the opposite. This oath was ta|ken on the fifteenth of the month
of Herakleios, | when the king was Apollodoros, (son) of Herogei|tes,
10   and when the secretary was Herodotos, (son) of Hero‖dotos. *vv* The
oath which King Pharnakes swore | when the envoys Matrios and
Herakle[i]os went to him: | I swear by Zeus, Ge, Helios, all the
Olympian gods | and goddesses. I will be a friend to the Chersonesitans
for all | time, and if the neighboring barbarians should make an
15   expedition ‖ against Chersonesos or the land controlled by the
Cherso|nesitans or should commit an act of injustice against
Chersonesitans, and if they call up|on me, I will help them just as if
mine were the cri|sis, and I will not plot against the Chersonesitans in
20   any | way, nor will I make an expedition against Chersonesos, nor ‖ will
I stockpile weapons against Chersonesitans, nor will I do | anything
with respect to Chersonesitans which would tend to harm | the people
of the Chersonesitans, but I will as|sist in guarding democracy with all |
25   my power, as long as they remain in friendship with m‖e and have
sworn the same oath | and maintain their friendship with the Romans |
and do nothing contrary to them. | May it be good for me swearing a
true oath and for me swearing a false oath the oppo|site. This oath was
30   taken in ‖ the one hundred and fifty-seventh | year, in the month of
Daisios, as King Pharnakes | *vv* reckons (time).[1] *vv*

---

1   The defensive alliance, as sworn to by both parties here, was previously dated to
180–179, but it has recently been shown that the era used in lines 30–1 cannot be
one which began with the accession of Mithridates II to the throne of Kios in 337/6,
as previously thought, but must be the Seleucid era of 312/11, which produces a
date of 155 when applied to our document. Thus, a recognized condition of

friendship had been established between Rome on the one hand and both Pharnakes and the city of Chersonesos on the other sometime prior to 155. That friendship also seems to have been recognized soon after 179, when Rome became reconciled with Pharnakes at the conclusion of the Pontic War (183–179). See Burstein, *loc. cit.*

78   Elis honors Lucius Mummius. Olympia, 146. Gray limestone statue base, second-century lettering.

I. Olympia 319 with drawing; *SIG^3 676.

The city of the Eleians (honors) Lucius Mummius,[1] son of Lucius, | consul of the Romans,[2] for his excellence and the benevolence which | he continues to have for it and the other Greeks.

1   For dedications by Mummius at Olympia from the Achaian War see Pausanias 5.24.4 and 8.
2   Consul in 146.

79   Elis honors Polybius, son of Lykortas. Olympia, after 146. Yellow limestone statue base, second-century lettering.

I. Olympia 302 with drawing; *SIG^3 686; cf. Polybius 39.5; Pausanias 8.30.8–9, 37.2, 48.8.

The city of the Eleians (honors) Polybius, | son of Lykortas, from Megalopolis.[1]

1   This is one of a number of monuments set up by Peloponnesian cities to honor the historian for his role in the Roman settlement of Greece after the Achaian War.

80   Dossier concerning the arbitration of a land dispute between Messene and Sparta by Miletos. Olympia, about 138. The inscription is inscribed on the base of a statue of Victory, second-century lettering.

I. Olympia 52 with drawing; *SIG^3 683; cf. Tacitus, *Annals* 4.43.1–6.

M. N. Tod, *International Arbitration amongst the Greeks* (Oxford 1913) 7; C. A. Roebuck, *A History of Messenia* (Chicago 1941) 106–7, 118–21; S. Accame, *Il dominio romano in Grecia dalla guerra acaica ad Augusto* (Rome 1946) 130, 135, 146.

I

Judgement concerning land | between the Messanians and the

Lakedaimonia[ns]. | Ambassadors having arrived from the city | of the
5 Messanians, Menodoros, son of Dionysios, ‖ Apollonidas, son of
Nikandros, Charetidas, son of Dor|konidas, and having handed over
letters in which it was made | clear that they had renewed the existing
kinsh|ip and friendship of the cities[1] with each other, they proposed |
10 that the city be permitted to record at Olympia ‖ the judgement
rendered to their city against | the city of the Lakedaimonians concern-
ing land.[2] | The ambassadors handed over also a letter from the
Milesians | that had been sealed and contained the judgement *that had*
15 *been rendered,* | and *in addition, the* ambassadors spoke *in accorda‖nce with*
what had been written. It was resolved by the councillors that answ|er
shall be given to the effect that the kinship and friendship exi|sting
with the city of the Messanians be renew|ed and further strengthened.
With regard to the permis|sion to record at Olympia the judgement
20 render‖ed to their city against the city of the Lakedai|monians concern-
ing the land by the Milesian People, | (it was resolved) that permission
be granted just as the city of the Messanians | has requested in its letter
and the ambassadors urged. They shall praise | also the ambassadors
25 both for their visit and the man‖ner in which they have conducted
(themselves), and there shall also be given to them by Philoni|kos, the
treasurer, the hospitality gifts of the finest quality (allowed) by the
laws, | and they shall invite them and the archons to the public | table.

II

30 The prytaneis of the Milesians and the security officials ‖ to the archons
and councillors of the Eleians, greeting. There having | come to us as
ambassadors from the Messenians, | Menodoros, the son of Dionysios,
Philoites, the son of Kratias, and | they having urged us to give to them
35 a copy for y|ou of the judgement rendered to the Messenians and ‖ the
Lakedaimonians in accordance with the decree of the senate; and the |
Boule and the People having granted the aforementioned (request)
and | instructed us to give them the judgement, we, having at|tached it
to the letter, have given it to the ambas|sadors in order that they might
40 transmit it to you *seal‖ed* with the *public* seal.

III

In the year in which the stephanephoros was Eirenias, the son of
Asklepiades, month | Kalamion,[3] second (day), and, as *wrote* the Praetor
Quin|tus Calpurnius,[4] son of Gaius, the *fourteen|th* month and eleventh
45 day according to the moon from the [day the] ‖ decree was passed, a full
assembly was convened in [the] *thea|tre* on the aforementioned day, just

as the La[kedaimoni]|ans and Messenians agreed. There was selected
by lot | from the whole People the largest tribunal (permitted) by the |
laws, six hundred jurors. The case was brought to trial in accordance
50   both ‖ with the letter of the aforementioned Praetor and | the decree of
the se[nat]e *concerning* [the] *dispu*|*te between* the [L]akedai[mon]i[a]ns
[and the Messenians, namely, that] *which*|*ever* party *possessed* the land
55   [when Lucius] | Mummius was consul or proconsul [in that] *pro*‖*vince,*[5]
they, therefore, should have possession of it. | The water *was divided*
between them by [measure; for the] | first speech [the Milesians]
measured out to each *fif*|*teen* (measures of water) and for the second
speech [the Milesians measured out] | five just as they agreed. *There*
60   *spoke* ‖ in observance of the water for the Lakedaimoni|ans Eudamidas,
the son of Euthykles, and for the Messenians Nik(i)|s, the son of Nikon,
and after the speeches had been delivered by ea|ch, it was decided that
the land was in the possession of the Messenians when | Lucius
65   Mummius was consul or proconsul in th‖at province and that, there-
fore, | they should possess it. The votes by which it was decided that
there *had been possession of* | the land by the Messenians and that they,
therefore, *should pos*|*sess* it were five hundred eighty-fou|r; for possession
70   by the Lakedaimonians ‖ sixteen.

The dossier contains three items, a decree of Elis granting permission for the publication of the decision at Olympia, a cover letter from Miletos to Elis and the decision
proper.
1   Messene and Elis.
2   The dispute concerned the Dentheliatis, a district between Messenia and Sparta on
    the western slopes of Mt Taygetos that was the supposed site of the outbreak of the
    First Messenian War (Strabo 8.4.9–10, C 362; Pausanias 4.2.2–3) and had been
    turned over to Messenia by Philip II of Macedon after the battle of Chaironeia in
    337. The dispute was settled finally in favor of Messenia by the Emperor Tiberius
    in 25 AD.
3   Last month of the Milesian calendar, approximately equivalent to June.
4   Probably A. Calpurnius Piso, consul in 135. Assuming that he had a normal career,
    his praetorship and these events would have taken place in 138.
5   Achaia was his consular province in 146 and his proconsular province in 145.
    According to Tacitus, he awarded the territory to Messene.

81   Heading for a list of Athenians who held the office of gymnasiarch on Delos. Delos, about 112/11. Marble stele.

A. Plassart, *BCH* 36 (1912) 395 with photograph; *SIG*[3] 657; *I. Delos* 2859.
W. S. Ferguson, *CP* 8 (1913) 220.

Phokion, son of Aristokrates, from Melite, | having held the office of
gymnasiarch,[1] had inscribed (the list of) | those who were gym-

5   nasiarch | from the time the people, through the Romans, recovered ‖ the island.[2]

1   On Delos where Athenian gymnasiarchs took over the management of the gymnasia after the Romans returned the island to Athens in 168.
2   A list follows of the gymnasiarchs from 167/6 to 112/11, together with fragments of its continuation.

82   Delphi honors the harpist Polygnota of Thebes and her cousin, Lykinos. Delphi, 86. Inscribed on a block of the right side of the pillar erected in honor of Eumenes II of Pergamon by the Aitolians.

SIG[3] 738; *I. Delphi* 3.3.249–50; **Nouveau Choix* 10.

L. Robert, *BCH* 53 (1929) 34–9; L. Robert, *Études épigraphiques et philologiques* (Paris 1938) 36–8; S. B. Pomeroy, *AJAH* 2 (1977) 54.

Gods. Good Fortune. | [The archon being Habr]omachos (86), month Boukatios,[1] the councillors <for the first [six-|month (period)> being Strat]agos, Kleon, Antiphilos, Damon. Resolved by the city of the | [Delphians]. *Since* Polygnota, daughter of S(o)krates, a harpist from
5   Thebes, was staying at Del‖[phi] *at the time* the Pythian games were to be held, but because of the present | [war],[2] the games were not held, on that same day she performed without charge and contributed (her services for) the day; and, *having* | *been asked* by the magistrates and the citizens, she played *f|or*[3] three days and earned great distinction in a manner worthy of the god | [and] of the Theban people and of our city,
10   and we reward‖ed her also with [[five hundred drachmas;]] *with good fortune,* (the city) shall | praise Polygnota, daughter of Sokrates, a Theban, for her reverent attitude toward the god *and* | her piety and her conduct with regard to her manner of life and art; and there *shall be given* | by our city to her and to her descendants the status of a proxenos,[4] priority in consulting the oracle, priority of | trial, inviolability, exemption from taxes, a front seat at the contests which the city
15   holds, ‖ and the right to own land and a house, and all other honors such as belong to the other *proxenoi* | and benefactors of the city, and it shall invite her to the *pryta|neion* to the public table; and it shall provide her with a sacrificial victim to offer to [Apol]‖lo. God. Good Fortune. | Resolved by the city of the Delphians. Since Lykinos, son of Dorotheos,
20   a Theban, *visited* ‖ our city with his cousin Polygnota[5] and behaved during his vis|it in a manner worthy of his own people and our city, it has | been resolved by the city that it praise Lykinos, son of Dorotheos, a Theban, and that he have [together with] | his descendants the status

of a proxenos, priority in consulting the oracle, priority of trial, inviol-
ability, exemption from taxes, a front | seat at the contests which the
25   [city holds] and other honors such as belong to the other ‖ proxenoi and
benefactors of the city; and that it invite him also to | the common table
of the city. The archon being Habromachos, the son of Athambos, the
councill|ors being Damon, Kleon, Stratagos, Antiphilos.

1   The second month of the Delphian calendar, approximately equivalent to August–
    September.
2   The First Mithridatic War. The games were not held because of Sulla's campaign in
    central Greece in 86.
3   Dittenberger: 'for three *additional* days'.
4   See Glossary.
5   Pomeroy suggests that he was his cousin's chaperone.

Chapter 5
PERGAMON

83 The Pergamene Chronicle. Pergamon, second century AD.
Three non-contiguous white marble wall blocks, second-century AD lettering.

I. Pergamum 613 with drawing; *OGIS* 264; *FGrHist* 506.

Jacoby, *FGrHist* 3b, pp. 422–3; Hansen, *Attalids*[2] 10–11; M. J. Osborne, *Historia* 22 (1973) 515–51; Allen, *Attalid Kingdom* 161–3

a

[A]rchias[1] [persuaded (the People)] that *prytaneis*[2] *be elected* [for the | city] each year, and the first *to hold the office of pryta|nis was* [Archi]as, and from him until now[3] | *they continue being governed by prytaneis.* And Orontes,
5   the son of Artasy‖[ros], *by race* a Baktrian,[4] having revolted from Artaxer|[xes], the King of the [Pers]ians, gained control of the Perga|[menians and] *resettled* them again on the *hi|ll* [at] the *old* city. Then Orontes, | *having turned over* [the city] to Arta]xerxes, died.[5]

b

10   [---]*having married* Anaxip‖[pe, --- she bore Eu]ippos, [and] Euippos |
     [--- | ---] *also* Daskylos, | [and they had one] *sister,* [Th]ersippe, | [and
15   she, having married---], a Paphlagonian ‖ [by race, bore ---], *and after these thing|s* [---].[6]

c

     [--- | ---] E[u]me[nes (II), already] *having shared* [while alive the rule] |
     with [At]ta[los (II), his brother, died] *leav|ing* the [kingdom to his own
20   son] | Attalos (III), [with his brother] *as guardian.* [And he][7] ‖ gave over
     the [kingdom on dying to Attalos], the son of Eumen[es --- | ---] *having ruled* [---].

1   Probably to be identified with the Archias who introduced the cult of Asklepios to Pergamon from Epidauros.
2   An annually elected magistrate similar to the archon at Athens.
3   The ornate letter forms with pronounced apices suggest a Hadrianic date for the inscription.
4   For Orontes and his family see Osborne.

5   These events have been dated to 354, but Osborne has shown that they are to be
connected with the 'Satraps' Revolt' of the 360s against Artaxerxes II (404–358; cf.
Diodorus 15.90–1 and Trogus, *Prolog* 10).
6   Fragment **b** dealt with the genealogy of Philetairos; cf. Pausanias 1.8.1, Athenaeus
13.577b, and Strabo 12.3.8, C 543.
7   Attalos II (159–138).

84   Delphi honors the family of Philetairos. Delphi, 282–263. Two
fragments of a gray limestone column.

I. Delphi 432.

Holleaux, *Études* 2.9–16; Hansen, *Attalids²* 19.

Gods. | The Delphians have granted [to Philetairos[1] and to his] *son*
At⁺alos[2] | and to his brother [Eumenes,[3] citizens of Perga]mon, the
status of proxenos, | the right of first consultation (with the oracle), the
5   privilege of *a front seat, priority of trial, inviolability,*[4] || and *such other things* as
(have been granted) also *to the other* proxenoi and *bene|factors. The archon
is* [---,] the councillors are | Ainesilas, Mena[ndros, Timo]genes,
Zakynthios, | Nikodamos.

1   The founder of the dynasty of Pergamon (282–263). Presumably he and his family
were honored for some gift to Delphi similar to those attested for Delos and
Thespiai.
2   Attalos I (241–197).
3   The father of Eumenes I (263–241) who is probably to be identified with the ruler of
the north Anatolian city of Amastris during the late 280s and early 270s (cf.
Memnon, *FGrHist* 434F9.4).
4   Immunity against individuals seeking to exercise their right of personal reprisal in
satisfaction of damages due to them.

85   Victory monument of Attalos I. Pergamon, last quarter of the
third century. Seven marble fragments of a long statue base set up in
the sanctuary of Athena at Pergamon to celebrate the victories won by
Attalos I during the first fifteen years of his reign. The lettering imitates
fourth-century forms.

I. Pergamum 21–8 with drawings; *OGIS* 273–9; cf. Polybius 18.41.7; Strabo 13.4.2,
C 624; Pausanias 1.25.2.

Hansen, *Attalids²* 31–5; Will, *Histoire* 1².298; Allen, *Attalid Kingdom* 195–9; H. Heinen,
CAH² 423–4, 428–32.

273) King Attalos from battles in war | (dedicated) thank-offerings to Athena.
274) [From the] battle [in] Helles|[pontine Phr]ygia | against A]ntiochos.[1]
275) [From the] battle [by the (temple)] | of Aphrodite against the Tolistoagioi | [and the Tektosa](g)ian Galatians and Antiochos.[2]
276) From the battle near the *sources* of the Kaikos River | against the T[olis]toagian Galatians.[3]
277) From the battle *by* [---] *against* L[y]sias,[4] | and the *strategoi* of Sel[eukos] (III).
278) [From the] *battle* [near Kol]oe | [against Antiochos].[5]
279) [From the battle by Harpassos in K]aria | [against Antiochos].[6]

1 Antiochos Hierax, the younger son of Antiochos II and Laodike I (about 241–227). Except for *OGIS* 276 these inscriptions seem to refer to events of the years 229–227.
2 Probably near Pergamon (cf. Livy 32.33.51). Trogus (*Prolog* 27) places the battle at Pergamon. Allen suggests that it was as a result of this battle that Attalos assumed the title 'King' and the epithet 'the Savior'. For these Galatian tribes see no. 16.
3 Allen dates this and the preceding battle to the period immediately following the Battle of Ankyra in 240 or 239.
4 Restored on the basis of *OGIS* 272. Lysias was probably a local dynast in Asia Minor.
5 Restored on the basis of Eusebius, *Chronicle* 1.253 (Schoene), who locates the battle in Lydia and dates it to 229.
6 Restored on the basis of *OGIS* 271 and Eusebius (*ibid.*) who dates the battle to 228.

86 Dedication of booty by Eumenes II and his allies. Pergamon, 195. Fragments of two marble statue bases.

I. Pergamon 60–1 with drawing; **SIG*[3] 595 = Sherk, *TDGR* 7.

Will, *Histoire* 2.149–50; Hansen, *Attalids*[2] 70–4.

A

[King Eumenes (II) from] the booty [derived from] the campaign | [which he conducted with the Roma]ns[1] *and the other allies* against Nabis, the Lakonian,[2] | [who had subdued the Argi]v[es[3] and] the Me[s]s[e]nians,[4] (dedicated) these first fruits to Athena, Bringer-of-Victory.

B

[(This statue of) King Eu]menes (has been dedicated) *for* his excellence | (by) *those* who sailed *with him* | [to Gr]eece *as soldiers* | [and sailors]
5 for the war against Nabis, || [the Lakon]ian.

1   195.
2   Last king of Sparta (207–192).
3   Argos was occupied by Nabis in 197 with the consent of Philippos V of Macedon (cf. Livy 32.38).
4   This is inexact as Messene was independent in 196 (cf. Livy 32.34.16); the reference is probably to his attack on Messenia in 202/1.

87   Amphiktiones honor Eumenes II and recognize the Nikephoria. Delphi, 182. Inscription on a limestone pillar dedicated by Attalos I, second-century lettering.

Holleaux, *Études* 2.63–72; *SIG^3 630; *I. Delphi* 261 with photograph.

M. Segre, *RFIC* 60 (1932) 446–52; Daux, *Delphes* 293–8; McShane, *Foreign Policy* 174; Hansen, *Attalids*[2] 448–50.

[The archon in Delphi] was Demosthenes. Decree of the Amphik[tiones. King] | Eumenes (II), [having inherited] from his father, King Attalo[s (I), with regard to the gods] | *piety* [and] with regard to the Amphiktiones good will, and *maintaining* [with the Romans] | friendship, continues always to be the cause [of some] *good* for the

5   Greeks, [and having shared] ‖ the same *risks* for their common security with many of the [Greek] *cities*, | *he has given* gifts for the maintenance of [their] present *good order*. Where|fore, the Ro[man]s, observing his attitude, *have increased his* kingdom, | thinking [it necessary] both that those kings, who plot against [the Gre]eks, ought to meet with | suitable

10   punishment and that those, who are the *cause* of no evil, ‖ *are worthy* of their fullest confidence.[1] He has sent *also sacred envoys* | to urge the Amphiktiones that, with regard to the precinct of Athena B[ringer-of-Vict]ory,[2] | they join with him in proclaiming it to be inviolate, and that, with regard to the contests,[3] which he has decided to establish as wreathed, | they recognize the musical as equivalent to the Pythian and the athletic and the *equestrian* as equivalent to the Olympian. | The

15   sacred envoys also described the *good will* of the king, which ‖ he continues to have *generally* for all the Greeks and individually for the cities. | (Since these things are so), [in order, therefore, that also the Am]phiktiones will be seen attending to those who are worthy | [and taking thought for] all kings who maintain toward the Romans – the common | [benefactors][4] – friendship (and) are always the cause of some good for the Greeks; with [good] fortune, | [it has been resolved] by the Amphiktiones that they praise King [Eu]menes, son of King

20   ‖ [Att]alos, [and] that *they crown* him with a laurel wreath in the temple of [A]pollo | [Py]thios, where it is *traditional* to crown their benefactors,

for his excellence | and good will toward the Greeks, and that they also
set up a bronze statue of him (seated) on a horse | in Delphi; and that
they proclaim the sanctuary of Athena Bringer-of-Victory at |
Pergamon to be inviolate for all time according as King Eumenes deter-
25   mines its boundaries, ‖ and that *no one is to be taken from* the defined area
either in war or peace | [---][5] and they recognize *also* the [two wreathed]
contests, | [just as the king requests], that, with regard to the [ages and
the honors for the vic|tors, the] *musical shall be equivalent to the Pythian*
[and] *the athletic* and the equestrian *to the Olympian.* | [They shall inscribe
30   the] *decree* in D[elphi on the base of] the statue [of the king ‖ in front of
the temple] and at P[ergamon in the sanctuary of] Athena [Bringer]-of-
Victory. | [And they shall proclaim the king's] *wreath* [and the] *inviol-
ability* of the sanctuary at the *contests* [of the | Pythia and the Soteri]a.

1   An allusion to the gains made by Eumenes at the expense of Antiochos III in the
    Peace of Apameia in return for his support of Rome in the 190s.
2   Cf. Strabo 13.4.2, C 624.
3   The Nikephoria (cf. *SIG*[3] 629) was established by Eumenes to commemorate his
    victory over Prusias I of Bithynia and the Galatians in 184/3. The contests were
    trieteric, that is, held every third year.
4   Restored by Dittenberger.
5   Dittenberger suggested: 'according [to a separate agreement].'

88   Letter of Eumenes II to the Ionian League. Miletos, 167/6. Four marble blocks from a circular statue base.

OGIS 763; *I. Didyma* I 9 with photograph; *Welles, RC* 52.

Holleaux, *Études* 2.153–78; McShane, *Foreign Policy* 182–6; Hansen, *Attalids*[2] 120–3.

(IA) King Eu[menes (II) to the League of the Ionians,[1] greeting]. | Of
your ambassadors, Menekles | did not meet with me, but Eirenias[2] and
5   Archelaos, | finding (me) at Delos,[3] conveyed to (me) ‖ the fine and
courteous decree[4] in which | you noted at the beginning that I, having
chosen from the start the finest | deeds and having revealed myself as
the common | benefactor of the Greeks, undertook many | great
10   struggles against the ‖ barbarians, *exerting* every effort and forethought |
in order that the inhabitants of the Greek *cities* | might for all time live
in peace and the best circumstances; | [and] that I, being reconciled
[to] the | (IC) *subsequent* danger and *choosing* to be [assiduous and
15   zea‖lous in] matters [involving the] league in accor|dance with the
policy of my father, have on many occasions given clear | indications
concerning these matters both publicly | and privately to each of the
cities that I was benevolently | inclined (toward them) by joining in

20   organizing many of those things that lead to fame ‖ and repute | for
     each, so that through deeds both my fame | [---]⁵ and the gratitude of
     the league; | wherefore, *you resolved*, in order that you might always
25   appear | awarding worthy honors to your benefactors, ‖ to crown us
     with a gold wrea|th of valor and to set up a gold statue in whatever |
     place in Ionia I wished, and to proclaim the honors | both in the contests
30   conducted by you | and city by city in those held in each one, ‖ (ID) [and
     to convey greetings to] *me* from the league [and to express its pleasure]
     | that I and my relatives⁶ *were in good health* | and that my affairs were in
     order, and to urge [me, on observing] | the gratitude of the People, to
     make *suitable pl|ans* through which the League of the I[onians] *might be*
35   *strengthen‖ed* and for all time *exist* in the *best* [condition]. | For, thus,
     afterwards I [would receive] *all* things that | lead to honor and repute.
     And in accordance [with all] | that has been granted, *the ambassadors* also
40   [with] even grea|ter zeal *described the whol‖e* People's *most earnest* [and] |
     sincere good will toward us. The honors *I accept in a friendly manner* | and,
     not ever having failed, in so far as [it was in my] | power, always to do
     [for all together] | and for each individual city something conducive to
45   [honor and repute], ‖ (IIB) I shall try also now | not to retreat from this
     purpose. | Would that events proceed in accordance with my desire!⁷ |
50   For thus, | you will receive even more through the deeds a true ‖ demon-
     stration of my attitude. | And in order that also in the future during the
     festival | of the Panionia by celebrating a day named | for us you may
     conduct the whole festival more brilliantly, | *I shall assign* to you
55   sufficient revenues ‖ from which you will be able *to give*⁸ to us fitting |
     commemoration. As for the gold *sta|tue, I shall have it made myself*, as I
     prefer that | [the] gift be *wholly without cost to the league*. | (IIC) And [I
60   wish] it to be set up in the ‖ *precinct voted* to us by the Miles[ians]. | For
     while you were in this city celebrating | the festival, you voted the honor
     to us, | (and) since this city alone of the Ionians until the | present has
65   assigned a precinct to us ‖ and since it is considered our kin through the
     Kyzikenes⁹ | and has done many things which are notable and memor-
     able on behalf of the | Ionians, I consider it to be most appropriate | that
     the (statue) be erected in it. What in | detail concerning our good will
70   both ‖ toward all of you together and toward each city | the ambassadors
     have heard, they will make known | to you. Farewell. *vv*

1   Cf. no. 8 n. 1.
2   Cf. no. 40 for this embassy.
3   On the basis of this reference and that to a war against the barbarians (1. 10), i.e. the
    Galatians, Holleaux dated the letter to the period immediately after Eumenes'
    rebuff by the Senate in 167 because of his attempt to mediate the Third Macedonian
    War (Polybius 30.19).
4   Lines 6 to 37 are a close paraphrase of this decree.

5   Welles notes that the missing word must be a verbal form meaning 'to show', but no
    satisfactory restoration has been proposed.
6   In the extended sense of members of the royal court.
7   Note the personal tone of the wish.
8   A Milesian decree (T. Wiegand, *Abhandlungen der Königlich preussischen Akademie der
    Wissenschaften*, Phil.-hist. Klasse (Berlin 1911) Anh. Abh. I.27–9, lines 2–3) suggests
    that the revenues were to be derived from money given by Eumenes to Miletos for
    investment.
9   Miletos founded Kyzikos, the home of Apollonis, Eumenes' mother.

89   Delphi honors Attalos II for establishing an educational endowment. Delphi, 160/59. Inscribed on the base of an equestrian statue of Attalos II.

SIG[3] 672; *Choix* 13.

Daux, *Delphes* 502–4; Hansen, *Attalids*[2] 459–60.

Resolved by the city of the Delphians in full assembly with lawful votes. |
Since King Attalos (II), son of King Attalos (I)[1] – we having | sent to
him previously as ambassadors Praxias, son of Eudokos, Kallias, son of
Eume|nidas, concerning the education of the children, and again
5   Praxias, son of Eudokos, ‖ Bakchios, son of Agron – being an ancestral
friend and favorably inclined toward the city | and being piously and
reverently disposed in matters concerning the gods, having listened
enthusias|tically to the requests, sent to the city for the children's
educa|tion eighteen thousand Alexander drachmas[2] in silver | and for
the honors and sacrifices three thousand drachmas; in order that the
10   gi‖ft might last for all time in perpetuity and the salaries for the teachers
be paid | regularly and that there be funds for the honors and sacrifices |
from the interest on the money loaned out, with good fortune, it has
been resolved by the | city that the money be dedicated to the god and
that it not be permitted either to a magistrate | or to any private citizen
15   to employ it for anything else in any other ‖ way either by decree or
resolution; and if anyone of these does such a thing, | be he magistrate
or private citizen, he shall be subject to condemnation for theft of
sacred monies, | and the mastroi[3] shall record against him according to
the decree or other|wise exact eight times the money, and the decree or
resolu|tion shall be invalid and without force. And if there is any
20   surplus from the interest, ‖ after payment of their salaries has been
made to the teachers just as has been ordained, it shall be referred to |
the probouloi[4] and the People, and what is resolved shall be binding. |
And three men who have been chosen as managers by the People shall
loan out the money | at one-fifteenth interest in the month Amalios[5] in

the archonship of Amphistratos.[6] Those wi|shing to receive a loan shall
25 register with the managers, who have been installed, ‖ (and they) shall
offer land as security. The land shall be worth double the money being
loaned, and there shall be loan|ed not less than five minas, and, further,
those taking out the loans shall designate guarantors whom also the
mana|gers approve, and the guarantors and securers shall offer
pledges. | And when they have made the loans, having listed those
taking out the loans and their pledges | on two whitened boards, they
30 shall read them aloud in the assembly. And the ‖ pledges shall be determined to be of sufficient value and free of claims. And they shall place
one board | in the temple[7] and the other board in the public records
office; and the expens|es and the travel money shall be appropriated at
the rate of exchange, and those managing it | shall render account to
the city. But in the future, the appointment of the managers and the
man|agement shall be as follows: The interest from the eighteen
35 thousand (drachmas) shall be expended for [the] ‖ teachers and from
the three thousand (drachmas) the honors and sacrifices shall be
offered by the managers of the | Attaleia[8] as follows: the magistrates for
the year shall nominate in writing | in the month Poitropios[9] in a lawful
assembly each year managers | (to the number of) three from those
proposed whom the People will select by vote. And after being
inst|alled, the managers shall swear as also the other magistrates, and
40 having exacted ‖ the interest on the money in the month
Enduspoitropios[10] before the fifteenth (day), | they shall deposit the
money for the teachers in the temple in the | month Herakleios,[11] and
during the rest of the year they shall pay the teachers | monthly, and
they shall render account to the city. And if they do not do as *has been
specified* [---][12] |

1 This decree was passed during the brief period at the end of Eumenes II's reign
  when Attalos bore the royal title as his brother's co-regent.
2 I.e. coins of Attic weight as had been those issued by Alexander.
3 'Seekers', judicial officials charged with investigating and punishing in matters of
  public interest such as, e.g., the scrutiny of magistrates.
4 A body of officials elected by the Delphians and charged with the responsibility of
  drafting decrees and resolutions.
5 Seventh month of the Delphian calendar, approximately equivalent to January.
6 Probably 160/59.
7 Presumably that of Apollo.
8 A festival in honor of Attalos II established in 160/59 together with one for his
  brother Eumenes II.
9 Sixth month of the Delphian calendar, approximately equivalent to December.
10 Tenth month of the Delphian calendar, approximately equivalent to April.
11 Eleventh month of the Delphian calendar, approximately equal to May.
12 Omitted are lines 45 to 87 which provide for: (1) the celebration of the Attaleia,

i.e. a festival in honor of Attalos II, (2) the publication of this decree and (3) the treatment of debtors defaulting on debts contracted under this decree as public debtors, that is, as subject to loss of citizenship.

90   Letter of Attalos II praising Aristo[---], tutor of Attalos III. Ephesos, about 150–140. Marble block, second-century lettering.

D. Knibbe, *JOAI* 47 (1974) Beiblatt 1–6 with photograph; *I. Ephesos* 202.

J. and L. Robert, *REG* 81 (1968) 95–6; Hopp, *Untersuchungen* 108.

[King Attalos] (II) to the Boule and people of the Ephesians, greeting. Aristo[--- | ---], your fellow citizen, having been judged worthy by us *to be in charge* of Attalos (III), [the son of] our *brother*,[1] | was summoned, and having been introduced to him, *provided* for the appropriate education. |
5   He was appointed by us especially because not only in his *acquain‖tance* with [and] *teaching* of oratory did he excel many, but also because in his whole character he appeared worthy of | *praise* and most fitted to associate with a youth, for (the fact) that the manners | of [their] over-seers are emulated by those youths who are naturally of noble character is evident to all. Wherefore, [indeed], he, having met not only from us but also from Attalos himself with an exceedingly gracious | reception, gained deserved distinction with us and with him.

1   Eumenes II (197–160).

91   Decree of Pergamon on citizenship after the death of Attalos III. Pergamon 133. Stele of white marble with a break running from the top center to the middle of the right side, broken at the bottom.

OGIS 338 = Sherk, *TDGR* 39; *Inscriptiones Graecae ad Res Romanas Pertinentes* (ed. Cagnat) IV 289. For the will of Attalos III cf. Livy, *Per.* 58–9; Strabo 13.4.2, C 624; Velleius Paterculus 2.4.1; Plutarch, *Tiberius Gracchus* 14; Pliny, *Nat. Hist.* 33.148; Appian, *Mithridatic Wars* 62; Justin 36.45.

T. R. S. Broughton, *Roman Asia, An Economic Survey of Ancient Rome*, ed. T. Frank (Baltimore 1938) 4.505–11; Magie, *RRAM* 1.147–50 and 2.1035 n. 5; F. Carrata Thomes, *La rivolta di Aristonico e le origini della provincia romana d'Asie* (Turin 1968) 35–41; Hansen, *Attalids*[2] 151–9; Hopp, *Untersuchungen* 121–38; G. Delplace, *Athenaeum* n.d. 56 (1978) 21–8.

In the priesthood of Menestra[tos], (son) of Apollodoros, | on the nineteenth of the month Eumeneios,[1] it was decreed by the | People on the motion of the strategoi: since King Attalos | Philometor and

5   Euergetes [passed away] from me‖n and left our *city* free, | having
included in it the territory which he judged to be *civic territory*,[2] | and
(since) his will must be ratified by the Romans, and (since) it is
[necessa|ry] for the common safety that the below lis|ted[3] peoples
10   share in the citizenship because of the whole-hearted good‖will that
they exhibited toward the People (of Pergamon), – with good luck, let
it be decree|d by the People to give citizenship to the *follow|ing*: those
registered in the lists of resident | aliens and of the soldiers living in the
ci|ty and its territory, and likewise the Macedonians and My[sians]
15   ‖ and those who are registered in the fort and [the] | old [city] as col-
onists, and the Masdyenoi[4] and [---] | and the police and the other [free
| men][5] living or owning property [in the city] | or the territory, and
20   likewise (their) wives and children. ‖ To the (class of) resident aliens
(etc.).[6]

When King Attalos III died in 133, naming the Romans as heirs to his kingdom and
granting the city of Pergamon the status of a free city – all subject, of course, to con-
firmation by Rome – a pretender to the throne called Aristonikos began a revolt that
lasted three years and was brought to an end by the combined forces of Rome, Greek
cities, and the kings of Pontos, Bithynia and Kappadokia. His appeal to classes such as
slaves, serfs, some royal soldiers, and non-Greeks was so great that the Pergamenes, in
order to forestall further defection to his cause, passed the present decree granting
citizenship to large numbers of the inhabitants who had not possessed it, with the hope
that the action would win their loyalty to the city.

1   No precise equivalent in the Julian calendar is possible.
2   Greek cities regularly controlled the adjacent countryside with its smaller com-
munities for some distance out from the city limits proper. P. Foucart, *Mémoires de
l'Académie des Inscriptions et Belles-Lettres* 37 (1904) 300, has suggested the phrase 'cities
and' for 'civic territory', thus: 'having included in it both *cities and* a territory which
he determined'.
3   Hansen translates the phrase as 'subordinate classes', and Delplace as 'les peuples
soumis'.
4   The Macedonians, Mysians and Masdyenians were colonists or settlers within
Pergamene borders. The soldiers previously mentioned were mercenaries of the
king.
5   Restoration by L. Robert, *Villes d'Asie Mineure*[2] (Paris 1962) 55 n. 6. Prott and Kolbe
in *Ath. Mitt.* 27 (1902) 109 n. 1, suggest '[auxiliary troops]'.
6   The text continues on for seventeen more lines, listing the classes of individuals
who are to be transferred to the class of resident aliens and depriving certain others
of their civic rights who had left the city or who may hereafter leave it. The stone
breaks off at a point where further provisions are being made about the granting of
citizenship.

Chapter 6
PTOLEMAIC EGYPT: KINGDOM AND EMPIRE

92   Decree of the League of the Islanders recognizing the Ptolemaieia. Amorgos, about 280–278. Marble stele, third-century lettering, found at Nikuria but originally from Amorgos.

IG XII 7.506 with drawing; *SIG*[3] 390.

Tarn, *JHS* 31 (911) 251–9; Tarn, *JHS* 53 (1933) 61–8; Rostovtzeff, *SEHHW* 1.139; P. M. Fraser, *BCH* 78 (1954) 55–60; P. M. Fraser, *HTR* 54 (1961) 141–5; J. Bosquet, *BCH* 82 (1958) 77–82; I. Merker, *Historia* 19 (1970) 141–60; J. Seibert, *Historia* 19 (1970) 337–51; Fraser, *Ptolemaic Alexandria* 1.231–2; Shear, *Hesperia* Supp. 17 (1978) 33–7; E. Turner, *CAH*[2] 138–9.

Resolution of the delegates of the Islanders,[1] concerning the matters (about which) | [Philokle]s, the king of the Sidonians,[2] and Bakchon, the Ne‖[siarch],[3] *wrote* to the cities, namely, that *they dis|patch* delegates
5   to Samos[4] *to* ‖ *deliberate* about the sacrifice and *sacred en|voys* and the contest, which King Pt[o|le]maios has established in honor of his father in Alexandria *as equivalent to the Olympi|c*, [and (which) now] with those who had come from the cities as *dele|gates* from the cities who were
10   present Philokles and Bakchon *discussed. It has been re‖|solved* by the assembly of delegates that, since the | king and savior, Ptolemaios,[5] was the cause of so many | great good things for | both the Islanders and the
15   other Greeks, | having freed the cities and returned their laws ‖ and re-established the ancestral constitution for all | and relieved (them) from eisphora;[6] and now, since King | Ptolemaios, having received the kingdom from | his father,[7] is continuing to display the same good will
20   and concern | for the Islanders and ‖ the other Greeks; and (since) he is offering a sacrifice in honor of his father | and has established contests equivalent to the Olympic – athletic and | musical and equestrian – and, preserving both his *piety* toward the gods | and maintaining his
25   good will toward his *ances|tors*, is urging in regard to these matters ‖ that the Islanders and the other Greeks *vo|te* that the contest be equivalent to the Olympic;[8] *it is pro|per* for all the Islanders, who were the *first*[9] to honor | the savior Ptolemaios with honors equal to those of a god | [both] *because* of his *public* [benefactions] and because of their *individual*
30   ‖ [obligations to King Pto]lemaios, who *urg|ed* [them on other occasions] to join with him, that they now | *vote* in accordance with [his decision with all] enthusiasm | [---] and [--- | ---] *to be given* worthy honors
35   ‖ [--- of] their good will, | *to recognize* the sacrifice and *to dispatch* sacred

117

envoys | for all time at the *ap|propriate* [times] just as the king has
written; | *and* the contest shall be equivalent to the Olympic and, as for
40   those victors, ‖ [who are Islanders], they shall receive the same honors
as those which | have been [specified] in the laws of each of the
Islanders | for victors in the Olympic games; and they shall also crown |
King Ptolemaios, son of the king and | savior, Ptolemaios, with a *gold*
45   wreath *of val‖or* (valued at) a thousand *staters* because of his excellence
and *good* | *will* toward the Islanders, and the *delegates* shall inscribe | this
decree on a stone stele and | [set it up on] Delos next to the altar of the
savior | [Pt]ole[mai]os. And, [accordingly], let there be passed by vote
50   this ‖ decree also by the cities that are members of the coun|cil, and let
them inscribe it on stone stelae | and place them in the sanctuaries in
which also the other hon|ors have been recorded in each. *And* there
shall be chosen | also by the delegates three sacred envoys who, *when*
55   *they arri‖ve* in Alexandria, shall offer sacrifice both on behalf of the |
league of the Islanders to Ptolemaios the savior and | shall present [the]
wreath to the king. And the | money for the wreath and for traveling
costs and *expen|ses* for the sacred envoys shall be furnished by cities, *each*
60   ‖ [according to its] *assessment*, and turned over to whomever Bak[chon |
designated]. Chosen as sacred envoys were Glaukon from Kyth[nos, |
---] from Naxos, Kleokritos from Andros.

1   The League of the Islanders was founded by Antigonos and Demetrios in 315/14
   (Diodorus 19.62.9) as a framework for controlling the Aegean and was then taken
   over by Ptolemaios I about 287. Its exact extent is unknown but probably included
   most of the Cyclades.
2   Philokles, son of Apollodoros, king of Sidon, is attested as nauarch (admiral), that
   is, commander of Ptolemaic naval forces in the Aegean with supreme authority over
   the islands, first under Ptolemaios II. All attempts to reconstruct his earlier career
   are hypothetical (cf. Merker and Seibert).
3   Bakchon, son of Niketas, a Boiotian, Nesiarch (governor of the islands), was the
   resident Ptolemaic representative to the League of the Islanders, albeit with military
   authority.
4   The date of the founding of the Ptolemaieia and, hence, of this decree, rests on two
   facts: (1) that Samos belonged to Lysimachos in 282 (cf. no. 12), and (2) that the first
   celebration of the Ptolemaieia occurred prior to the restoration of the Panathenaia
   in the summer of 278 (cf. no. 55).
5   Ptolemaios I was deified as Soter (Savior) by Rhodes in 304 (Diodorus 19.100.3)
   and by his son Ptolemaios II in 282.
6   Extraordinary levies in addition to regular tribute, probably demanded by
   Demetrios Poliorketes. Dittenberger refers these events to 310–308 although 287 is
   possible also.
7   The allusion is probably to Ptolemaios II's accession in 282 as sole king following
   his father's death and not to his association as co-regent in 285.
8   The festival was penteteric, that is, celebrated every four years.
9   *IG* XII 7.506 reads '*previously him . . .*'. Dittenberger suggests that the allusion was to
   Ptolemaios I's cruise of the Aegean in 308 (Diodorus 20.37.2).

93   Alexandrian sacred law concerning sacrifices to Arsinoe Philadelphos. Oxyrhynchos, Egypt, law dated about 267. Selections from a papyrus containing fragments of a work by the late third-century Peripatetic, Satyros of Kallatis, *On the Demes of Alexandria.*

P. Oxy. 27 (1967) 2465 as corrected by L. Robert, *Essays Welles* 192–210.

Hauben, *Callikrates* 41–6; Burstein, 'Arsinoe II' 201–2; E. Turner, *CAH*[2] 169.

[---] let no one walk [--- | ---] the kanephoros[1] [--- | --- of A]r[si]noe
10   Philadelph[os --- ‖ together with the] prytaneis and the priests *and* [the
      magi|strates] and the ephebes[2] and the *rodbearers.* | [As for those] who
      wish to sacrifice to Arsin[oe Phila|de]lphos,[3] let them sacrifice before
15   *their own do|ors* or on their *houses* or *by* [the] ‖ road along which the
      kanephoros *walks.* | Let all sacrifice either a bird [or whateve|r] *each*
      wishes except a male go|at and a female goat.[4] Further, *let the* altars be
20   made | by everyone of *sand;*[5] but if some ‖ *have* altars made of bricks, let
      them | strew sand on them and [on] *th|is* let them place the fire wood on
      [which] | they will burn [the] pulses [---].

1 'Basket-bearer', the title of the priestess of Arsinoe Philadelphos, first attested in
   267. Lines 7 through 11 of the law deal with organizing the procession in honor of
   Arsinoe Philadelphos.
2 See Glossary.
3 Probably deified posthumously, although Turner has again restated the case for a
   date during her lifetime.
4 Robert has shown that the law presupposes the identification of Arsinoe with
   Aphrodite. The prohibition on the sacrifice of goats would differentiate her from
   Aphrodite Pandemos, Aphrodite of the Whole People, the patroness of prostitutes,
   to whom they were sacred.
5 The sand altars are to be connected with Arsinoe's identification with Aphrodite
   Euploia, Aphrodite of the Fair Voyage, the patroness of sailors, in which form she
   was worshipped in the temple dedicated to her at Cape Zephyrium near Alexandria
   by the admiral, Kallikrates of Samos. Probably also to be connected with these sand
   or brick altars are the small plaques inscribed 'Of Arsinoe | Philadelphos' (*OGIS* 39)
   which have been found in various places in the Aegean basin.

94   Allocation of the apomoira to the cult of Arsinoe Philadelphos. Fayum, 263/2. Extract from a papyrus containing revenue regulations.

C. Ord. Ptol.[2] 17.

M. Rostovtzeff, *A Large Estate in Egypt in the Third Century B.C.* (Madison 1922) 17, 165;
Rostovtzeff, *SEHHW* 1.283; D. J. Crawford, *Studies on Ptolemaic Memphis* (Louvain 1980)
23–7.

[--- in order that] *it happen in accordance with the written* (instructions).[1] | *vv*
Farewell. (year) 23 (263/2), Daisios 5. | The royal secretaries of the
nomes *in the countryside*, | each for the nome of which *he is secretary*, shall
5   record ‖ both the number of aroura of vi|nes [and] of orchards, and the
yields from these, | farmer *by farmer*, since (year) 22 (264/3), separating
out | the *sacred land* and the yields from it, | in order that [the] remainder
10 [---] from which the sixth[2] is to be collected ‖ for the [Phi]la[delphos],[3]
and they shall turn in a list of these | to the agents of [Satyro]s.
Likewise, | the *kleruchs*[4] also, who have *vineyards* | or *orchards* on the
military allotments which they received from the ki|ng and all the rest
15 who possess ‖ vineyards or orchards, either having them on gift (land)[5]
or cu|ltivating them in any fashion, shall each | record his own both as
to the extent of the land and the yi|elds and shall give the sixth of the
yields | to [Ars]inoe Philad[el]phos for the sacrifices and the *drink
offerings*.

1 The reference is to the general law concerning the apomoira (cf. n. 2), one of whose
   provisions this text implements.
2 The apomoira, a tax of one sixth on vineyards, which was collected by the temples
   prior to the promulgation of the regulation contained in this document which
   assigned it to the cult of Arsinoe Philadelphos.
3 The deified sister-wife of Ptolemaios II whose cult in all Egyptian temples the
   apomoira was to support.
4 Greek and Macedonian soldiers paid with land allotments intended to provide their
   economic support (see Glossary).
5 Estates conditionally granted to royal officials for the purpose of bringing them
   under cultivation or improving their management.

95   Letter of Ptolemaios II to Miletos. Miletos, about 262. Marble
stele.

I. Didyma 139;*Welles, *RC* 14.

G. de Sanctis, *Atti dell' Acc. c. di Torino* 49 (1913–14) 122–4; W. W. Tarn, *JHS* 46 (1926)
158–61; Bevan, *Ptolemy* 68–9, 386–7; Welles, *RC* pp. 72–6, 161–2; A. Momigliano and
P. Fraser, *Classical Quarterly* 44 (1950) 108–18; A. D. Roos, *Mnemosyne*[4] 3 (1950) 59–63; J.
Crampa, *I. Labraunda* 98–199; Hauben, *Callicrates* 52–7; J. Seibert, *Chiron* 1 (1971) 159–
66; Bagnall, *Administration* 173; Burstein, *The Ancient World* 3 (1980) 77–9; H. Heinen,
CAH[2] 418–19.

King Ptolemaios (II)[1] to the Boule and the people of the Milesians,
greeting. | Previously I exerted myself greatly on behalf of your city, |
both giving it land[2] and taking care in other matters, as was proper, |
because I saw that our father toward the city was also favorably
5   dis‖posed and had been the cause of many good things for you, having

relieved you of tributes | which were harsh and irksome and from transit
duties which certain | of the kings had imposed;[3] and now, as you have
properly preserved both the city and | friendship with us and the
alliance – for | the son[4] and Kallikrates[5] and the other friends who are
10   among you have written to me (and described) what a d‖emonstration
of your good will toward us you have made – and we ourselves,
agree|ing, praise you very greatly and we shall try to repay the Peo|ple
by conferring benefits. In the future also we urge | you to maintain the
same attitude toward us, in order that we also, you being such people,
even greater | care for the city may exercise. But we have instructed
15   Hegestra‖tos to speak further concerning these matters and to extend
to you greetings from us. Farewell.[6]

1   Tarn's date of 276/5 has not found acceptance. About 262 is based on the identification of Peithenous, proposer of the answering Milesian decree (*I. Didyma* 139, line
22) with the stephanephoros of 261/60.
2   Cf. no. 25.
3   The refusal to mention any enemy by name is common. The kings in question have
been variously identified with Asander, Antigonos Monophthalmos, Demetrios
Poliorketes and Seleukos I, and Lysimachos; and Ptolemaios I's benefactions have
been dated to 314, 308, the early 290s and 294–287 (cf. Seibert and Burstein).
4   Ptolemaios the Son, co-regent with Ptolemaios II from about 267 to 259. He died in
a revolt at Ephesos (Athenaeus 13.593a–b). He has been identified with Ptolemaios,
the son of Lysimachos and ruler of Telmessos under Ptolemaios III (cf. no. 100), a
son of Ptolemaios II and Arsinoe II or an otherwise unattested illegitimate son of
Ptolemaios II. For various reasons only the latter identification appears to fit (cf.
Welles, Roos and Crampa).
5   Kallikrates, son of Boiskos, from Samos, nauarch (admiral) under Ptolemaios II
from the 270s until the 250s.
6   There follows the answering Milesian decree (*I. Didyma* 139, lines 16–51) which
refers to the present military threat to Miletos, Ptolemaios having arranged peace
for the city because of its loyalty, and the decision of the Milesians that annually the
ephebes and the other citizens would swear an oath of loyalty to Ptolemaios and his
house.

96   Letter of Ptolemaios II concerning the revenues. Fayum, 259. Papyrus.

B. P. Grenfell and A. S. Hunt, *The Amherst Papyri* 2 (London 1901), no. 33 (with plate IX);
C. Ord. Ptol.[2] 23.

Rostovtzeff, *SEHHW* 2.1094.

King Ptolemaios (II) to Apollonios,[1] greeting. Since some | of the
advocates listed below are intervening in | fiscal cases to the detriment
of the revenues, issue instructions | that those advocates shall pay to

5   the crown twice ‖ the additional tenth[2] and that they shall no longer be
allowed to serve as advocates in an|y matter. And if any of those, who
have harmed the revenues, | be discovered to have served as advocate
in some matter, have him | sent to us under guard and have his property
| assigned to the crown. (Year) 27, Gorpaios 15.[3]

1 Dioiketes, that is, chief fiscal officer and by extension head of the civil administration, under Ptolemaios II from about 261 to about 246 (see Glossary).
2 A fine levied at the conclusion of a case on the loser at the rate of one-tenth the
   amount at issue.
3 6 October 259.

**97   Demotic copy of an order of Ptolemaios II concerning the
preparation of a comprehensive survey of Egypt. Thebes, Egypt,
258.** Terracotta ostrakon. The translation is based on the Italian
version of an unpublished Demotic Egyptian text which is itself a
translation of a lost Greek original.

*E. Bresciani, *Das ptolemäische Aegypten* 31–7 with photograph.

E. Turner, *CAH*² 135–6.

Inventory of the royal domain. The inventory of which a written copy
was ordered to be made so that it would be (possible) | to conduct an
audit. Everything connected with it was delivered to Phoinix (P3 njk),[1]
the chief treasurer (mr-ḫtm),[2] in the 28th year, in the month of Thoth,[3] |
of the king who was victorious over the Philopersian king[4] | when he
entered Syria. His scribes and district officials compiled it, from
5   ‖ Elephantine to the Mediterranean, in detail nome by nome, altogether
36 provinces.[5] They declared and | reported concerning the water,
(noting) when the basins (are full) and the flooded fields | are green,
enumerating their water sources and levees. A census of Egypt was
ordered, | specifying field by field, their irrigation possibilities, their
location, their quality, their arable | portions, their relation to the
property of the protector gods, their (common) borders with the fields
10   ‖ of the benefices themselves and of the royal fields, specifying area by
area, the size of the parcels | and vineyards, noting when the fields of
the area are dry – likewise the pastures – and the water channels, the
fields | that are free and vacant, the high fields and the fields that are
(artificially) irrigated, | their basins, and the embankments that are
ploughed and cultivated, specifying orchard by orchard the trees with
their fruits, the gardens, the high fields and the low parcels, | their foot-
paths, the list of leased parcels with their equipment, the decisions

15   concerning price in connection with them, ‖ the emoluments of the
priests, the emoluments of the dependents of the reigning king, and, in
addition, their taxes, | the total of the expenditures for the welfare of
Egypt and its sublime freedom, of its cities | and of its temples.

1   Since Apollonios was still dioiketes in 258, Bresciani suggests that Phoinix, first
    attested in office in 242, temporarily occupied the post during an absence from
    Egypt by Apollonios in 259/8.
2   The first attestation of the Egyptian equivalent of the title dioiketes.
3   First month of the Egyptian calendar, equivalent to November 258 since in Egyptian
    documents Ptolemaios II's regnal years were counted inclusively from the begin-
    ning of his co-regency with his father in 285.
4   Depending on whether the First or Second Syrian War is intended, the reference is
    to Antiochos I (281–262) or Antiochos II (262–246). The description of him as the
    'Philopersian King' is an attempt to capitalize on the hostility of the Egyptians to
    their former Persian rulers. Turner, indeed, suggests that the purpose of the survey
    documented by this text was to provide the basis for raising revenue needed to fight
    the Second Syrian War.
5   The text differentiates provinces, that is administrative districts, from the tra-
    ditional 42 nomes that formed the basis of the Pharaonic organization of Egypt and
    were responsible for the furnishing of military forces and provisions for royal
    undertakings; cf. R. O. Faulkner, *JEA* 39 (1953) 32–47. As the scribe entered an
    interlinear correction of the numeral to 39, Bresciani suggests that three new
    districts had been created shortly before the decree was issued.

98   Report on the Third Syrian War, possibly by Ptolemaios III. Gurob, Egypt, about 246/5. Papyrus, third-century script.

P. Petrie 2.45, 3.144; L. Mitteis and U. Wilcken, *Grundzüge und Chrestomathie der Papyrus-kunde* (Leipzig 1912) l. 1; F.Bilabel, *Die kleineren Historikerfragmente auf Papyrus* (Bonn 1923) 9; *FGrHist* 160; Holleaux, *Études* 3.281–315; cf. *Daniel* 11.7–9, Justin 27.1.5–9, Polyaenus 8.50, and Porphyry, *FGrHist* 260F43.

Bevan, *Seleucus* 1.184–6; G. de Sanctis, *Atti dell' Acc. di Torino* 47 (1911–12), 801–8; A. G. Roos, *Mnemosyne* n.s. 52 (1923) 262–78; Bevan, *Ptolemy* 192–203 with photograph; G. Downey, *A History of Antioch in Syria from Seleucus to the Arab Conquest* (Princeton 1961) 89–90; Will, *Histoire* 1².248–54; H. Heinen, *CAH²* 420–1.

I

20   [---][1] and afterwards, [having given] a pledge ‖ [to them and] *appointed*
Epigenes to be in charge of the | [citadel and turned over to him] the
city, at sunrise, | [---] after sending a message, he withdrew. | [---] At the
25   same time and | [with the ---] *15* boats of the sister, ‖ [---]

II

[---] and they sailed | along the coast to Soli in [Kilik]ia and *took on board*
5   the | *monies* that were stored *there* and transported them to ‖ Seleukeia,
1500 (talents) of [silver, | which] Aribazos, the *strategos* in Kili<ki>a
had intended to send | to Ephesos to the supporters of Laodike (I). An
agreement, however, had been made | among themselves by the citizens
of Soli and <the> soldiers | *there*, and *strong support* was provided by
10   ‖ Pythagoras and Aristokles [---]. | Since they were all good men, it
happened that | these monies were seized and the city and the | citadel
came into our hands [---] Aribazos fl|ed, but when he had reached the
15   vicinity of the pass through the Tauros (Mountains), ‖ some of the
natives cut off his *head* | and *brought* it to Antioch. [Meanwhile, after
we][2] | *had readied* the *ships*, at the beginning of the first | watch, we
embarked on as many ships as | the harbor at Seleuk[eia][3] would be able
20   to accommodate, and sailed along the coast ‖ to the fortress called
[P]osideion and dropped anchor | about the *eighth hour* of the day. In the
morning we set sail from there | and arrived at Seleukeia; | and the
priests, *archons* and *the* other citizens, | the commanders and soldiers,
25   (all) wearing ‖ wreaths, came to the harbor | to meet us.

III

[---] good will [toward] *us* | [---] to the city | [---] *the* sacrificial victims *set*
5   *out* | [on the] *altars* that *they* ‖ *had prepared* [---] and the honors at the mart |
were proclaimed by [---] *on this same* | *day* [---] and on the next day | [---] as
10   much as was possible | [---] on which (ships) *we recei*‖*ved* [---] *all* those |
[who had sailed] with us [and] the satraps [from] the region together
with the *strategoi* [and other] commanders who *were not* | *stationed* [---] *in*
15   the city and the | [citadel ---] | *the garrison* ‖ [---] for they were amazing |
[---] *Afterwards* to Antioch[4] | [---] such preparations [--- | ---] *we found* so
that [we] were astonished. | For [there came to meet] us outside the
20   gate ‖ the [---], the satraps, the other *com*|*manders* [and the] *soldiers*
together with the priests and the magistrates | and [all the] young men
from the gymnasium and the rest of the | *populace* [---] *wearing wreaths*;
and the ritual objects | had been brought out by them to the road in
25   front [of the gate]. Some *welcomed* (us) ‖ and others [greeted us] with
applause and shouting. |

IV

15   [--- | ---][5] by each house | [---] they continued doing ‖ [---] While there
were many things for us | [---] by nothing were we so pleased *as* | *by their*

zeal. Afterwards, | the sacrificial victims that had been set out [---] |
20   an\<d\> those of the private citizens we sacrificed. As it already ‖ was
nearly sunset, we immediately went | in to the sister.[6] Afterwards, | we
dealt with affairs, received the | commanders, soldiers and others | in
25   the area, and deliberated ‖ and made plans about *everything*. In addition
to these matters, for *some* days | [---].

1   Lines 1 to 19 of Col. I deal with the capture of a city in Kilikia but are too fragmentary for translation.
2   Probably Ptolemaios III (246–222).
3   Seleukeia in Pieria, the port of Antioch, which was occupied by Ptolemaic forces from 246 to 219.
4   Occupied by Ptolemaic forces from 246 to 244.
5   Twelve lines are missing.
6   Berenike, the sister of Ptolemaios III, whose appeal to her brother for aid against the forces of Laodike and her children was the ostensible cause of the Third Syrian War. The simple reference to her as 'the sister' and the constant use of the first person plural by the author in referring to himself are the main reasons for assigning this work to Ptolemaios III himself. The apparent contradiction between this text which suggests that Berenike was alive at the time of her brother's arrival in Antioch and the unanimous evidence of the literary sources that she was already dead is probably to be resolved, as Holleaux proposed, on the basis of Polyaenus 8.50, namely, that Ptolemaios found her dead but co-operated in maintaining the fiction originally devised by her attendants that the attack on her had failed.

99   The Adulis Inscription of Ptolemaios III. 246–222. An inscription originally set up in Adulis, modern Massawa, on the Red Sea coast of Ethiopia and preserved in a copy made by the sixth-century AD traveler Cosmas Indicopleustes (*Christian Topography* 2.58–9). Line divisions are conventional only.

OGIS 54; Cosmas Indicopleustes, *Topographie chrétienne*, ed. W. Wolska-Conus (Paris 1968) 1.364–86; cf. Appian, *Syriaka* 65, Justin 27.1.9 and Porphyry, *FGrHist* 160F43.

Bevan, *Seleucus* 1.181–90; Bevan, *Ptolemy* 192–3; Fraser, *Ptolemaic Alexandria* 2.344 n. 106; H. H. Scullard, *The Elephant in the Greek and Roman World* (London 1974) 126–37; Will, *Histoire* 1².250–4.

The great king, Ptolemaios (III), son of King Ptolemaios | and of Queen Arsinoe,[1] the gods Adelphoi, the children of King | Ptolemaios and of Queen Berenike,[2] the gods Soteres, | descended through his father
5   from Herakles, the son of Zeus, and through his mo‖ther from Dionysos, the son of Zeus,[3] having inherited from his father | dominion over Egypt and Libya and Syria | and Phoinikia and Kypros and Lykia and Karia and the | Cycladic Islands,[4] he marched out into Asia[5] with |

10   infantry and cavalry forces and a fleet ‖ and elephants – Troglodytic[6]
     and Aithiopian[7] – which his father │ and he first hunted in these
     countries, │ and, having brought them back to Egypt, trained for │
     military use.[8] And having become master of all the countries on this
     side of the Euphrates │ and of Kilikia and of Pamphylia and of Ionia and
15   of the Hel‖lespont and of Thrace and of all forces in these countries │
     and of Indian elephants; and having made the rulers in │ these places
     all subjects, he crossed the Euphrates │ River; and, after having made
     Mesopotamia and Babylonia and Sousi│ana and Persis and Media and
20   all the rest as far as ‖ Baktriana his subjects;[9] and after having sought
     out all │ the sacred objects which had been taken from Egypt by the
     Persians and return│ed (them) together with the other treasures from
     these places to E│gypt,[10] he sent his forces through the can│als [---].[11]

1   Actually he was the son of Ptolemaios II (285–246) by his first wife, Arsinoe I, and
    was later adopted by Arsinoe II at the instigation of his father (cf. scholion on
    Theocritus 17, line 128).
2   Ptolemaios I (305–282) and Berenike I.
3   Not quite correct since both Ptolemaios II and Arsinoe II claimed descent from
    Hylas, the son of Herakles, the son of Zeus and Deianeira, the daughter of
    Dionysos (cf. Satyros, *FGrHist* 631F1 = Theophilus *Ad Autol.* 2.7 for the genealogy
    of Ptolemaios IV).
4   Cf. Theocritus 17, lines 85–92.
5   In 246 at the beginning of the Third Syrian War (246–241); cf. no. 98.
6   Manuscript reading. The correct form is Trogodytic.
7   Elephants from Trogodytike, the coastal regions of the Red Sea, and Aithiopia,
    the interior of the Sudan.
8   Cf. Diodorus 3.18.4 and 40–1, Strabo 16.4.14, C 773–4.
9   Appian says he advanced as far as Babylon. According to Porphyry he appointed
    two governors, Antiochos, one of his friends, for Kilikia, and Xanthippos for the
    Trans-Euphrates areas.
10 Porphyry says that he brought back 40,000 talents of silver and 2500 sacred vessels
    and divine images that had been looted from Egypt by Kambyses.
11 Justin and Porphyry attribute his return to a revolt in Egypt. His route is disputed.
    If the canals are those of Babylonia, he returned by sea around Arabia; if they are
    those of the Nile, then he returned the same way he had come.

**100   Telmessos honors Ptolemaios, son of Lysimachos. Telmessos,
240/239.** White marble stele broken down the middle, from Makri,
Turkey.

M. Bérard, *BCH* 14 (1980) 162–7; *OGIS* 55; **TAM* 2.1 (with drawing).

C. Préaux, *L'économie royale des Lagides* (Brussels 1939) 421; Holleaux, *Études* 3.365–404;
Magie, *RRAM* 2.762–4.

vv With good fortune. *vv* | In the reign of King Ptolemaios (III), the son of Ptole|[ma]ios and of Arsinoe, the gods Adelphoi, | *seventh* year, in the
5   month Dystros,[1] in the year in which the priest[2] is Theodo||[to]s, son of Herakleides, on the second day, *ma*|*in* assembly, it was resolved by the Telmessian | city. Since Ptolemaios, the son of Lysima|[cho]s,[3] having received the city from Kin|g [Pt]olemaios, the son of Ptolemaios, in a
10   poor || *state* because of the wars,[4] both in | [other matters] *continues* caring publicly for the | [citizens] and for each privately, and, seeing that they were in every way | *distressed,* he has granted that they be *exempt* from
15   (the levies on) *woo*|*d, fruits* and pasturage; and he caused the || tax on *grain,*[5] on pulses of all kinds and on *keg*|*chros* and *elymos*[6] and sesame and lupines, which *for*|*merly* was levied unfairly, | to be levied according to the *law,* calculating the tithe [---][7] | both [to the] farmer and the
20   tithe-farmer; and as for the *remaining items* || connected to the grain *tax,*[8] he granted that they be exempt from all of them; it has been resolved by the Te|[lmes]sians that they praise Ptolemaios Epig[--|-]s[9] for the good will he continues to have for the | *city* of the Telmessians and that
25   there be set up || *on his behalf* an altar to Zeus the Savior in the market place in | *the* most prominent place, and that they sacrifice year|ly in the month of Dystros on the eleventh day a *three-year-old* bull | and that there shall be an assembly of all the *cit*|*izens* together with the paroikoi[10] for
30   the sacrifice. [But] if || the archon[11] and the citizens do not perform the | *sacrifice* every year, they shall be (considered) sinners | (against) all the *gods* and the archon shall pay a sacred fine | to Zeus the Savior of one thousand drachmas, *un*|*less* because of war *he is prevented from performing*
35   the sacrifice. || This decree shall be inscribed by the *ar*|*chon* on a stone stele and he shall set it up in the | sanctuary of Artemis in the most prominent *pla*|*ce,* and, as for the expenses incurred, they shall be borne | by the city. *vv*

1   About February or March 240/39.
2   Bérard suggested the priest of Alexander and the Ptolemies.
3   The son of Lysimachos and Arsinoe, he had escaped being murdered by Ptolemaios Keraunos by fleeing first to the Illyrians (Trogus, *Prolog* 24) and thence to Egypt. Attested as a Friend of Ptolemaios II with connections to Telmessos sometime between 265/4 and 257/6, he received the city as a gift estate from Ptolemaios III shortly before the date of this inscription.
4   Presumably the Third Syrian War (246–241) is meant.
5   Restored by Dittenberger on the basis of line 20.
6   Two kinds of millet.
7   A corrupt word follows.
8   These taxes probably ante-date Ptolemaic rule of Telmessos instead of being the result of the introduction of the Ptolemaic fiscal system from Egypt. The 'remaining items' are probably illegal surcharges demanded by the tithe-farmers.
9   Holleaux restored 'Epi[gono]s' ('After-born') and interpreted it as an epithet

identifying Ptolemaios as belonging to the generation following that of
Alexander's successors (*TAM* = 'in [all | ways]').
10   Resident aliens.
11   The chief magistrate of Telmessos.

101   Selections from a memorandum of instructions by a dioiketes to an oikonomos. Tebtunis (Fayum), Egypt. Papyrus, third-century script. Dated by script and internal evidence to the reign of Ptolemaios III (246–222).

*P. Tebt. 703.

D. J. Crawford, *Das ptolemäische Aegypten* 195–202; E. Turner, *CAH²* 147–52, 158.

During your tours | of inspection,[1] try, *while making your rounds*, to
encourage each individual | and to make them bolder. Do this not only
45   by word | but also, if some of them ‖ lay a complaint against the village
scribes or komarchs[2] | concerning some matter pertaining to farming, |
look into it and, so | far as you can, put an end to such situations. | And
50   when the sowing has been completed, ‖ it would not be a bad idea if you
made a careful inspection; | for, thus, you will accurately observe the
sprouting, | and you will easily identify the (fields) that have been
improperly sown | or not sown at all;| and *you will learn* [from] this those
55   who were careless ‖ and you will know [if some] | have employed the
seeds for other purposes. | In addition, the | sowing of the nome in
60   accordance with the plan for planting | is to be one of your ‖ prime
concerns. And if some are | suffering because of their rents or | even
have been completely ruined, do not *allow* this to be *un\examined*. Also,
65   make a list | of the oxen involved [in] farming, ‖ both *royal and* private, |
and exercise due care | that the *calves* of the royal cattle, | when they are
70   ready to eat hay, | *are sent* to the *calf-rearing* ‖ barns.[3]

It is your responsibility | also that the designated | provisions *are trans-*
85   *ported* to Alexan\dria – of these we are sending you a list – on ‖ schedule,
(and) [not] only in the proper amount, | but *also tested* and | suitable for
consumption. Go | also to the weaving sheds in which the | linen is
90   woven and take special ‖ care that *as many as possible* of the lo\oms are in
operation | and that the weavers are completing | the amount of fabric
95   specified | in the plan. If | some are behind in their assigned ‖ work, let
them be fined | for each category the sche\duled price. Moreover, to the
end that the linen | be usable *and* have the number of threads specified
in | the regulation *pay careful attention.*[4] As for looms that are not | in
115   operation, have all of them transported to the ‖ nome metropolis[5] and

stor|ed in the storerooms under | seal. Conduct an audit also of the |
revenues, if it is possible, | village by village, and this seems to be not
120 im‖possible if you zealously | apply yourself to the task; | but if not, then
toparchy[6] by | toparchy, accepting in the audit | with regard to money
125 taxes ‖ only what has been deposited at the bank;[7] | and with regard to
the grain taxes and | oil produce what has been measured | (and
received) by the sitologoi.[8] If | there is any deficiency in these, *compel* |
130 the toparchs[9] and the tax farmers[10] ‖ to pay to the banks | for arrears in
the grain tax the price specified | in the schedule and for arrears in the
oil | produce by wet measure according to each category.[11]

As the revenue from the pasture dues is | among the most significant, it
will be particularly increased | if *you conduct* the census in the best way. |
The most suitable time for | *it* is around the month of Mesore,[12] for, at
170 ‖ this time, because the [whole] land is covered by the | flood waters,
the herdsmen send their *herds* to | the highest places, | as they are unable
175 to disperse them to *other pl|aces.* You should also take care that *g‖oods* are
not sold for more than the speci|fied prices. As for those goods without
set | prices and for which the vendors | *may charge* what they wish,
180 examine | this carefully and, having determined a mod‖erate profit for
the merchandise being so|ld, compel the | [---] make the disposition.[13]

Make a list also of the | royal houses and of the | gardens associated
with them and who | is supposed to care for each, | and inform us.
215 ‖ Further, it should be your concern also that affairs regarding the |
machimoi[14] be handled in accordance with the mem|orandum which *we*
drafted concerning | persons who had absconded from their | tasks and
220 [---] sailors in order that to ‖ [---] the prisoners be confined until their |
transportation to Alexan|dria.[15] Take particular care that no | fraud
225 occur or any other | wrongful act, ‖ for it ought to be clearly understood
| by everyone living in the countryside | and believed that all such |
matters have been corrected and | that they are free from the former
230 evil conditions, ‖ since *no one*[16] has the power | to do what he wishes but
everything is being managed | in the best way. (Thus) you will create
security in the countryside | and (increase) the revenues sig|nificantly.[17]

260 The reasons I sent you to the nome, | I told you, ‖ but I thought it would
be good also to send you a written copy of them in this memorandum.[18]
Afterwards, | *you should behave well* and be upright in your | duties, not
275 *become involved* with bad | company, avoid *any* involvement ‖ in corrup-
tion, believe | that if you are not accused of such things, | you will merit
promotion, have | this memorandum at hand | and write concerning
280 each matter as re‖quired.

1   The tone of the document as a whole and the context of line 258 in particular suggests that its author was a dioiketes (cf. Glossary) and that it was addressed to an oikonomos (steward), his representative in a nome.
2   Village headman. In Egypt the komarch was in charge of the civil administration of a village and was responsible to his superiors at the toparchy (cf. n. 6) and nome level for his village's compliance with the economic demands of the government; cf. Preisigke, *s.v.* Komarchos, *RE* 11 (1922) 1129–31.
3   Omitted are lines 70 to 81.
4   Omitted are lines 100 to 112.
5   The capital of a nome.
6   An administrative subdivision of a nome comprising several villages.
7   In the metropolis of each nome and in some villages there were branch banks of the royal bank at Alexandria which had as their main function the receipt of all payments and taxes due the king.
8   The managers of the royal granaries in the various nomes.
9   The governor of a toparchy.
10 Not tax collectors but individuals who purchased contracts from the government requiring them to act as guarantors for the accurate collection of taxes and promised them a share of any surplus collected as their profit.
11 Omitted are lines 135 to 165.
12 Twelfth month of the Egyptian calendar, approximately equivalent to June–July.
13 Omitted are lines 183 to 210.
14 The native Egyptian military caste.
15 Turner notes that the suggestion that this alludes to recent unrest connected with the uprising that caused Ptolemaios III to return from his Asian campaign in 241 (cf. no. 99 n. 11) has recently been confirmed by the similar remarks concerning sailors found in *P. Hibeh* II 198, which is dated to shortly after 243/2.
16 I.e. no government official.
17 Omitted are lines 234 to 257.
18 Omitted are lines 261 to 270.

102   Narrative of the establishment of the cult of Sarapis on Delos. Delos, about 200. Marble column, late third- or early second-century lettering.

*SIG*³ 663; P. Roussel, *Les cultes égyptiens à Délos du IIIe au Ier siècle av. J.-C.* (Paris 1915–16) 71–83; *H. Engelmann, *The Delian Aretalogy of Sarapis* (Leiden 1975).

A. D. Nock, *Conversion* (Oxford 1933) 51–3; T. A. Brady, *The Reception of the Egyptian cults by the Greeks (330–30 B.C.)* (Columbia 1935) 31–5; P. M. Fraser, *Opuscula Atheniensia* 3 (1950) 22–3.

The priest Apollonios recorded (this) in accordance with | the command of the god.[1] For our grandfather, | Apollonios, being an Egyptian,
5   (one) of the priests,[2] | arrived from Egypt with the god[3] ‖ and continued serving (him) as was traditional, | and he is thought to have lived ninety-seven years. | My father, Demetrios, having succeeded | and
10 likewise served the *gods*, | was honored for his piety by ‖ the god with a

bronze statue, which is set up in the temple | of the god; and he lived sixty-one years.[4] | And after I took over the rites and atten|ded scrupulously to the services, the god infor|med me in a dream that a
15   Sarapieion ‖ of his own must be dedicated to him, and that it should not be in lea|sed (quarters) as before, and that he would find the place | himself where it was to be built, and that he would indicate the | place And this happened. For this place was | full of dung; it was listed for
20   ‖ sale on a little notice on the path through the | market place; and as the god wished, the sale took | place and the temple was built quickly | in six months.[5] But some men conspired against | us and the god and
25   brought a public charge against the temple ‖ and myself about what penalty should be suffered or what fine paid,[6] but | the god promised me in a dream that we would win. | And the trial having been completed and we, having won | in a manner worthy of the god, praise the gods, rendering proper thanks. | And Maiïstas also wrote on behalf of the temple on this subject.[7]

1   Sarapis.
2   A member of the priestly caste (cf. Herodotus 2.38. Diodorus 1.88). According to the hymn of Maiïstas (lines 37–8) he came from Memphis.
3   He brought the statue of Sarapis.
4   On the basis of the lettering the inscription is dated to the end of the third or the beginning of the second century. Combined with the data in lines 6 and 11, this indicates that the cult of Sarapis was introduced to Delos sometime during the first third of the third century.
5   Serapaeum A (cf. Roussel 19–32; and Engelmann 42 for details).
6   The formula in Attic law defining the juror's choice of penalty. Engelmann suggests that the charge was introducing foreign gods. The identity of the accusers and the course of the trial are unknown. Maiïstas' hymn (lines 66–8) describes them as 'evil men motivated by envy' whom Sarapis miraculously silenced during the trial. Cf. no. 75 for the final resolution of this affair.
7   Maiïstas' 65 line hexameter aretalogy of Sarapis follows.

103   The Rosetta Stone: selections from the Greek version of a trilingual decree (Greek, Hieroglyphic (= Middle Egyptian) and Demotic) passed by a synod of the priests of Egypt at Memphis on the occasion of the coronation of Ptolemaios V (204–180) as king of Egypt. Rosetta, Egypt, 27 March 196. Black granite stele, letter forms typical of the third and early second century.

OGIS 90; E. A. Wallis Budge, *The Rosetta Stone in the British Museum* (London 1927) 17–169 with photograph, text and translations of all three versions of the inscription.

Bevan, *Ptolemy* 261–8; C. Préaux, *Chronique d'Égypte* 11 (1936) 527–53; E. Bikermann, *Chronique d'Égypte* 28 (1940) 126–8; Rostovtzeff, *SEHHW* 2.712–15; M. Alliot, *Revue belge de Philologie et d'Histoire* 29 (1951) 421–43; P. W. Pestman, *Chronique d'Égypte* 40 (1965) 157–70; Will, *Histoire* 2.161–3; Walbank, *Commentary* 3.203–4.

In the reign[1] of the young (god) who received the kingship from his father, Lord of crowns, great of fame, who established Egypt, and toward the | gods is reverent, victorious over his enemies; who improved the life of men, lord of the thirty-year cycle[2] just as Hephaistos the Great,[3] (and) king just as Helios;[4] | great king of the upper and lower lands, son of the gods Philopatores, whom Hephaistos approved, to whom Helios gave victory, living image of Zeus;[5] son of Helios, Ptolemaios, | living forever, beloved of Ptah.[6] Ninth year,[7] in which Aetos, son of Aetos, is priest of Alexander and of the gods Soteres and of the Gods Adelphoi and of the gods Euergetes and of the gods
5   Philopatores ‖ and of the god Epiphanes Eucharistos, and in which the athlophoros of Berenike Euergetes is Pyrrha, the daughter of Philon, the kanephoros of Arsinoe Philadelphos is Areia,[8] the daughter of Diogenes, the priestess of Arsinoe Philopator is Eirene, | the daughter of Ptolemaios. Fourth day of the month Xandikos[9] and the eighteenth day of the Egyptian month Mecheir.[10]

Decree

The high priest and prophets and those who enter the sanctuary for the robing of the | gods, and the feather bearers and the sacred scribes and all the other priests, who, having come from the temples in the country to Memphis to be with the king for the celebration of the coronation | of Ptolemaios, living forever, beloved of Ptah, Epiphanes Eucharistos, successor of his father, and having met in the temple at Memphis on this day, introduced the following motion. | King Ptolemaios, living forever, beloved of Ptah, Epiphanes Eucharistos, son of King Ptolemaios and Queen Arsinoe, Gods Philopatores, has conferred
10   benefits in many ways on the temples ‖ and their staffs and on all those subject to his rule, as he is a god from a god and goddess just as Horos, the son of Isis and Osiris, the defender of his father Osiris; (and) being in matters concerning the gods | benevolently inclined, he has assigned to the temples revenues in money and grain; and he has undertaken many expenses for the purpose of making Egypt prosperous and establishing the temples. | With his own resources he has assisted everyone; and of the imposts and taxes in Egypt, some he has remitted entirely and others he has lightened in order that the people and everyone else may live in | prosperity during his reign; and debts owed the crown by those in Egypt and the rest of his kingdom he has cancelled; and those being held in jails | and those who had been detained because of accusations for a long time he has freed of charges.[11] | Likewise also he distributed justice to all just as Hermes the Great; and he gave orders

that those of the machimoi[12] who had returned together with the others
20 ‖ who had been disaffected during the period of disturbances should
remain in their own homes. He also provided that cavalry and infantry
forces and ships be sent against those attacking | Egypt by sea and land,
undertaking great expenditures of money and provisions so that the
temples and all in Egypt might be secure.[13] And having arrived | at
Lykopolis in the Bousirite (nome), which had been seized and had been
readied for a siege with an abundant store of weapons and all other
provisions since | the conspiracy had been prepared over a long period
of time by impious men who had gathered together in it and who had
committed many evil (acts) against the temples and the inhabitants of
Egypt, he enc|amped opposite it and surrounded the city with mounds
and ditches and wondrous walls. As the Nile flood in the eighth year
25 was great and normally covered the ‖ plains, he restrained it by blocking
in many places the mouths of the canals, having spent not a little money
on these things; and, having stationed cavalry and infantry to guard |
them, in a short time he took the city by force and destroyed all the
impious men in it,[14] just as [Herm]es[15] and Horos, the son of Isis and
Osiris, dealt with the rebels[16] in these same | places[17] formerly. Those
who had led the rebels in the time of his own father and caused [dis-
order] in the land and desecrated the temples, when he arrived at
Memphis to avenge | his father and his realm, he punished all of them
fittingly[18] at the time he arrived to perform the rites connected with his
coronation.[19] |
(Since these things are so), with good fortune, it has been resolved by
the priests of all the temples in the land that [all] *honors* belonging to |
King Ptolemaios, the eternal, beloved of Ptah, god Epiphanes
Eucharistos, and likewise also those of his parents, the gods Philo-
patores, and those of his grandparents, the gods Euergetes, [and
those] | of the gods Philadelphoi and those of the gods Soteres, shall be
increased greatly; and they shall set up a statue of King Ptolemaios, the
eternal, god Epiphanes Eucharistos, in each temple in *the most prominent*
[place], | which shall be called (the image of) 'Ptolemaios the Avenger
of Egypt', and beside which shall stand the chief god of the temple, and
there shall be given to it a weapon of victory prepared [in Egyptian]
40 ‖ style, and the priests shall perform cult service to these images three
times a day and dress them in sacred apparel and perform all the other
ritual acts just as (is done) for the other gods in [the native] *festivals*.[20]

---

1   Ptolemaios V had actually become king in 205/4 (cf. Polybius 15.25–33 and Justin
    30.2).
2   The Sed festival which was normally celebrated after thirty years of rule to
    rejuvenate a king.

3   Ptah, chief god of Memphis.
4   Re.
5   Amon.
6   The five names and epithets that constituted Ptolemaios V's Egyptian titulary.
7   186.
8   Athlophorus, 'prize-bearer', is the title of the priestess of the deified Berenike II. For the kanephoros see no. 93 n. 1.
9   Sixth month of the Macedonian calendar, equivalent to 27 March 196.
10 Sixth month of the Egyptian calendar.
11 Omitted are lines 14 to 18 which provide for the cancellation of unsettled debts and the guarantee of the fiscal privileges of the Egyptian priesthood and temples.
12 The Egyptian military caste (cf. Diodorus 1.73.7–8). Ptolemaios IV's inclusion of them in the army that defeated Antiochos III at Raphia in 217 was followed by revolts (Polybius 5.107.1–3).
13 The reference must be to the Fifth Syrian War (about 202–200) despite the fact that it ended with Antiochos III's occupation of Koile Syria.
14 Fall 197. Compare Polybius' (22.17.1–2) characterization of the treatment of the captured rebels as cruel with the congratulatory tone of the decree.
15 Thoth.
16 Seth, the brother of Osiris, and his supporters who, according to Egyptian myth, killed his brother and seized the throne of Egypt.
17 Osiris was originally the god of Bousiris where his tomb was supposed to be located (Diodorus 1.88.5).
18 An exaggeration since from 207 to 186 a large part of the Thebaid was controlled by two native kings, Harmakis and Ankhmakis.
19 Omitted are lines 29 to 37 which provide for the remission of taxes paid by the temples and the granting of gifts to them by the king.
20 Omitted are lines 41 to the end which provide for the offering of cult to images of Ptolemaios V in Egyptian temples and the annual celebration of his birthday and accession days.

104   Testament of Ptolemaios VIII Euergetes II, leaving his kingdom of Cyrene to the Romans. Cyrene 155. Stele of white marble perfectly preserved, second-century lettering.

G. Oliverio, *Documenti antichi dell'Africa Italiana* I: *Cirinaica* fasc. 1 (Bergamo 1932) 11ff. with photographs; *SEG* 9 (1938) 7 = Sherk, *TDGR* 31.

Oliverio, *op. cit.* 11–84; M. N. Tod, *Greece and Rome* 2 (1932) 47–51; P. Roussel, *REG* 45 (1932) 286–92; E. Bickermann, *Gnomon* 8 (1932) 424–30; W. Otto, *Abhandlungen der Bayerischen Akademie der Wissenschaften*, Phil.-hist. Abteilung n.s. 11 (1934) 97–119; Th. Liebmann-Frankfort, *Revue Internationale des Droits de l'Antiquité* 13 (1966) 73–94; B. A. Kouvelas, *Platon* 24 (1972) 300–4.

In the fifteenth year,[1] in the month of Loos. | With good luck. This is the testament of King | Ptolemaios, (son) of King Ptolemaios | and of
5 Queen Kleopatra, gods ‖ manifest, the younger (son).[2] Of this another copy | has been sent to Rome.[3] May it be mine | with the good will of

the gods to take vengeance | worthily upon those who have organized
10   against me | the unholy plot and have deliberately chosen ‖ not only of
my kingdom but also | of my life to deprive me. But if anything happens
to me, | in accordance with human destiny, before successors | are left
(by me) for my kingdom, I bequeath | to the Romans the kingdom
15   belonging to me,[4] ‖ for whom from the beginning friendship and |
alliance have been preserved by me with all sincerity. | And to the same
(Romans) I entrust my possessions | for them to protect, appealing to
them by all the gods | and by their own good reputation that, if any
20   persons ‖ attack either my cities or my territory, they may help, | in
accordance with the friendship and alliance which {toward} | toward
each other we (now) have and (in accordance with) | justice, with all
their power. | And I make witness to these (dispositions) Jupiter
25   ‖ Capitolinus and the Great Gods | and Helios and the Founder
Apollo,[5] to whose (custody) the text of these (dispositions) is also
consecrated. | With good luck.

1   From 170 to the summer of 163 Ptolemaios IV Philometor and his younger brother
     Ptolemaios VIII ruled Egypt jointly. The fifteenth year of their reign is 155. Dissen-
     sions between them caused Roman intervention and a division of the realm: the
     older brother retained Egypt and Cyprus, the younger only the Cyrenaica, to which
     he withdrew in 163. For all details see Will, *Histoire* 2.262–75 and 2.302–6.
2   The 'younger (son)' is Ptolemaios VIII Euergetes II, who was nicknamed *Physkon*
     ('Pot-belly').
3   No literary sources mention the existence of this will. Its terms were never carried
     out, since Ptolemaios VIII eventually had children and recovered Egypt, seizing the
     throne after the death of his brother in 145. He died in 116. Bickermann argues that
     we have before us not an authentic will at all, but rather an official extract, published
     in 155, of an earlier will. Roussel accepts Bickermann's main conclusions.
4   He probably considered Kypros as much as part of his kingdom as Cyrene.
5   Apollo was considered the founder of Cyrene.

105   Persecution of intellectuals by Ptolemaios VIII.

*Menecles of Barca, *FGrHist* 270F9 = Athenaeus 4.83.

H. I. Marrou, *A History of Education in Antiquity*, trans G. Lamb (New York 1956) 243–5;
Fraser, *Ptolemaic Alexandria* 1.86, 1.517–18, 2.745 n. 198.

For do you not know that Menecles, the historian from Barca,[1] and also
Andron of Alexandria[2] in his *Chronicles* record that the Alexandrians are
the ones who educated all the Greeks and barbarians, general education[3] having failed because of the continual disturbances in the
period of Alexander's successors? There was again a renewal of all
education at the time of the seventh Ptolemaios (VIII)[4] to rule Egypt,

the one usually called by the Alexandrians Malefactor. For he, having killed many of the Alexandrians and also driven into exile many of those who were ephebes[5] during the reign of his brother,[6] caused the islands and the cities to be full of men who were grammarians, philosophers, geometers, musicians, painters, gymnastic trainers and doctors and many other skilled men who, because of poverty, taught what they knew and made many men notable.

1   *FGrHist* 270. Jacoby suggests a mid second-century date.
2   *FGrHist* 246. Date unknown.
3   General education (*egkuklios paideia*) refers either to the basic education required of a gentleman or that considered preparatory to advanced studies. In either case it consisted essentially of the subjects that made up the seven liberal arts of the Middle Ages – grammar, rhetoric, dialectic, geometry, arithmetic, astronomy and music.
4   Ptolemaios VIII Euergetes (Benefactor) II (145–116). Athenaeus refers to him as the seventh member of his dynasty because he has omitted the brief reign of Ptolemaios VII Neos Philopator, who ruled jointly with his uncle before the latter murdered him in 144.
5   Youths 18 or 19 years of age enrolled in gymnasia from whom the citizen body was recruited.
6   Ptolemaios VI Philometor (180–145). The persecution took place shortly after the accession of Ptolemaios VIII in 145.

106   An Egyptian apocalypse: the 'Oracle of the Potter'. Third century AD. Papyrus. Original text dated to about 130 by allusions to historical events.

*L. Koenen, *ZPE* 2 (1968) 178–209 with plates III–VI; cf. Josephus, *Contra Apionem* 1.230–50.

C. C. McCown, *HTR* 18 (1925) 397–401; S. K. Eddy, *The King is Dead* (Lincoln, Nebraska 1961) 292–323; L. Koenen, *ZPE* 2 (1968) 178–209 (commentary); *idem, Proceedings of the 12th international Congress of Papyrology*, ASP 7 (Toronto 1970) 249–54; *idem, ZPE* 13 (1974) 313–19; A. B. Lloyd, *Historia* 31 (1982) 50–5; L. Koenen, *Egypt and the Hellenistic World: Proceedings of the International Colloquium Leuven, 24–26 May 1982* (Leuven 1983) 174–89; *idem, ZPE* 54 (1984) 9–13.

The river,[1] [since it will not have] *sufficient* water, [will flood], but (only) a little so *that scorched* will be | [the land ---] but unnaturally. [For] in the [time] of the *Typhonians*[2] | [people will say] 'Wretched Egypt, [you have been] maltreated ‖ by the [terrible] malefactors who have committed evil *against* you.' | And the sun will darken as it will not be willing to observe the evils in Egypt. | The earth will not respond to seeds. These will be part of its | blight. [The] *farmer* will be <du>nned for taxes <for> wh<at> he did not plant. | There will be *fighting* in Egypt because *people* will be in need of food. ‖ What one plants, [another] will *reap* and carry off. When this happens, | there will be [war and slaughter] which [will kill] *brothers* and *wives*. | For [these things will happen] when the great god *Hephaistos*[3] will desire | *to return* to the [city],[4] and the Girdlewearers[5] will kill each other as they | [are

15 Typhonians. ---] evil will be done. And he will pursue (them) on foot || [to the] *sea* [in] wrath and destroy many of them | because [they are] impious. <The king>[6] will come from Syria, he who will be hateful to all | men, [---] . . . and from Aithiopia[7] | *there will come* . . . He (together with some) of the unholy ones (will come) to Egypt, and he will | *settle*

20 [in the city which] later will be deserted. [--- || ---]. |[8] Their children *will be made weak*, and the country will be in *con|fusion, and many* of the inhabitants of Egypt will *aba|ndon* their homes (and) travel to foreign places. <Then there will be slaughter among friends>; and *people will lam|ent*

25 their own problems although they are less than those of others. *M||en will die at the hands of each other*; two of them | will come to the same place *to aid one*.[9] Among women | who are pregnant death will also be common. The Girdlewearers will kill themselves | as they also are Typhonians. Then Agathos Daimon[10] will | abandon the city that had

30 been founded and enter Memphis, and || the city of foreigners,[11] which had been founded, will be deserted. This will happen | at the end of the evils (of the time) when there came to Egypt a cr<owd>[12] | of foreigners. The city of the Girdlewearers will be abandoned like | my kiln[13] because of the crimes which they committed against Egypt. | The *cult images*, which had been transported there, *will be brought back* again

35 to || Egypt;[14] and the city by the sea will be a *refuge* for fishermen because | Agathos Daimon and Knephis[15] will have gone to Memphis, | so that passersby will say 'All-nurturing was this city | in which every race of men settled.' Then will Egypt | flourish when the generous fifty-five year[16] || ruler appears, the king descended from Helios,[17] the giver of

40 good things, the one in|stalled by the greatest {Isis}, so that the living will pray | that the dead might arise to share th(e) | prosperity. Finally the leaves will fall. The Nile, which had lacked water, | will be full and winter, which had changed its orderly ways, || will run its proper course

45 and then summer will resume its own | track, and normal will be the wind's breezes which previously | had been weak. For in the <time> of the Typhonians the sun will | darken to highlight the character of the evils <and> to reveal the greed of the | Girdlewearers.[18] And Egypt

50 [---]. Having spoken clearly up to this point, he fell sil||ent. King Amenophis,[19] who was grieved by the many disasters | he had recounted, buried the potter in Helio|polis and placed the book in the sacred archives there and | unselfishly revealed it to all men. | Speech

55 of the potter[20] || to King Amenophis, <translated> as accurately as | possible, concerning *what will happen* in Egypt.

'The Oracle of the Potter' is a rare example of a text originally composed in Egyptian that is now extant only in Greek translation. Its author used a traditional Egyptian literary form, the prophecy, to express hostility toward Greco-Macedonian rule in Egypt. As is typical of such texts, 'The Oracle of the Potter' consists of two parts, namely a frame story – preserved in fragmentary form in *P. Graf* 29787 of the second century AD – in which a popular king of the Egyptian past is confronted by a prophet, in this case a potter arrested on a charge of sacrilege, and his prophecies, that is, a description of a future time of troubles uttered by the prophet during an ecstatic trance. The latter, which are preserved in slightly different recensions in two third-century AD papyri, *P. Rainer* 19813 and *P. Oxy.* 2332, are couched in the form of a series of generalized images of disruption of the natural and social orders that are intended to characterize a period of domination by the followers of Typhon/Seth, the mythical opponent of Osiris and Horus, which, the prophet promises, will end when a true king, a genuine son of Helios/Re, appears. The version of the prophecies translated below is that found in *P. Rainer*, a papyrus of the third century AD.

1 The Nile.
2 Followers of Typhon, that is, of Seth, the Egyptian god of the desert, storm and foreigners, and brother and mortal enemy of Osiris.
3 Ptah, chief god of Memphis.
4 Memphis, the earliest Egyptian capital. The prominence of Memphis suggests a possible Memphite origin for this text.
5 The Greeks and Macedonians who are identified with the followers of Typhon/Seth.
6 Preserved in *P. Oxy.* 2332, line 30. The reference is probably to the invasion of Egypt by Antiochos IV in 170/69.
7 The reference is unclear. In the similar text paraphrased by Josephus the savior king is to come from Nubia, but here another evil ruler seems intended. Koenen suggests an allusion to Harsiesis, leader of an uprising in the Thebaid in 131 and 130, who might have been a Nubian.
8 Two fragmentary lines follow that may contain a reference to the two year reign of Harsiesis. *P. Oxy.* 2332 adds at this point 'but he will not be our (king). The fifty-five year (king) who will be ours, however, will <bring upon> the Greeks the evils which the lamb prophesied to Bacharis (= Bochchoris = Bekenrinef, last king of Dynasty 24, about 715). Tyche (Fortune) will be taken away from this race.'
9 To assist him in the commission of a crime?
10 The 'Good Daimon', the patron god of Alexandria who was identified with Shay, the Egyptian god of fate.
11 Alexandria.
12 The word translated as 'crowd' actually refers to the leaves shed by trees in the autumn, a curiously inappropriate metaphor in an Egyptian context.
13 In *P. Graf*, lines 13–16, there seems to be a reference to the emptying of the potter's kiln and the destruction of its contents.
14 An allusion to Alexandria officially not being part of but 'next to' Egypt.
15 A form of the Theban god Amon.
16 Koenen notes that the savior king is given a reign one year longer than that of Ptolemaios VIII when his reign is counted from his proclamation as king in Alexandria in 170, thus indicating that our versions of the 'Oracle of the Potter' reflect a revision made about 116.
17 The sun god Re whose son the king was believed to be in Egyptian tradition.
18 Reversal of the natural and social orders (cf. lines 8–22), which it was the duty of

a true king to maintain, is typical of descriptions of times of troubles in Egyptian prophetic texts.
19 As in the prophetic text in Josephus, the potter is made to address one of the Amenhoteps of the 18th dynasty (about 1575–1308).
20 The choice of a potter instead of a scribe or sage to play the role of prophet is unusual in Egyptian prophet texts. An incarnation of the god Khnum, who creates men on a potter's wheel, may have been intended.

107   Amnesty decree issued by Ptolemaios VIII and his co-regents Kleopatra II and Kleopatra III. Fayum, Egypt, 118. Papyrus.

P. Tebt. 5 with photograph; Hunt and Edgar, *Select Papyri* 2.210; *C. Ord. Ptol.*[2] 53 (selections).

Bevan, *Ptolemy* 312–19; C. Préaux, *L'économie royale des Lagides* (Brussels 1939) 131–2, 394–5, 402, 405; Rostovtzeff, *SEHHW* 2.878–82; L. Koenen, *Eine Ptolemäische Königsurkunde* (Wiesbaden 1957) 1–4; Will, *Histoire* 2.366–8; H. J. Woelff, *Proceedings of the 16th International Congress of Papyrology* (Chico, Calif. 1981) 313–18; E. Turner, *CAH*[2] 155.

Col. I

[King] Ptolemaios and Queen Kleopatra, the sister, | [and Queen] Kleopatra, the Wife,[1] pardon[2] those *subject to* | *their rule*, all of them, for errors, *wrongful acts, ac|cusations*, <condemnations>, charges of all sorts up to the 9th of Pha[rmouthi of the] 52nd[3] (year) | except [those] *guilty*
5 *of willful murder* and sacrilege.[4] || *They have given orders* also that those who have fled [because of being accused of] | *theft* and other charges[5] shall return to [their own (homes)] | (and) resume their former occupations, [and that they shall recover] | whatever of their property still *remains* unsold from that [which had been seized as security] because of *these matters.*[6]

Col. II

They have given orders also that all those having land allotments and all those | in possession of sacred land and other released land, | who have intruded into royal land and others | who possess more land than is proper,[7] having with|drawn from all ex<ce>ss they possess and having
40 declar||ed themselves and paid a year's rent in kind, shall be for|given for the period up to (year) 51 (119) [--- and] | they shall have full possession.[8]

Col. III

No one is to take away anything consecrated to the gods *by force* | nor to apply *forceful persuasion* to the managers of the sacred revenues, | whether villages or land or other sacred revenues, nor are taxes on *associations*[9] or crowns[10] or artaba-taxes[11] | to be collected (by anyone) from property consecrated to the *gods* nor are the sacred (lands) to be placed under
60   patronage[12] ‖ on any pretext, but they are to allow them to be managed by the priests themselves.[13]

Col. IV

77   *They have given orders* that the (costs) for the burial of Apis[14] and Mnevis[15] are to be sought from the royal treasury | *as* also in the case of those who have been deified. Likewise, also the costs of the other sacred | anima<!>s.[16]

Col. VIII

They have given orders that strategoi and | other officials are not to
180   seize | any of those living in the countryside ‖ for their private purposes nor are their animals | to be requisitioned for any of their personal (needs) nor | are their cattle to be seized nor are they to be forced to raise sacred animals | or geese or birds or pigs | or to furnish grain at a
185   (low) price or (in return) for ‖ renewals of their leases nor to compel tasks | to be performed (by them) as a gift on any pretext.[17]

Col. IX

They have given orders also concerning suits of Egyptians[18] | against Greeks and concerning (suits) of Greeks against | Egyptians or of Egyptians against Greeks of all categories | except those of persons farming royal land and of those bound to government tasks and of
210   ‖ others connected with the revenues, | that those | Egyptians who have made contracts in the Greek manner | with Greeks shall be sued and sue | before the chrematistai.[19] All Greeks who make contracts in the
215   Egyptian manner[20] ‖ shall be sued before the laokritai[21] in accordance with the | laws of the country. The cases of Egyptians against | <E>gyptians are not to be usurped by the chrematistai, | but they are to allow them to be settled before the laokritai in accordance with the | laws of the country.[22]

1   Ptolemaios VIII Euergetes II, Kleopatra II, his sister and former wife, and
    Kleopatra III, his niece and wife.
2   This text contains extracts from a Philanthropa, a general amnesty decree. Such
    decrees were issued at critical points during a reign such as the accession of a king.
    In this particular instance, the edict was intended to bring to an end the period of
    disorders resulting from the civil war that divided Egypt between the supporters
    of Ptolemaios VIII and Kleopatra II from 132 to 124.
3   28 April 118. Ptolemaios VIII's years of rule are counted from his accession as
    joint ruler of Egypt with his brother Ptolemaios VI and his sister Kleopatra II in
    170.
4   This is apparently a traditional exclusion since it also occurs in the Philanthropa
    of Ptolemaios VI from 163 edited by Koenen in *Eine Ptolemäische Königsurkunde.*
5   This is probably a euphemism for members of the factions of Ptolemaios VIII and
    Kleopatra II who were being invited to return to their normal pursuits.
6   Omitted are lines 10 to 35.
7   Kleruchs, priests and other officials who had exploited the confusion of the civil
    war to increase their own holdings at the expense of the crown were to return the
    appropriated land in return for forgiveness of back rent and guaranteed possession
    of their previous holdings.
8   Omitted are lines 44 to 56.
    Originally a tax paid in cash by kleruchs and priests, by the end of the second
9   century it had been transformed into a land tax paid in kind.
10 Ostensibly a gift, it was from the end of the third century an annual land tax levied,
    as this text shows, even on temple land.
11 A grain tax levied at a rate of one artaba (see Glossary) per aroura (= 100 cubits
    square).
12 The reference is to the practice of civil or military officials arrogating to themselves
    the role of protector of various temples to the detriment of the royal interest.
13 Omitted are lines 62 to 76.
14 Ptah, god of Memphis, incarnate as a bull.
15 The sacred bull of Heliopolis which was worshipped as the incarnation of the sun
    god Re-Atum.
16 Omitted are lines 79 to 176.
17 Omitted are lines 188 to 207.
18 For the considerable practical difficulties involved in the application of this
    section see Turner.
19 A board of three judges who formed a Greek language itinerant court dealing with
    royal affairs and open to both Greeks and Egyptians.
20 As this passage indicates, law in Egypt was not personal. Rather, Greeks or
    Egyptians were free to employ Greek or Egyptian law as they deemed best.
21 Egyptian judges who administered Egyptian law in Egyptian.
22 Omitted are lines 219 to the end.

108   Petition of the priests of Isis at Philae. Philae, 145–116. Three
inscriptions, the first inscribed and the latter two, which are translated
below, painted on the base of a granite obelisk in front of the propylon
of the temple of Isis at Philae; second-century lettering.

OGIS 137–9; **I. Philae* 19 with drawing; *C. Ord. Ptol.*[2] 51–2.

King Ptolemaios (VIII) and Queen Kleo|patra (II), the Sister, and
Queen Kleopatra (III), the Wife,[1] | to [Lo]chos,[2] our brother, greeting.
Of the *petition* [given] to us | by the *priests* [on the Abat]on[3] and [at
15 || Phil]ae of Isis *we have attached below* [for you] a copy. | You will do well
to issue instructions, [just as they request], that *no* | *one* harass them [--- |
---]. Farewell. |

20 To King Ptolemaios and Queen Kleopatra, || the Sister, and Queen
Kleopatra, the Wi|fe, gods Euergetai, greetings from the priests on the
Aba|ton and at Philae of Isis, the greatest goddess. Since those
travel|ing to Philae – strategoi and epistatai[4] | and Thebarchs[5] and
25 basilikoi grammateis[6] and epistatai phy||lakiton[7] and all other officials
and their ac|companying escorts and the rest of their retinues – com|pel
us to extend hospitality to them against our will, | whence it has come
to pass that the sanctuary is impoverished and | we are in danger of not
30 having the resources necessary to offer || on behalf of you and your
children the sacrifices | and offerings, we ask of you, greatest gods, if |
it seem (best to you), to instruct Noumenios, your kinsman and
episto|lo graphos[8] to write to Lochos, your kinsman and strategos of the |
35 Thebaid, not to harass us in these ways nor to || permit anyone to do the
same thing, and to give to us | the appropriate documents concerning
these matters, including | permission for us to set up a stele on which
we will inscribe | (a record) of the benefaction conferred on us by you
regarding these matters | in order that your kindness shall exist in
40 everlasting memory before her[9] for || all time. And if this happens, we
also in | these matters and the temple of Isis will have experienced your
kindness. | May you have good fortune.

1 Omitted are lines 1–10 which contain a brief letter from Ptolemaios VIII and his
  consorts informing the priests of Isis that their petition has been granted.
2 General of the Thebaid (cf. below line 33).
3 'The untrodden place', Bigah Island near Philae, the site of the supposed tomb of
  Osiris.
4 'Governors', probably of the individual nomes and cities that composed the Thebaid
5 Dittenberger suggests that the reference is to the military governor of Thebes itself.
6 Royal scribes.
7 Police commanders.
8 Letter-writer.
9 Dittenberger's reading. He understands the reference as being to Isis before whose
  temple the documents were inscribed.

109   Letter of Ptolemaios X Alexander I (101–88) granting the right of asylum to the temple of Horos at Athribis. Benha, Lower Egypt, 25 March 96. Stele bearing a trilingual decree in Greek, Hieroglyphic (= Middle Egyptian) and Demotic.

OGIS 761; **C. Ord. Ptol.*[2] 64.

Rostovtzeff, *SEHHW* 2.899–903.

vv King Ptolemaios (X) who is also Alexander.[1] *vv* | Since Ptolemaios, the kinsman and dioiketes, has reported to us that all | the temples in Egypt already have been granted greater benefits by our ancestors, | and that some of the principal ones have also the right of asylum,[2] but
5   that ‖ the (temple) of Harkentechthai[3] in Ath[rib]is, one of the first in rank and notable, as it is very ancient and most | famous, although it possesses most of the other privileges, lac|ks the right of asylum, we have ordered that there be granted also to this temple | the right of asylum within its circuit wall[4] just as is the situation at Memphis and Bou|siris and elsewhere with regard to other temples. Let it happen, therefore, accordingly.

1   The Hieroglyphic text gives the date as 'year 18, Phamenoth 11' or 25 March 96.
2   This is the earliest example of a grant of asylum to an Egyptian temple, a privilege which allowed individuals to take refuge within the temple precinct, but, even more importantly, also permitted the priests to deny entry to anyone including royal officials.
3   A form of Horos identified with Khentekhtay, a crocodile god.
4   Meaning clear although the text is corrupt at this point, probably because of an error by the cutter.

110   Act of obeisance to Isis by Kallimachos, governor of the Thebaid. Philae, 62. Inscribed on the south face of the south pylon of the temple of Isis.

OGIS 186; **I. Philae* 52; cf. Strabo 17.1.73, C 798.

Hutmacher, *Ehrendekret* 2–3; J. H. Thiel, *Eudoxus of Cyzicus* (Gröningen 1966) 50–1; G. Geraci, *Aegyptus* 5 (1970) 19, 123; J. Bingen, *Chronique d'Égypte* 45 (1970) 371–7; L. Mooren, *Ancient Society* 1 (1970) 17–24; *idem, Ancient Society* 3 (1972) 128–33; Fraser, *Ptolemaic Alexandria* 2.315 nn. 400–1; J. David Thomas, *The Epistrategos in Ptolemaic and Roman Egypt* (Opladen 1974) 106–8.

I, Kallimachos,[1] | kinsman and epi|strategos[2] and strate|gos of the
5   Indian ‖ and Erythraean Sea[3] | have come to the mistress, Isis, | and

have made an act of obeisance[4] | for the lord king, the god Neos |
10   Dionysos Philopator ‖ [and Phil]adelphos,[5] | year 18, Pachon 8.[6]

1   Probably the same individual as the honorand of no. 111.
2   Of the Thebaid. The office made him governor of all the nomes of Upper Egypt.
3   Here Erythraean Sea refers to the modern Red Sea instead of, as usual in ancient
    geographical texts, the Indian Ocean and its gulfs. Kallimachos was responsible for
    the supervision and protection of shipping on the Red Sea and Indian Ocean.
4   The inscription itself is the proskynema or act of obeisance and not a commemor-
    ation of a religious act performed in the sanctuary.
5   Ptolemaios XII (80–58, 55–51).
6   14 May 62.

**111   Honorary decree for Kallimachos, governor of the Thebaid.
Thebes, March 39.** A bilingual inscription, Greek and Demotic,
inscribed on a re-used black granite New Kingdom stele.

OGIS 194; *Hutmacher, *Ehrendekret* 18–25 with photograph.

Bevan, *Ptolemy* 369–71; H. Volkmann, *Cleopatra*, trans. T. J. Cadoux (New York 1958)
74–5; J. P. V. D. Balsdon, *Historia* 7 (1958) 85–7; *idem, Classical Review* 74 (1960) 68–71;
H. Heinen, *Historia* 18 (1969) 181–203; D. Bonneau, *Le Fisc et le Nil* (Paris n.d.) 148–9,
231.

[In the reign of Kleop]atra (VII), goddess [Ph]ilopat[or and of
P]tolemaios, who is also the son of Kaisar,[1] god Philopator, god
Philometor, | [year 13,[2] Art]emisios 18, Phamenoth 18.[3] It has been
resolved by the priests from Diospolis the Great,[4] (priests) of the |
[greatest god, Amo]nrasonther,[5] both the elders and all the others.[6]
Kallimachos, the kinsman, | [and strategos and] revenue officer for the
district of Thebes,[7] and gymnasiarch and *cavalry-commander*, previously
5   *having taken* ‖ *over* the city, which had been ruined [as a result of]
manifold [disastrous] circumstances,[8] tended it carefully | [and main-
tained it] unburdened [in] complete peace. Moreover, he reverently
outfitted the sanctuaries of the great ancestral gods, and the lives | [of
those in them he saved]; and, in general, he made all[9] [---]. | In addition,
he restored everything [to its former] *prosperous state and strengthened*
truth and justice.[10] And, indeed, | [he displayed] his goodness of heart,
and *in beneficence* those *who excel in generosity* [---].[11] And *further, now* [---][12]
10   ‖ [--- the] severe famine caused by a crop-failure like none hitherto
recorded, and when the city had been almost crushed by | [need], he,
having devoted himself wholeheartedly, voluntarily contributed to the
salvation of each of the local inhabitants. Having labored | [as a father
on behalf] of his own fatherland and his legitimate children, with the

good will of the gods, in continuous abundance of | [food] he maintained *nearly* everyone; and [he kept them] unaware of the circumstance from which he furnished the abundance. | The famine, however, con
15   tinued in the present year[13] and became even worse and [--- ‖ ---] *a failure of the flood* and misery far worse than ever before reigning throughout the *whole* | [land] and the condition of the city being wholly critical and [---][14] | and all having become weak from want and virtually everyone *seeking everything*, but [no | one] *obtaining it*, he, having called upon the greatest god, who then stood at his side, | [Amonrasonth]er, and having nobly shouldered by himself the burden again, just as a
20   bright star and a good daimon,[15] ‖ he shone upon [everyone]. For he dedicated his life wholly [---][16] | [---] for the inhabitants of the district of Thebes, and, having nourished and saved everyone together with their wives and children, just as from | [a gale and] *contending* winds, he brought them into a safe harbor. But the chief and greatest (indication) | [of his piety] (was the fact that), *being* in charge of everything connected with the divine, to the greatest degree possible he reverently and sleeplessly | took thought [for the sacred rites] so that from the
25   time his grandfather,[17] Kallimachos, the kinsman and epistrategos, ‖ [renewed them], the processions of the lord gods and the festivals *have been held* in a most holy and *excellent* manner just as in | [ancient times]. (Since these things are so), with good fortune, he shall be addressed as savior of the city, which is ancient [--- | ---] on his birthday in important places in the sanctuary of the great god, Amonrasonther; | [three statues of him, one] of hard stone the priests and two, one of bronze and the other likewise of hard stone, the city (shall set up); | [and every year they shall celebrate] this same day as his nameday and offer
30   sacrifice to the lord gods and wear wreaths and hold a feast, ‖ [just as is customary]; and they shall inscribe the decree on a stone stele in both Greek and native letters [18] | [and set it up on] the floor of the temple[19] so that publicly he shall share in the [good will] of the greatest god, | [Amonrasonther], in order that for all time his benefactions shall exist in everlasting memory.

In preparing the stele for Kallimachos' inscription, the relief showing an Egyptian king and queen sacrificing to Amon and Montu, the chief gods of Thebes, was retained, but the hieroglyphic inscription identifying them was erased. Originally erected at Thebes, the stele is now in the Turin museum.

1   Ptolemaios [Kaisarion], the alleged son of Kleopatra VII and Julius Caesar, who reigned as her co-regent from 44 until his murder by Octavian in 30. For the controversy concerning his paternity see Balsdon (against) and Volkmann and Heinen (for).
2   39. Dittenberger restored year 10, but see n. 13.
3   At the end of the second century the Macedonian and Egyptian calendars were synchronized so that the seventh month of the Macedonian calendar, Artemisios

(equivalent to March), here is equated with Phamenoth, the seventh month of the Egyptian calendar.

4　Thebes.

5　Amon-Re, King of the Gods, the chief god of Thebes.

6　Following Dittenberger in construing 'elders and all the rest' as defining 'priests' instead of as a reference to three distinct groups – priests, elders and laity – as suggested by Hutmacher.

7　In the Ptolemaic period Thebes and its immediate environs formed a separate administrative district with its own governor.

8　The reference may be to the damage suffered by Thebes when a revolt in the Thebaid was suppressed in 88 (cf. Pausanias 1.9.3).

9　Omitted is an obscure reference to Kallimachos' personal expenditure at this time.

10　'Truth and justice' together renders Egyptian Ma'at whose maintenance was the main obligation of an Egyptian king.

11　A phrase meaning 'he excelled' probably should be restored at this point.

12　This phrase marks the transition from the summary description of the early years of Kallimachos' governorship of Thebes to the detailed account of his actions from 42 to 40.

13　According to Seneca (*Natural Questions* 4.2.16), 42 and 41 were years of abnormally low Nile floods. The famine years, therefore, were 41 and 40 and the decree was passed in March 39.

14　Untranslatable phrases follow from a clause Hutmacher suggests was to the effect that 'all despaired of life and no helper appeared'.

15　Kallimachos is here likened to the Agathos Daimon, the patron deity of Ptolemaic Alexandria (cf. Fraser, *Ptolemaic Alexandria* 1.209–11).

16　An untranslatable phrase follows.

17　This suggests that the governorship of Thebes was virtually hereditary in the family of Kallimachos.

18　The Greek inscription is preceded by an unfortunately undecipherable twelve-line Demotic inscription. In format, style and content, this inscription parallels such earlier royal inscriptions as no. 103, thus reflecting the fact that in Thebes Kallimachos had virtually usurped the role of the king.

19　Of Amon at Thebes, that is, Karnak.

112　'Praises of Isis'. Kyme in Aiolis. White marble stele with gable from the temple of Isis, late first-century BC or first-century AD lettering (although the inscribed text is earlier since its beginning is quoted by Diodorus writing in the third quarter of the first century BC).

A. Salac, *BCH* 51 (1927) 378–83; *IG* XII 14; **I. Kyme* 41 with photograph; cf. Diodorus 1.27.3–5.

R. Harder, *Karpokrates von Chalkis und die memphitische Isispropaganda, Abh. Berlin*, 14 (1943) 18–52; A. D. Nock, *Gnomon* 21 (1949) 221–8; J. Bergman, *Ich bin Isis* (Lund 1968) 172–240, 297–300; R. E. Witt, *Isis in the Graeco-Roman World* (London 1971) 100–10; V. F. Vanderlip, *The Four Greek Hymns of Isidorus* (Toronto 1972) 42–7; F. Solmsen, *Isis among the Greeks and Romans* (Cambridge, Mass. 1979) 42–7.

Demetrios, the son of Artemidoros, who is also (called) Thraseas, a Magnesian | from (Magnesia on the) Maeander, an offering in fulfillment of a vow to Isis. | He transcribed the following from the stele in Memphis which | stands by the temple of Hephaistos:[1]

5   I am Isis, ‖ the tyrant[2] of every land; and I was educated by | Hermes,[3] and together with Hermes I invented letters, both the hieroglyphic | and the demotic, in order that the same script should not be used | to write everything. I imposed laws on men, | and the laws which I laid

10 down no one may change. ‖ I am the eldest daughter of Kronos.[4] I am the wi|fe and sister of King Osiris. I am she who discovered (the cultivation of) grain | for men.[5] I am the mother of King Horos. | I am she who rises in the Dog Star.[6] I | am she who is called goddess by women.

15 By me the city of Bubastis[7] ‖ was built. I separated earth from sky. | I designated the paths of the stars. The sun and the moon's | course I laid out. I invented navigation. | I caused the just to be strong. Woman and man I | brought together. For woman I determined that in the tenth

20 month she shall deliver a baby into ‖ the light. I ordained that parents be cherished by their children. | For parents who are cruelly treated | I imposed retribution. | Together with (my) brother Osiris I stopped

25 cannibal|ism. I revealed initiations to men. ‖ I taught (men) to honor the images of the gods. I | established precincts for the gods. The governments of tyrants | I suppressed. I stopped murders. I | compelled women to be loved by men. I | caused the just to be stronger than gold

30 and silver. ‖ I ordained that the true be considered beautiful. | I invented marriage contracts. Languages | I assigned to Greeks and barbarians. I caused the honorable and the shameful | to be distinguished by Nature.[8] I | caused nothing to be more fearful than an oath. He who

35 unjustly ‖ plotted against others I gave into the hands of his vic|tim. On those who commit unjust acts | I imposed retribution. I ordained that suppliants be pitied. | I honor those who justly defend themselves. |

40 With me the just prevails. Of rivers and winds ‖ and the sea am I mistress. No one becomes famous | without my knowledge. I am the mistress of war. Of the thunder|bolt am I mistress. I calm and stir up the sea. | I am in the rays of the sun. I sit beside the | course of the sun.

45 Whatever I decide, this also is accomplished. ‖ For me everything is right. I free those who are in bonds. I | am the mistress of sailing. The navigable I make unnavigable when|ever I choose. I established the boundaries of cities. | I am she who is called Thesmophoros.[9] The

50 island from the *dep|ths* I brought up into the light. I ‖ conquer Fate. Fate heeds me. | Hail Egypt who reared me.

---

1 Ptah, the chief god of Memphis. On the basis of this note Harder argued that this text and its parallels from Ios (*IG* XII 14), Thessalonike (*IG* X 2, 1.2543), Andros (*IG*

XII 739) and in Diodorus were based on a lost Greek translation of an Egyptian original. For the view that the original text reflected in these later versions was Greek see Nock.

2 Diodorus' version had 'Queen' at this point.

3 Thoth, the Egyptian god of Wisdom and writing and messenger of the gods.

4 Geb, god of the earth. Traditionally the king of Egypt was held to be the incarnation of the sky god Horos, the son of Osiris, King of the Dead, and his sister Isis, the children of Geb.

5 Isis is here identified with Demeter.

6 Sirius, whose heliacal rising, that is, when Sirius first becomes visible at the eastern horizon at dawn, on 19 July marked the beginning of the new year.

7 A city in lower Egypt sacred to the goddess Bastet. Bergman (40 n. 1) suggested an identification of Isis and Bastet was implied based on an etymology of Bastet as 'Soul of Isis'.

8 The goddess Ma'at, the personification of the natural order.

9 'The Law-Bearer', a title borne by several goddesses – Isis, Hera, Demeter, Selene – but here, suggests Bergman, possibly a reference to Egyptian portrayals of gods bearing small statues of Ma'at who was also goddess of law.

GLOSSARY

Agonothetes. Magistrate at Athens and elsewhere responsible for the organization and conduct of public festivals. At Athens the replacement of the choregoi who undertook such tasks as liturgies by an elected agonothetes who employed public funds was one of the most lasting reforms of Demetrios of Phaleron. The practice of agonothetes supplementing state monies with their own funds to carry out properly their responsibilities tended increasingly, however, to give the office the character of a liturgy. See Busolt-Swoboda, *Staatskunde* 2.929–30.

Agora. The open square at the heart of a Greek city, where people could gather for political or commercial activity. In it were located the main public buildings.

Amphiktiones ('Those dwelling around'). These were religious associations or unions connected with temples and their cults. Largest and most important politically was the Amphiktionic League, the council of which, composed of representatives (Hieromnemons) from twelve Greek states, each of which had two votes, met at Delphi. From the early third century until the settlement of the Aitolian War in 189 the Delphic amphictiony was controlled by the Aitolian League. See Ehrenberg, *Greek State* 108–12.

Archon (eponymous). Title of the magistrate at Athens and elsewhere, notably Delphi, who gave his name to the year. During the Hellenistic period the Athenian archon continued to be responsible for various routine judicial and civil functions including from 327/6 on the arrangement of the contests at the Thargelia and Dionysia. Following the expulsion of Demetrios of Phaleron in 307/6 the archon was again chosen by lot. The high proportion of otherwise unknown persons attested as archons during the Hellenistic period suggests that the office was of limited political importance. See Geagan, *Athenian Constitution* 6–12.

Aroura ('tilled land'). In Egypt a land measure equal to about 2/3 of an acre (0.275 hectares).

Artaba. An Egyptian grain measure. Although exact values vary in the papyri, one artaba was equal to 40 choinikes – i.e. scoopfuls – or, in the Roman period and probably before also, about 43 litres. See J. Shelton, *ZPE* 42 (1981) 99–106.

Boule ('Council'). Best known is the one at Athens, which in classical times consisted of 500 members selected by lot from the demes, each of the ten tribes being represented by 50 men in the Boule. Its chief task was to prepare the agenda for the Ekklesia ('assembly'). The increase in the number of tribes to twelve in 307/6 raised the membership to 600. The relationship of the Boule and the Ekklesia, however, remained essentially unchanged until 83 when Sulla granted the Boule the power to make decisions without the approval of the Ekklesia. Outside Athens Greek cities with constitutions that were democratic, at least in form, had Boules or equivalent institutions with similar functions although there was considerable variation in their membership, term of office, etc. For Athens see Rhodes, *Boule*, *passim*, and Geagan, *Athenian Constitution* 62–91. For other cities see Busolt-Swoboda, *Staatskunde* 1.456ff.

Glossary

Deme. The basic meaning of the term is village. In Classical and Hellenistic Athens, however, deme also denoted the lowest unit in the Athenian tribal system as reformed by Kleisthenes in 508/7. In this latter sense a deme was a territorial unit with an administrative center that might include within its boundaries one or more villages. The exact number of such demes that existed is unknown – according to Strabo (9.1.16,. C. 396) different authorities said there were 170 or 174 – but in the Hellenistic period, as before, registration in a deme was required of all citizens. See C. W. J. Eliot, *Coastal Demes of Attika* (Toronto 1962) 3–5; and J. S. Traill, *The Political Organization of Attica* (Princeton 1975) *passim*.

Dioiketes ('Administrator'). Chief financial official and head of the administration in Egypt. By both Pharaonic tradition and right of conquest all Egypt belonged to the king and was, therefore, treated by the Ptolemies as their personal estate. Its administration was organized accordingly. As on an estate, the head of the administration was a dioiketes, who was appointed directly by the king, served at his pleasure and exercised through delegation from him the royal authority in all areas dealing with fiscal affairs in Egypt and her overseas possessions. He appointed, supervised, disciplined and, if necessary, removed all governmental officials with fiscal functions, that is, virtually all administrative officials. It should, however, be noted that there is evidence that suggests that some time between the end of the reign of Ptolemaios II and the beginning of the first century BC the experiment was briefly tried of abolishing the single office of *dioiketes* and replacing it with a system involving the simultaneous existence of several *dioiketai*, each responsible for the administration of a particular region. See A. Bouché-Leclerq, *Histoire des Lagides*, 4 vols. (Paris 1903–7), 3.381–6; Ehrenberg, *Greek State* 181–3; J. D. Thomas, *Das ptolemäische Aegypten* 189–92; E. Turner, *CAH*[2] 143–4.

Dionysia (Greater). Athenian festival in honor of the god Dionysos celebrated in the city of Athens during March. The festival lasted for five days and was attended by persons from all over Greece. During the Hellenistic period, in addition to new tragedies and comedies, revivals of earlier plays, both tragic and comic, were often produced. At Athens and elsewhere the plays were performed by professional actors who traveled from city to city and were organized into guilds such as the Synodos of Dionysiac Artists in Athens. The guilds were patronized by various kings, had a quasi-political organization and enjoyed numerous privileges and immunities. See A. Pickard-Cambridge, *The Dramatic Festivals of Athens*[2] (Oxford 1968) 57–101, 279–325.

Drachma. A standard of weight as well as of silver coinage. The smallest unit of weight and coinage was the obol (on the Attic-Euboic standard about 0.72 g). There were six obols to a drachma, 100 drachmas to a mina, and 60 minas to a talent. Its value in the Hellenistic period varied greatly from city to city.

Ephebia. At Athens the ephebia was the period of trial a boy had to pass through before being accepted as a fully privileged citizen. As reorganized by Lykourgos shortly after the battle of Chaironeia in 338/7, it was a two-year period of mandatory military, moral and civic instruction required of all 18-year-old Athenian males during which the ephebes as part of their training manned the five frontier forts that made up Athens' outer defensive perimeter. Sometime after the mid third century BC the ephebia was made voluntary, the term of service shortened to one year spent in Athens, with the primary emphasis being placed on the cultural rather than the military training of the ephebes. The result was that it became essentially a state organized institution of higher education for Athenian and, after 119/18, non-Athenian aristocrats as well. In this form the ephebia was widely imitated in the Hellenistic world, most notably in Alexandria where at some point, perhaps as late as the reign of the Emperor Augustus (27 BC–AD 14), full citizenship was limited to those who had completed the ephebate. See Aristotle, *Athenian Politeia* 42.2–5; C. Pélékidis, *Histoire de l'ephébie attique* (Paris 1962) *passim*; H. I. Marrou, *A History of Education in Antiquity*, trans. G. Lamb (New York 1964) 151–9; Fraser, *Ptolemaic Alexandria* 1.77; and Rhodes, *Commentary* 502–10.

Epiphanes. Epithet associated with kings of both the Ptolemaic and Seleucid dynasties as well as with those of lesser dynasties in Asia. In non-religious contexts epiphanes means little more than 'illustrious'. In connection with the gods and, by extension, the Hellenistic kings it refers to the manifestation in them either of divine traits (as, for example, in the case of Demetrios Poliorketes at Athens (cf. no. 7)) or of a new divinity. See Martin P. Nilsson, *Geschichte der griechischen Religion*[2], 2 vols. (Munich 1967–74) 2.183–4; and Cerfaux and Tondriau, *Culte des Souverains* 422.

Epistates ('Foreman'). In general, the term designates a person or persons charged with responsibility for a particular sphere of activity. At Athens and elsewhere the epistates par excellence was the chairman of the committee of the Boule – the prytaneis, proedroi or their equivalent – which presided over meetings of a city's assembly. Finally, in the Hellenistic kingdoms epistates refers to the administrator of a Greek city appointed by the king to which the city was subject. See Rhodes, *Boule* 23–4, 124–5; and Ehrenberg, *Greek State* 195–6.

'Friends' (Philoi). 'Friend of the king' (*philos tou basileos*) in the Hellenistic kingdoms was a court title indicating, not that a person enjoyed a personal relationship with a king, but that an individual so described was officially a member of the king's personal entourage with the privilege of personal access to the ruler. Such 'friends' were the king's closest associates in peace and war, and from them were drawn his advisers and officials. A king appointed whomever he felt qualified to the position of 'friend' and employed them in whatever office he chose, irrespective of either their previous careers or any special qualifications other than his own confidence in them. In addition, the title 'Friend' in similar titles such as 'First Friend' and 'Honored Friend' formed part of a graded hierarchy of honorific titles which a king could grant to individuals and officials. Such honorific titles admitted individuals to particular ranks in the complicated social hierarchies of the Hellenistic courts but did not entail specific functions or membership in the royal entourage. See E. Bikerman, *Institutions des Séleucides* (Paris 1938) 40–50; L. Mooren, *The Aulic Titulature of Ptolemaic Egypt: Introduction and Prosopography* (Brussels 1975) 1–7; and G. Herman, *Talanta* 12–13 (1982) 103–49.

Kleruch. In Egypt a kleruch was an immigrant soldier, usually Macedonian or Greek, who received as part of his pay for military service a grant of an allotment of land, which varied in size depending on his rank. In the third century BC such grants were potentially revocable at the pleasure of the king, but as time passed, they tended to become hereditary, *de facto*. Because kleruchs were often away on campaign, many did not work their land directly but leased it to local peasant tenants. See Rostovtzeff, *SEHHW* 1.284–6.

Medimnos. A Greek dry measure. The value of the medimnos varied from city to city, but at Athens the medimnos was equal to 48 Athenian choinikes – one choinix was the equivalent of a man's grain ration for one day – approximately 50 litres.

Nikator ('Conqueror') and Kallinikos ('Gloriously Victorious'). These epithets, which emphasize military prowess, are associated primarily with the cults of kings of the Seleucid dynasty but are also found in the dynastic cults of kingdoms composed of former Seleucid territory such as that of Kommagene.

Panathenaia. An Athenian festival dedicated to Athena which took place in midsummer beginning on the 28th day of Hekatombaion and lasting for an unknown number of days (four in the second century AD). The festival was celebrated annually, and its highlight was a procession to the Akropolis at the climax of which a splendidly embroidered new dress, the *peplos*, was presented to Athena. Every fourth year a more elaborate version of the festival was celebrated, characterized by the addition to the program of athletic and musical contests. This special form of the festival, which was known as the Great Panathenaia, attracted contestants from all over the Greek world, although it ranked in prestige below the four major athletic festivals – the Olympian, Isthmian, Nemean and Pythian. See Parke, *Festivals* 33–50.

People (Demos). The citizen body of a Greek city. The protocol of a decree at Athens normally indicates that it was passed by the Boule and the People, that is, the assembly (ekklesia). In the Hellenistic period until Sulla in 83 gave the Boule the power to make decisions without consulting the People, the assembly acted on the agenda prepared for it by the Boule and presented to it by the proedroi, approving, amending or rejecting the motions presented to it. Outside Athens the institution is found in all Greek cities with constitutions that were democratic in form, although there was considerable variation in the organization and procedures of assemblies from city to city. See Rhodes, *Boule, passim*, and Busolt-Swoboda, *Staatskunde* 1.442ff.

Philadelphos ('Brother-loving'), Philometor ('Mother-loving') and Philopator ('Father-loving'). Epithets emphasizing dynastic solidarity associated primarily but not exclusively with the dynastic cults of members of the Ptolemaic dynasty in Egypt. Closely related in emphasis is the cult of Theoi Adelphoi ('the Fraternal Gods'), that is, the joint cult of Ptolemaios II and his sister-wife, Arsinoe II.

Phratry ('Brotherhood'). The origin of the Athenian phratries is unclear. Although structured as kinship groups, for a number of reasons it seems clear that this was a secondary development, and that in the archaic period a phratry originally consisted of the male members of a *eupatris genos* ('noble clan') and the *genos'* dependents and followers. During the fifth and fourth centuries BC the phratries had their own meeting places, assemblies, officials and priests and were responsible for a number of religious functions of which the most important was conducting during the month of Pyanepsion the festival of the Apatouria at which fathers presented their male infants to the phratry for acceptance as members. As a result the presence of a person's name in a phratry's membership register was important evidence should his citizenship be questioned. After the early Hellenistic period, however, the phratries declined in importance and eventually disappeared. See H. T. Wade-Gery, *Essays in Greek History* (Oxford 1958) 116–34; A. Andrews, *JHS* 81 (1961) 1–15 and *The Greeks* (New York 1967) 79–86; and Parke, *Festivals* 88–92.

Proedroi ('Presiding officers'). A sub-committee of the Boule in Athens consisting of nine members. From the early fourth century BC onwards the prytaneis no longer presided over the Ekklesia and introduced its agenda, but instead at the beginning of each meeting of the Ekklesia the epistates of the prytaneis chose by lot for that purpose proedroi – one from each tribe not on prytany duty that day – and designated one of the nine to be epistates for that day. A person could serve as proedros once in each prytany and as epistates once a year. See Rhodes, *Boule* 25–8.

Proxenos. A citizen of a Greek city could be made proxenos ('public friend' or state 'guest') to represent the interests of a foreign state in his own city. He would be chosen to act as proxenos by the foreign state and would usually be granted certain honors and privileges in return. It was a status much respected in the fifth and fourth centuries BC throughout the Greek world, but already in the fourth century it had begun to lose some of its original significance. In Hellenistic times it gradually degenerated into a reward for previous actions, often only as a conventional honor granted to important foreigners, although occasionally it was still felt to exist for its original purpose. See F. Geschnitzer in *RE s.v.* Proxenos, Supplement XIII (1973) cols. 629–730.

Prytaneis. Title of various governmental agencies in different cities. Prior to the year 307/6 the civil calendar of Athens consisted of ten periods during each of which the prytaneis, the fifty representatives from each tribe, served as a standing committee of the Boule. Their primary duties were to convene the Boule and the Ekklesia and to set the agenda for the Boule. During their term of office the prytaneis met in the prytaneion, the town hall of Athens. The increase in 307/6 of the number of Athenian tribes from ten to twelve, however, resulted in a redivision of the civil calendar into twelve periods which it retained throughout the Hellenistic period. At Miletos the prytaneis were not a committee of the Boule but an independent college of magistrates closely associated with it which possessed important civil and police powers including the right to draft bills for submission to the Boule and assembly. Finally, at Pergamon and elsewhere in Anatolia prytanis was the title of the eponymous magistrate. For Athens see Rhodes, *Boule* 16–25. For other cities see Busolt-Swoboda, *Staatskunde* 449, and Müller, *Volksbeschlüsse* 29–39.

Soter and Euergetes ('Savior' and 'Benefactor'). Originally applied to the gods by the Greeks, the term *soter* was later used to describe men who were thought to have saved or delivered their city or people from some danger. *Soter* was often coupled with the term *euergetes* to add still greater honor. Although by themselves these terms did not necessarily imply divinity, cities could offer persons so designated honors and cult similar to those accorded heroes. In the Hellenistic period these epithets were most often used of kings in Ptolemaic Egypt and elsewhere in the Greek East in recognition of the fact that, like the gods, such rulers were pre-eminent in their ability to confer benefactions on both their subjects and the Greek cities. This conception of the king as the benefactor of man par excellence and worthy for that reason of receiving cultic honors was popularized by the third-century BC utopian writer Euhemerus, who claimed that the gods had, in fact, been humans who had been deified because of the great benefits they had conferred on mankind. See A. D. Nock, *Essays on Religion and the Ancient World*, ed. Z. Stewart (Cambridge, Mass. 1972) 1.720–3; Habicht, *Gottmenschentum, passim*; and Fraser, *Ptolmaic Alexandria* 1.289–94.

Stater. The chief unit in precious metal weight and coin systems. The specific weight and value of a stater varied from city to city. In Athens, and cities and kingdoms which based their silver coinages on the Attic standard, the stater was the tetradrachm = 4 drachmas.

Stele. A square or rectangular slab of stone, placed in an upright position for public viewing, with a smooth front surface for the engraving of epitaphs, decrees, laws or other material of a public or private nature. A stone stele containing an important document often reproduces in miniature the architrave of a temple with acroteria, pediment and molding, and may contain engraved reliefs or painted scenes of various kinds. Like the lettering itself, these stelai show patterns of style and development along geographical and chronological lines. See J. Kirchner, *Imagines*

Inscriptionum Atticarum[2] (Berlin 1948); and, for the archaeological criteria, Möbius in *RE s.v.* Stele, cols. 2307–20.

Stephanephoros ('Wreath-bearer'). Title of the eponymous magistrate at Miletos and other Ionian cities. See no. 25.

Strategos ('General'). From very early times the strategos was a most important official in almost every Greek city-state, and in Athens during the fifth century he had political as well as military power. During the Hellenistic period the ten Athenian generals no longer formed a unified college with similar responsibilities. Each instead had specified duties including: Hoplite general, General for the district of Eleusis, General for the Coastal district, General for Piraeus, General for the Fleet and General for Preparedness. Elsewhere, particularly in Asia Minor, boards of Strategoi, which originally had been in charge of military affairs, were transformed into civil officials whose duties varied from city to city. Strategoi were also the chief magistrates in the Aitolian and Achaian leagues. In the Hellenistic kingdoms strategoi with a variety of military responsibilities are attested. In addition, strategoi with combined military and civilian powers governed provinces in the kingdom of Lysimachos and in the Seleucid kingdom from the reign of Antiochos III on. Finally, in Ptolemaic Egypt strategoi replaced the traditional Egyptian nomarchs as governors of the nomes that formed the administrative framework of Egypt. See Rhodes, *Commentary* 676–82; Geagan, *Athenian Constitution* 18–21; and Bengtson, *Strategie, passim.*

Theos. God. The most notable instance of the epithet Theos in connection with a living ruler concerns the Seleucid king, Antiochos II. The application of the epithet to him, however, derives not from a dynastic ruler cult but, like the epithets *soter* and *euergetes*, from the Greek cities' practice of conferring quasi-divine honors on benefactors, in his case by Miletos for Antiochos' role in freeing the city from the rule of the tyrant Timarchos about 260 (cf. Appian, *Syriaka* 65). See Cerfaux and Tondriau, *Culte des Souverains* 238.

Thesmothetai. The six junior archons who together with the three archons proper (the Archon, Basileus and Polemarchos) and their secretary made up the college of archons at Athens. Their functions were primarily judicial in nature and included the responsibility for assigning courts and trial dates to magistrates as well as presiding over various categories of cases themselves. Their special area of judicial responsibility involved cases concerning in some way the state. Thus, they conducted the preliminary scrutiny of the qualifications of candidates for office as well as introducing cases dealing with the deposition of magistrates still in office and the constitutionality of laws. They ratified foreign commercial agreements and introduced cases connected with them, and, in a closely related area, they also brought before juries the scrutiny of honors awarded to foreigners by the Athenian assembly. See Aristotle, *Athenaion Politeia* 59; Rhodes, *Commentary* 657–68; and Busolt-Swoboda, *Staatskunde* 2.1096–8.

APPENDIX I

King lists
All dates are BC

EGYPT
Ptolemaios I Soter	305–282
Ptolemaios II Philadelphos	282–246
Ptolemaios III Euergetes	246–222
Ptolemaios IV Philopator	222–205
Ptolemaios V Epiphanes	204–180
Ptolemaios VI Philometor	180–145
Ptolemaios VII Neos Philopator	145–144
Ptolemaios VIII Euergetes II	145–116
Kleopatra III and Ptolemaios IX Soter II	116–107
Kleopatra III and Ptolemaios X Alexander I	107–101
Ptolemaios X Alexander I and Kleopatra Berenike	101–88
Ptolemaios IX Soter II	88–81
Kleopatra Berenike and Ptolemaios XI Alexander II	80
Ptolemaios XII Theos Philopator Philadelphos Neos Dionysos (Auletes)	80–58
Berenike IV	58–55
Ptolemaios XII	55–51
Kleopatra VII and Ptolemaios XIII	51–47
Kleopatra VII and Ptolemaios XIV	47–44
Kleopatra VII and Ptolemaios XV (Kaisarion)	44–30

SYRIA
Seleukos I Nikator	311–281
Antiochos I Soter	281–261
Antiochos II Theos	261–246
Seleukos II Kallinikos	246–225
Seleukos III Soter	225–223
Antiochos III the Great	223–187
Seleukos IV Philopator	187–175
Antiochos IV Epiphanes	175–164
Antiochos V Eupator	163–162
Demetrios I Soter	162–150
Alexander Balas	150–145
Demetrios II Nikator	145–140
Antiochos VI Epiphanes	145–142
Antiochos VII Sidetes	138–129
Demetrios II Nikator	129–125
Kleopatra Thea	126
Kleopatra Thea and Antiochos VIII Grypos	125–121
Seleukos V	125
Antiochos VIII	125–96
Antiochos IX Kyzikenos	115–95
Seleukos VI Epiphanes Nikator	96–95
Demetrios III Philopator	95–88
Antiochos X Eusebes	95–83
Antiochos XI Philadelphos	94
Philippos I Philadelphos	94–83
Antiochos XII Dionysos	87–84
Tigranes I of Armenia	83–69
Antiochos XIII Asiatikos	69–64
Philippos II	65–64

MACEDON
Kassandros	305–297
Antigonos I	306–301[1]
Philippos IV	297
Antipatros	296–294
Alexander V	296–294
Demetrios I Poliorketes	306–283[2]
Antigonos II Gonatas	283–239
Demetrios II	239–229
Antigonos III Doson	229–221
Philippos V	221–179
Perseus	179–168
Andriskos	149–148

1. Antigonos I never ruled in Macedon.
2. Demetrios I only ruled in Macedon from 294 to 287.

155

Appendix I. King lists

PERGAMON

Philetairos	283–263	Eumenes II Soter	197–160
Eumenes I	263–241	Attalos II	160–139
Attalos I Soter	241–197	Attalos III	139–133
		Aristonikos = Eumenes III	133–129

APPENDIX II

Chronology

The lack of a comprehensive narrative source for the Hellenistic period has resulted in the problem of accurately dating documents becoming one of the central concerns of Hellenistic historiography. For the major kingdoms of the Near East the problems are relatively minor, although in the case of any particular text there may be considerable difficulty in determining its exact date. Ptolemaic documents normally are dated by reference to three items: the year of a particular king's reign, and the month and day of the Macedonian and Egyptian calendars. Since the 365-day Egyptian calendar did not correct for the one-fourth of a day remaining at the end of a year, it and the Macedonian calendar diverged steadily during the third century until the two were synchronized during the fourth year of Ptolemaios V (205–180) as follows:

Dystros = Thoth	Gorpaios = Phamenoth
Xandikos = Phaophi	Hyperberetaios = Pharmouthi
Artemisios = Hathyr	Dios = Pachon
Daisios = Choiach	Apellaios = Payni
Panemos = Tybi	Audnaios = Epeiph
Loios = Mecheir	Peritios = Mesore

In 119/18 these equations were changed to:

Dios = Thoth	Artemisios = Phamenoth
Apellaios = Phaophi	Daisios = Pharmouthi
Audnaios = Hathyr	Panemos = Pachon
Peritios = Choiach	Loios = Payni
Dystros = Tybi	Gorpaios = Epeiph
Xandikos = Mecheir	Hyperberetaios = Mesore

Cf. E. J. Bickerman, *Chronology of the Ancient World*[2] (Ithaca, N.Y. 1980) 38–40; and for tables for the conversion of Egyptian to Julian dates see T. C. Skeat, *The Reigns of the Ptolemies* (Munich 1954). Unlike the Ptolemies, the Seleucids did not date by regnal years, but rather by reference to an era beginning at a fixed point in time, the return of Seleukos I to Babylon in late summer 312/11 (between 1 Loios and 1 Dios), from which all dates were calculated.

Unfortunately the situation is less straightforward with regard to the Greek mainland. Individual cities continued to use their independent calendrical and chronological systems, but of these the Athenian archon list is by far the most important, both because of the significance of Athenian sources in the reconstruction of Hellenistic history and because later chronographers used it in conjunction with the system of Olympiad dating to form a standard chronological framework for all of Greek history. It is, therefore, particularly unfortunate that no complete list of archons survives for the years after 292. Reconstruction of the archon list has understandably been a prime concern of scholars, and the dates used in this volume are based on the latest complete list, that of B. D. Meritt, *Historia* 26 (1977) 161–91. As is true of the lists hitherto proposed, the dates given by Meritt cannot claim absolute certainty in any individual case, especially since 'Ferguson's Law', the rule that during the Athenian civil year the secretary of the Boule was drawn successively from each Athenian tribe in accordance with the official order of the tribes, does not hold true for the third century as a whole, since it has been shown that on at least two occasions after 270 the secretary cycle was interrupted for unknown periods of time and then re-started again. The dates of individual archons, therefore, have been modified from those proposed by Meritt whenever later studies have shown this to be necessary. For most of the third century the official order of tribes on which the secretary cycle was based was as follows:

I	Antigonis	VII	Akamantis
II	Demetrias	VIII	Oineis
III	Erechtheis	IX	Kekropis
IV	Aigeis	X	Hippothontis
V	Pandionis	XI	Aiantis
VI	Leontis	XII	Antiochis

In 224/3 a thirteenth tribe was added, Ptolemaios, between Leontis and Akamantis; and in 201/0, probably because of hostilities between Athens and Philippos V of Macedo Antigonis and Demetrias, which had been created to commemorate the liberation of Athens in 307/6, were abolished. Almost at the same time, however, a new tribe, Attalis, was established in honor of Athens' ally, Attalos I of Pergamon, and placed at the end of the list, and this remained the official order of the tribes until the second century AD. For details see A. G. Woodhead, *The Study of Greek Inscriptions*[2] (Cambridge 1981) 112–16, and Habicht, *Untersuchungen* 116–21.

INDEXES

All references are to numbers of items and, where applicable, of numbered lines or sections of items. References to explanatory notes are marked 'n'.

I. Personal names

Achaios, 19, and n.6
Achaios, son of Andromachos, 19 n.6
Acilius, L., 70.119, and n.4
Acilius Glabrio, M'. (cos. 191), 71.10–11
Aemilius Lepidus, M. (cos. 187), 70.122, and n. 5
Aetos, son of Aetos, 103.4
Agasitimos, son of Timachidas, 46 A2
Agathokles, son of Antiphilos, 68.3
Agathon, 70.105
Agelaos, 31.1, and n.1
Agelochos, 46 C113
Agesidamos, 30.16
Agestratos, 46 C113–14, 122
Agon, 71.25
Agyrrhios, son of Kallimedon, 13.9
Ainesilas, 84.7
Alexander III (King), 23.22; 25 n.5; 46 C103–4; 103.4
Alexander of Epiros (?), 50 n.3
Alketas, 54
Ameinias, 5 II 9
Amenophis (King), 106.50,55
Amphistratos, 89.23
Anaxipolis, 46 D100,114
Anaxippe, 83.9–10
Anaxippos, son of Alexander, 27.2,17
Andragoras (satrap of Parthia), 51 A 7, and n.5
Andron, 105, and n.2
Andronikos, 72.1
Antenor, son of Xenaros, 25.37
Antialkidas (King of Taxila [?]), 53.5
Antigenes, 64.13
Antigonos I Monophthalmos (King), 4 n.1; 6.9; 11.18,28; 23.22; 25.4.22, and nn.2,4
Antigonos II Gonatas (King), 14 n.6; 15 n.5; 50 n.3; 57; 58; 60.13; 61.2,10,14; 63.1
Antiochis, mother of Attalos I, 19 n. 6
Antiochos I (King), 2; 15.2,26, and nn.8,10; 18 n.1; 19.1; 20.1,13; 21; 22; 23.1, and n.1; 25.36; 32.2.14,51
Antiochos II (King), 18 n.1; 19 n.6; 24.1; 32.3; 50 n.3; 57

Antiochos III (King), 15 n.8; 18 n. 1; 19 n.6; 29.148; 30 n.7; 32.4,5; 33.1–2,46; 35.138; 39B; 40 n.7
Antiochos IV (King), 38; 39B,C.1, and n. 5; 40.II.1, and n.7; 41.1,5, and nn.1,2,5–6; 42.258,259, and nn.5,6; 43 nn.2–5
Antiochos V (King), 41 n.6; 43.22, and nn.2,5
Antiochos VIII (King), 48.5–7
Antiochos I (King of Kommagene), 48.1–4
Antiochos Hierax, 85 passim
Antipater (Etesias, King of Macedon?), 14.8, and n.4
Antipater (archon 262/1), 58
Antiphilos, 82.3,27
Antiphon (archon 259/8), 61 n.3
Apama, wife of Seleukos I, 2 n.2
Apollodoros, 5 II 14
Apollodoros of Athens, 58
Apollodoros, son of Herogeites, 77.8
Apollodoros of Artemita, 51 C(a),(b)
Apollonidas, son of Nikandros, 80.5
Apollonides, son of Aggeliskos, 62.2
Apollonides, son of Glaukios, 54.3–4
Apollonios, 36.90
Apollonios (dioiketes), 96.1
Apollonios (governor of Judaea), 42.259, and nn.3,5
Apollonios I, father of Apollonios II, 102.2
Apollonios II, priest of Sarapis, 102.1
Apollonios, son of Kleombrotos, 68.2
Apollonis, wife of Attalos I, 38.32,45, and n.7
Apollodoros, son of Apollodoros, 61.2,12
Appian, 9 n.2
Archelaos, 88.3
Archestrate, 57
Archias, 83.1.3, and n.1
Areia, daughter of Diogenes, 103.5
Areus I (King), 56
Argeios, son of Kleinios, 56.58
Ariarathes V (King), 76.2, and n.3
Aribazos (strategos of Kilikia), 98 II 6,13
Aristaeus, 36.91
Aristarchos, 69.2

I. Index of personal names

Aristo, 30.6
Aristo[---], 90.1
Aristodama, daughter of Amyntas, 64.3
Aristodemos, son of Parthenios, 25.11, and n.4
Aristodikides, 21
Aristogeiton, 6.39
Aristokles, 98 II 10
Aristolochos, 25.3,47
Arnion, 54.6
Arrhenides (archon 261/0), 58; 59.10
Arrhidaios, 24.24
Arsaces I (King), 51 A6
Arsinoe II, wife of Lysimachos and Ptolemaios
  II, 3.1; 56 n.4; 93.3; 99.2; 100.3; 103.5
Arsinoe III, wife of Ptolemaios IV, 103.5
Artaxerxes II (King), 7 n.8; 83.5–6,9
Asander, 25 n.5
Asklepiades, son of Hekataios, 32.7–8
Aśoka, see Piodasses
Athanagoras, 46 C112–13
Athanokles, 71.13
Athenaios, 2.34
Athenaios (naval commander), 21.53
Athenaios, brother of Attalos II, 38.40
Athenodoros, son of Gorgippos, 55.6
Atrosokes, 52.3
Attalos I (King), 19 n.6; 30 n.7; 33.19–20,34;
  38.31,44; 84.2; 85.273.1; 87.2,19–20;
  89.2
Attalos II (King), 76.2, and n.3; 38.37; 83.17;
  89.2; 90.1
Attalos III (King), 83,19; 90.2,7; 91.3
Attinas, daughter of Alketas, 54

Bakchios, son of Agron, 89.5
Bakchon (nesiarch), 92.2–3,60
Banebelos, 19.6,27, and n.5
Berenike, wife of Antiochos II, 23 n.2
Berenike I, wife of Ptolemaios I, 3 n.1; 99.3
Berenike II, wife of Ptolemaios III, 103.5
Bhagabhadra, son of Kasi (King), 53.6, and n.4
Bias, 12.22, and n.7
Bottas, 23.2,21

Calpurnius, Q. (cos. 135), 80.42–3
Charetidas, son of Dorkonidas, 80.5–6
Charias, 5
Charixenos, 62.8, and n.6
Charmides (governor of Delos), 75.1
Chlidane, 54.6
Chremonides, son of Eteokles, 56.7, and n.2
Claudius, T., 75.20–1

Damon, 82.3,27
Daphnaios, [son of ---]krates, 71.24–5
Dareios III (King), 46 C104–5
Daskylos, 83.12

Demetrios I (King of Baktria), 51 B4,C(a), and
  n.10
Demetrios II (King of Baktria), 41 n.1
Demetrios I Poliorketes (King of Macedon),
  1.2, and n.1; 4 n.1; 5 n.6; 6.12,20; 7.3,
  and nn.4–5; 10 nn.2,3; 11.18,28, and
  nn.5,11; 15 n.8; 25.22, and n.5; 46 D.95;
  54.2, and n.1; 55; 63.1–2
Demetrios II (King of Macedon), 46 C129
Demetrios I (King of Syria), 44.31, and n.3
Demetrios, grandson of Demetrios of
  Phaleron, 58 n.1
Demetrios, son of Artemidoros = Thraseas,
  112.1
Demetrios, son of Dios, 15.2
Demetrios, son of Mnaseas, 70.78
Demetrios the Rhenaian, 75.5,23–4
Demochares, 7; 11 nn. 8,10
Demodamas, son of Aristeides, 2.1
Demophon, son of Lykideus, 32.31
Demosthenes, 87.1
Dexikrates, 70.99,102
Diogeitos, 26.3,46
Diogenes, 67.13, and n.4
Dion, 59.12
Dionysios, 34.8
Dionysios, son of Amyntas, 64.12
Dionysios, son of Apollo[---], 33.32
Dionysios, son of Bianor, 68.1–2
Dionysios, son of Hippomedon, 15.1
Diophanes, 71.13
Diotimos, son of Dionysios, 34 a2, b3
Diyllos, son of Phanodemos, 5 II 27, and n.9
Duris, 7

Eirene, daughter of Ptolemaios, 103.5–6
Eirenias, son of Asklepiades, 80.41
Eirenias, son of Eirenias, 40 I 2,9, II 12; 88.3
Epichares, son of Pheidostratos, 55.9
Epicurus, 14.1, and nn.1,2,5
Epigenes (strategos), 64.14
Epigenes, 98 I 20
Eraton, son of Amphitimos, 70.99
Eratosthenes, 57
Euboulos (archon 256/5 ?), 61.4, and n.3
Euchares, son of Euchares, 55.11
Eudamidas, son of Euthykles, 80.61
Euippos, 83.10
Eukratides (King), 51 B1, C(b), and n.8
Euktemon (archon 299/8), 4.1; 11.13
Eulaios, 39 B
Eumenes (father of Eumenes I), 84.3
Eumenes II (King), 38.31,50; 40 I 4; 83.16; 86
  A1, B1; 87.2–3,19,24; 88.1
Euremon, 71.21
Eurykleides, son of Mikion, 67 nn.1–2,4

I. Index of personal names

Euthios, son of Antiphon (archon 283/2), 11.1; 13.10,24
Euthydemos (King), 51 C(a), and n.15
Eutychides, 27.1

Fannius, C. (cos. 161), 44 n.3
Fonteius, M'., 75.22–3

Glauka, 54.6
Glaukon, 56 n.2
Glaukon from Kythnos, 92.61
Glaukos, 70.98,102
Gorgos, son of Phryni[---], 6.7
Gyges (King), 12 n.4

Habromachos, 82.2,26
Habron, son of Kallias, 70.106
Hagetas, 64.2
Harmodios, 6.39
Helenos, 19.4
Heliodoros, 38 n.1
Heliodoros, son of Dion, 53.2–3
Herakleios, 77.11
Herakleitos, son of Asklepiades, 60.10–11, and n.5
Herakleitos, son of Zoes, 32.6–7
Hermagoras, son of Epimenes, 33.33
Hermokles, 7 n.3
Herodoros, son of Ph[---], 6.8,24
Herodotos, 14.1, and n.1
Herodotos, son of Herodotos, 77.9
Hieromnemon, son of Teisimenos, 11.5
Hieron (King), 46 C121
Hippomachos, son of Theron, 25.2
Hippon, son of Kratistoteles, 59.10
Hipponikos, 31.6
Hippostratos, son of Hippodemos (strategos), 8
Hor, 39 n.5

Isaios (archon 284/3), 11.39

Judas Maccabaeus, 39 B
Julius Caesar (= Kaisar), C. (cos. 59), 111.1; 111 n.1

Kallias, 70.99,103
Kallias, son of Eumenidas, 89.3–4
Kallias, son of Thymochares, 55
Kallikles, 46 D96,111
Kallikrates (archon at Delphi), 70
Kallikrates, 95.9
Kallikrates, son of Theophanes, 70.110
Kallikrates, son of Theoxenos, 74.2, and n.2
Kallimachos (strategos), 110.1; 111.3
Kallimachos (epistrategos), 111.24
Karneades, 76.1, and n.1
Kassandros (King), 4.14; 5.3.21, and nn.2,11;

14 n.4
Kineas, 49 A4, and n.4
Klearchos, 49 A3, and n.3
Kleodamos, 70
Kleokritos, 92.62
Kleon, 69.2
Kleon (strategos), 82.3,27
Kleopatra I (Queen), 39 B, and nn.2–3
Kleopatra II, sister of Ptolemaios VIII, 104.4; 107.1; 108.12,19
Kleopatra III, wife of Ptolemaios VIII, 107.2; 108.13,20
Kleopatra VII (Queen), 111.1
Kleopatra Tryphaina, daughter of Ptolemaios VIII, 48 n.4
Kosmas, 54.4
Krateros, brother of Antigonos II, 14.12, and n.6
Kriton, son of [---], 71.25–6
Kydenor (archon 244/3), 61 n.3
Kydios, son of Hierokles, 36.1
Kylon, 64.14

Lachares (tyrant), 5.1.5,10, and nn.10,11
Lachares, son of Papos, 19.7–8,27
Laodike I, wife of Antiochos II, 19 n.6; 24; 98 II 7, and n.6
Laodike II, wife of Antiochos III, 33.36,47, and n.7; 36.3
Laodike Thea, mother of Antiochos I of Kommagene, 48.4–7, and n.4
Laodike, daughter of Antiochos III, 40 n.7
Lareta, 54.15
Lenaios, 39 B
Leonnorios (Galatian chieftain), 16.11.3
Leontis, son of Sokrates, 70.91–2
Lochos, 108.13,33
Loutourios (Galatian chieftain), 16.11.3
Lygdamis (King), 12
Lykos, son of Phileas, 70.125
Lysander, son of Kalliphon, 5 II 8–9
Lysias, 14.14, and n.7
Lysias (dynast), 85.277.1
Lysias (regent for Antiochos V), 43.22, and n.2
Lysimachos (King), 3.2; 8 I 2, and nn.3,6; 10, and nn.1,5,6; 11.10,16; 12.1; 14 n.5; 23 n.3; 25 n.6; 55 n.5
Lysimachos, son of Nausistratos, 4.9

Magas, 50 n.3
Maïstas, 102.29
Mantias, 69.2
Marsyas, 54.5
Matrios, 77.11
Meidogenes, son of Meidon, 13.32
Meleagros, 21.29
Meleagros (strategos), 20.6; 21.1,18,25,50

161

I. Index of personal names

Melesippos, son of Philo[---], 62.1
Menandros, 84.7
Menandros (King), 51.3a, and n.13
Menecles of Barca, 105
Menekles, 88.2
Menestratos, son of Apollodoros, 91.1
Menodoros, son of Dionysios, 80.4,32
Menon, 70
Metrodemos, son of Timokles, 20
Metrodoros of Lampsakos, 14 n.5
Metrophanes, 24.1, and n.1
Mikion, son of Mikion, 67.11,15
Mikkos, son of Hermias, 62.39
Minucius, Q., 70.15
Mithres, 14 n.5
Mithridates I (King of Parthia), 51.2.1
Mithridates Kallinikos (King of Kommagene), 48.3–4
Mnasiptolemos, 31.6
Mnason, 70
Moiragoras, son of Stephanos, 30.25,28
Mummius, L. (cos. 146), 78.1; 80.53,79

Nausimenes, son of Nausikydes, 11.2
Neon, 64.13
Nikagoras, son of Aristarchos, 1.2
Nikanor, 42.259, and n.4
Nikias (II) (archon 282/1), 13.2, and n.1
Nikis, son of Nikon, 80.61–2
Nikodamos, 84.8
Nikomedes I (King), 26.9
Nikomedes II (King), 16
Nikostratos (archon 295/4), 6.2
Noumenios, 108.32
Nymphis, son of Diotrephes, 15.1

Oineus, son of Phesinos, 62.39
Oinokrates, son of Oinobios, 13.7
Olympiodoros, 14.6, and n.3
Onasimos, son of Epikratides, 70.103
Orontes, son of Artasyros, 83.4–5,8
Orthon, son of Zopyros, 70.82
Ortyx, 54.5

Pausanias, 9 n.2
Peithias, 5 II 8
Peithodemos (archon 269/8 or 268/7), 56.2
Phaidros, son of Thymochares, 55 nn.1,3
Pharnakes (King), 77.10,31
Pheres, son of Pheres, 32.31–2
Philainetos, son of Philophron, 1.1
Phile, daughter of Apollonios, 45.1
Philetairos, father of Attalos I, 84.2
Philetairos, son of Attalos I, 38.40
Philippides, son of Philokles, 11.8.58, and nn.2,11

Philippides, son of Philomelos, 4.11
Philippos (King), son of Kassandros, 5 II 25,29
Philippos V (King), 30 n.7; 36 n.2; 46 C127,129; 65.1; 72.10–11
Philippos, son of Dia[---], 41.6, and n.6
Philiskos, son of Philios, 32.31
Philochoros, son of Kyknos, 57
Philodemos, 14 n.2
Philoites, son of Kratias, 80.32
Philokles, 59.12
Philokles (King), 92.2, and n.2
Philopoimen, son of Kraugis, 73.3,42
Phoinix (dioketes), 97.2, and n.1
Phokion, son of Aristokrates, 81.1
Phrad[mon], 68.55
Piodasses = Aśoka (King), 50.2, and nn.2–3
Plutarch, 7 n.8
Polemarchos, 31.2
Polianthes, 9.6,13, and n.4
Polybius, son of Lykortas, 79.1–2
Polygnota, daughter of Sokrates, 82
Pompeius, Gn., son of Hiroitas, Theophanes, 47.2–3, and nn.2,4
Porcius, P., 75.20
Porphyry, 39 B
Poseidippos, 9 n.1
Poseidippos, son of Bakchios, 4.15,20–1
Poseidonios, 17.1
Praulos, son of Phoxinos, 70.13
Praxias, son of Eudokos, 89.3–4
Ptolemaios I (King), 3.1, and n.1; 7 n.5; 46 C110–11, and n. 11; 46 D; 55; 99.3
Ptolemaios II (King), 15 n.4; 24 n.2; 25.39; 26 n.6; 46 C99, and n.8; 50 n.3; 55; 56; 57; 92; 95.1; 96.1; 99.1; 100.2
Ptolemaios III (King), 26.23; 67 n.5; 98 n.2; 99.1; 100.2,9
Ptolemaios IV (King), 30 n.7; 67 n.5
Ptolemaios V (King), 39 B; 103; 104.3
Ptolemaios VI (King), 39 B, and n.4
Ptolemaios VII (King), 48 n.4
Ptolemaios VIII (King), 104.2–3; 105; 107.1; 108.12,19
Ptolemaios X (King), 109.1
Ptolemaios XV (King), 111.1, and n.1
Ptolemaios, son of Lysimachos, 100.7–8,22, and n.3
Ptolemaios, son of Thraseas, 35.138, and n.2
Ptolemaios (dioiketes), 109.2
Pyrgoteles, 46 A9–10
Pyrrha, daughter of Philon, 103.5
Pyrrhos (King), 46 C114; 55 n.5
Pythagoras, 98 II 10
Pythes, 23.2,21
Python, son of Athanaios, 64.15
Python (archon at Delphi), 64.13

162

II. Index of gods and goddesses

II. Gods and goddesses

163

III. Index of geographical names

Ge, 22.1,24; 56.87; 77.11

Harkentechthai, 109.5, and n.3
Helios, 22.1,24; 28.44; 56.87; 77.11; 104.25
  (= Re), 103.2–3; 106.40
Hephaistos (= Ptah), 103.2–3; 106.12
Herakles, 99.4
Hermes (= Thoth), 103.26; 112.6
Hestia, 73.45
Horos, 103.10,26; 112.12

Isis, 103.10,26; 108.15,22,41; 110.6; 112.2,4

Jupiter Capitolinus, 104.24–5

Knephis, 106.36
Kronos (= Geb), 112.10

Mnevis, 107.77

Osiris, 103.10,26; 112.11

Oxos, 52.4

Poseidon, 7; 8.12,22, and n.3; 22.24; 28.44;
  56.88
Ptah, 103.4. *See also* Hephaistos

Sarapis, 72.4,11,20; 75.5–6,25; 102

The Great Gods, 3.2; 104.25
The Maiden, 7; 11.44
The Tauropolos, 22.26, and n.5
Typhon (= Seth), 106 n.2

Vasudeva (Vishnu), 53.1, and n.2

Zeus, 19.19,26; 22.124; 28.44; 56.87; 77.11;
  99.4,5; Hellenios, 42.261,263;
  Oromasdes, 48.54; the Savior, 71.26;
  73.10,42; 100.25,28; (= Amon), 103.3

III. Geographical names

Listing is by geographical designation, but no attempt is made to distinguish between country and inhabitants within separate entries.

Abaton, 108.14,21
Abdera, 28.24
Achaia, 30 n.7; 37 n.1; 56.24,38; 63 n.4
Acharnai (deme), 13.4; 55.6; 59.12
Agrinion, 69.4,11
Aigelioi, 27.2,26
Aithalidai (deme), 56.7
Aithiopia, 106.17
Aitolians, 7; 30 n.7; 31.9,13; 62; 64.1,6; 69.5,8
Akarnania, 30 n.7; 63 n.4
Akersekom, 73.30, and n.7
Akragas, 70.92
Alexandria (Egypt), 92.55; 93 (sacred law of);
  101.83,222; 105
Alexandria---, 32.113
Amphipolis, 20.10–11
Anakaia (deme), 59.10,12
Andros, 55.20; 92.62
Ankyra, 16.11.7
Antioch (Syria), 98 II 16
Antioch by [---], 32.112
Antioch in Persis, 30 n.7; 32.1,20,51
Apameia near the Sellas, 32.103–4
Apollonia, 70.96
Arachosians, 51 B3
Argives, 86.3
Ariana, 51 B3, C(a)
Arkadians, 73.33
Arsinoeia, 8.24, and n.6. *See also* Ephesos
Asia, 16.11.3,4; 17.14; 30.17; 46 C105; 99.8
Asioi, 51 D

Assos, 21.2,19,27
Athens, 5 I 3; 6.11,14,42; 7; 11.13,39,60; 13
  (decree of); 37 n.1; 38 (decrees of);
  55.91; 56; 57; 58; 59 (decree of); 60.13;
  67.27; 70.106; 75.27
Athmonea (deme), 60.10
Athribis, 109.5
Azenia (deme), 76.1

Babylon, 41; 99.18
Baktria, 51; 83.5; 99.20
Barca, 105
Batinetis, 12.12,24,28
Beroia, 54
Bithynians, 16.11.5; 26.1
Bizone, 68.26
Boiotia, 30.14; 63 n.4
Bousiris, 109.9
Bousirite Nome, 103.22
Bubastis, 112.14
Byzantion, 16

Chalkis, 30 n.7
Chersonesos, 77
Chians, 62.22,28
Cholargos (deme), 11.2
Corinth, 14.12
Cycladic Islands, 99.8
Cyrene, 104

164

III. Index of geographical names

Daphne, 38.57
Dardanians, 46 C130
Delos, 75.2,25; 81; 88.4; 92.48; 102
Delphi, 7 n.6; 31.22; 62.14,27; 69.3,9,16; 70.1;
 82.4,5,19; 84.2; 87.1,29; 89.1
Didyma, 2.7,28,42; 9.3; 24.32
Diospolis the Great, 111.2. *See also* Thebes
 (Egypt)
Dodona, 46 C116
Drangianians, 51 B 3

Egypt, 39 B; 97.7,16; 99.7,12,22–3; 102.4; 103;
 105; 106; 107; 109.3
Elateia, 71
Elephantine, 97.5
Eleusis (deme), 13.8; 56.69
Eleutherna, 34 A4
Elis, 56.23,38; 78.1; 79.1
Ephesos, 1.3,16; 24.31; 90.1
Epidamnos, 30 n.7
Epiros, 63 n.4
Erchia (deme), 55.9; 56.6
Erythraean Sea, 110.5
Erythrai, 23.1
Euphrates River, 99.12,17–18

Galatians, 16; 17.5; 19.14; 51 A 7; 85.275.2,
 276.2
Gergitha, 21.23
Greece, 7; 17.14,18; 34 B5; 48.30; 60.6; 62; 87;
 107

Halikarnassos, 37 n.1
Harpassos, 85.279.1
Hellespont, 99.14
Hellespontine Phrygia, 85.274.1–2
Hellespontine satrapy, 21.27–8
Herakleia (on the Pontos), 16.11.1,2
Herakleia by Latmos, 37
Hybandos River, 37.30,37
Hypanis River, 51 C(a)
Hyrcania, 51 A8

Iasos, 36.3
Ilion, 15 (decree of); 20 (decree of); 21.1,21;
 24.29
India, 51 B3,4, C(a),(b)
Indian Sea, 110.4
Ionia, 12.14; 64.3; 88.27; 99.14
Ipsos (battle of), 11.17
Isamos River, 51 C(a)
Istria, 68 (decree of)
Ithaka, 30 n.7

Jaxartes River, 51.4
Jerusalem, 44.22
Jews, 29.149; 35.138; 42; 43.24; 44.23,27,29

Judaea, 39 B

Kaikos River, 85.276.1
Kalchedonians, 16.11.2
Kallion, 64.2
Kaphyans, 55.25,39
Karia, 85.279.1; 99.7
Kephale (deme), 4.4; 11.8
Kerameikos, 59.11
Kiddios, 19
Kieros, 16.11.2
Kilikia, 98 II 2,6; 99.14
Kition, 59.10
Knidos, 37 n.1
Koile (deme), 11.6
Koile Syria, 39b; 39 n.3
Kollytos (deme), 13.10
Koloe, 85.278.1
Konthyle (deme), 55.11
Kos, 26.2; 27 (decree of)
Kretans, 56.25,39
Krokodilopolite nome, 39 C2, and n.6
Kypros, 55.51; 99.7
Kyrbissos, 28
Kythnos, 92.61
Kyzikos, 24.3; 37 n.1; 88.65, and n.9

Ladarma, 46 A12
Lakedaimonians, 56; 74.1; 80
Lakonian, 86.2,5. *See also* Lakedaimonians
Lamia, 64.3
Larisa, 65.1
Leontion, 74.2
Leukas, 70.100
Libya, 99.6
Lindos, 46
Lydia, 29.149
Lykia, 99.7
Lykopolis, 103.22
Lysimacheia, 22.11,13,17, and n.3

Macedonians, 5 III 29; 46 C129; 51 A5, C(b);
 63.2; 91.14
Magnesia on the Maeander, 10.5–6, and n.3;
 30.9,21,34,35; 31.4–5,14; 32, and n.5;
 37; 112.1–2
Maidoi, 46 C130
Mantineans, 56.24,38
Marathon (battle of), 7
Masdynoi, 91.16
Media, 99.19
Mediterranean (Sea), 97.5
Megalopolis, 73; 79.2
Melite (deme), 81.1
Memphis, 39 B; 103.7–8; 106.36; 109.8; 112.3
Mesopotamia, 99.18
Messenia, 30.16; 80; 86.3

IV. Index of subjects and terms

Xupetaion (deme), 59.10

Zeleia, 24.3

IV. Subjects and terms

IV. Index of subjects and terms

Decrees: (Egyptian), 103 *passim*; Greek, 23.3; 32.33; 46 A5,11; 62.4; 65.27; 80.45; 88.5; 89.15,19; 92.47; 100.35; of the Roman senate, 75.4,14; 80.35,51

Dedications, 3; 9.5,13; 46 *passim*; 52; 53; 60.3–5; 63; 72.14–15; 74; 76; 78; 79; 86 *passim*; 87 *passim*; 112.2

Deification: Kallimachos (temple-sharing), 111.31; Philopoimen, 73.4–5,42; Theophanes, 47

Deme, 6.34. *See also* Glossary

Democracy, 11.49; 16.11.4, and n.5; 22.8; 25.4; 55.82; 77.24

Diadem, 38.18; 48.103

Diagramma, 72.1–2

Dikaios (epithet of Antiochos I of Kommagene), 48.2

Dioiketes: Egypt, 92.2, and n.1; 96.1, and n.1; 101.258, and n.1; 109.2; Seleucid, 36.15–16, and n.3. *See also* Glossary

District Governor, 42.261 (Seleucid)

Divine manifestations: Artemis, 30.5,10; 32.35–6; Athena Lindia, 46 A7–8, D95–116; Sarapis, 102.14–26

Doctor, 20.5; 27.3 (public)

Dynastic cults, 10.18 (Lysimachos); 15.26 (Antiochos I); 33.51–2 (Antiochos III); 41.1 (Antiochos IV); 48 *passim* (Antiochos I of Kommagene); 92.27–8 (Ptolemaios I); 93 *passim* (Arsinoe II); 88.60 (Eumenes II); 103.37–40 (Ptolemaios I–V). *See also* Priests *and* Priestesses

Dystros (month), 100.4

Education, 59.10; 89 *passim*; 90.3–9; 105

Elaphebolion (month), 6.3

Elephants, 99.10–16

Embassies, 23.21; 33.30; 55 *passim*; 71 *passim*

Enduspoitropios (month), 89.40

Ephebes, 93.12; 95 n.6; 105. *See also* Glossary

Ephors, 56.91

Epimenios, 15.1, and n.1 (Ilion); 68.1 (Istria)

Epiphanes (epithet), 39 B; 41.1 (of Antiochos IV); 48.2 (of Antiochos I of Kommagene); 48.6 (of Antiochos VIII); 103.5,9,37–8; 104–5 (of Ptolemaios V). *See also* Glossary

Epistates, 15.1, and n.2 (Ilion); 72.23 (Thessalonike); 108.23–5 (Egypt)

Epistolographos, 108.32–3

Epistrategos, 110.2–3 (of the Indian and Erythraean Seas); 111.24

Estates, 19.9–10 (of Achaios)

Eucharistos, 103.5,9,37–8 (epithet of Ptolemaios V)

Euergetes (epithet), 103.4–5,37 (of Ptolemaios

III and Berenike II); 108.22 (of Ptolemaios VIII, Kleopatra II and Kleopatra III). *See also* Glossary 'Soter and Euergetes'

Eumeneios (month), 91.2

Eunuchs, 39 B

Exemption: from eisphora, 92.16; from garrison and tribute, 22.9–10; from taxes, 1.13; 2.39; 8.9; 29.151; 35.141–4; 37.52,57; 40 II 2; 71.6–7; 82.14,23; 100.13–16; from tribute, 23.23,27–8; 33.18–19,33–4

Exetastes, 4.30–2; 6.44 (Athens); 62.1,34 (Chios)

Exiles, 28.23–4; 71 *passim*; 74

Famine, 111 *passim*

Festivals: Asklepieia, 26 n.3; Attaleia, 89.35–6; Boadromia, 71.31; Dionysia, 11.62; 17.42; Ephesia, 1.10, and n.2; Leukophryenia, 32.25–59; Nikephoria, 87 *passim*; Panionia, 88.51–2; Ptolemaieia, 92 *passim*; Pythia and Soteria, 87.31–2; Soteria, 73.17. *See also* Games and contests *and* Glossary 'Dionysia' *and* 'Panathenaia'

Financial administrators: Athens, 6.56; 11.67–8,70–1; 13.41; 56.51–2,67; 59.11; Priene, 10.24

Fines, 46 A11; 54.20–4; 66 *passim*; 72.19; 89.16–18; 96.4–5,8–9; 100.33–4; 102.25

Fortresses, 11.36, and n.7; 28 *passim*; 37.42–3; 61; 91.15; 98 II 20

Foundation (of a colony), 29 *passim*; 32.14–16

Freedom, 11.31,35,45; 25.3; 56.18,73; 67.10; 91.5; 92.14; 97.11

Friends, 6.9–12; 8.2; 15.9,15,23; 33.23; 95.9. *See also* Glossary

Friendship, 31.6,10–11; 77.3–4,25–6

Friendship and Alliance: Antiochos I or II and Lysimacheia, 22 *passim*; Antiochos III and Iasos, 36.5; Athens and Sparta, 56 *passim*; Ptolemaios II and Miletos, 95.8; Rome and the Jews, 44.31; Ziaelas and Kos, 26.19,25

Friendship and good will, 32.50

Funds (special): decrees, 12.71; Galatian, 23.28; public, 32.67,74; sacred monies, 17.49–50; wall building, 8.39

Gamelion (month), 13.4

Games and contests, 1.12; 2.35–7; 11.42–5; 30.10–30; 32.25–30, 56–60,78–81; 34 *passim*; 62.9–11,15–18,21–2,23–5; 67.24; 71.31; 83.5–6,24; 87.12,26–7; 92.21–2,39–42. *See also* Festivals

Garrisons, 28 *passim*; 55.14,20; 58; 61.1,5,7

IV. Index of subjects and terms

Gerousia, 56.91
Gifts, 1.19; 11.12,14–15; 21 *passim*; 23.5,14;
  32.74; 36.10–25; 40 I 6–15;
  55.50–5,65–70; 61.6–7; 62.33–4; 80.26;
  95.3
Gorpaios (month), 65.39; 96.9
Governors, 51 A (Seleucid); 55.20,71
  (Ptolemaic); 75.1–2,27 (of Delos)
Gymnasiarch, 81.2–3 (Delos); 111.4 (Thebaid)

Hagneon (month), 37.91
Herakleios (month), 32.70; 77.7
Hieromnemonic vote, 31.22
Hieronomoi, 15.20
Hipparchos, 31.2 (Aitolian League); 56.87
  (Athens); 64.14 (Lamia)
Honors: for benefactors, 1.10–16; 2.30–42;
  6.27–40; 11.58–66; 19.21–3; 33.42–53;
  40 II 8–15; 55.90–3, and n.15; 59.11;
  60.8–11; 71.27–30; 88.25–41; for
  proxenoi, 64.8–13; 69.13–16; 82.13–25;
  84.4–7
Hypaspists, 66 A3,8
Hyperberetaios (month), 35.143; 41.5

Ides, 75.17
Inscriptions, 46. *See also* Steles
Inviolability, 26.7,45, and n.4; 30.9–10,30–5;
  31.11; 33.18,47–8, and n.3; 64.13; 71.28;
  84.4; 87.12,24–6
Isoteleis, 61 *passim*

Kallinikos (epithet), 32.3–4 (of Seleukos II);
  48.4 (of Mithridates of Kommagene);
  48.7 (of Antiochos VIII)
Kinship, 88.65
Kinship and Friendship: Chios and the
  Aitolians, 62.2–3; Magnesia on the
  Maeander and Antioch in Persis,
  32.11–13,22,34–5; Messene and Elis,
  80.7–8,16
Kinsman, 108.32–3; 109.2; 110.2; 111.3
  (Egypt)
Kleruchs, 39 C; 94.12–13. *See* Glossary
Komarchs, 101.45

Land: annexation of, 21 *passim*; 24.14,18–19;
  gift (Egypt), 94.15; 100.8–10; released
  (Egypt), 107.37; temple (Egypt), 94.7;
  97.9–10; 107.37. *See also* Royal land
Laokritai, 107.215,218
Law (Egypt), 107.206–19
Leagues: Achaian, 71.11,15–16; 73 *passim*;
  Aitolian, 31 *passim*; 64.1,5–6; 62
  passim; 69.5; Amphiktionic, 31.21;
  87.1,3,12; Hellenic, 63 nn.3–4; Ionian, 8
  passim; 88.1,34; Islands, 92 *passim*

Lenaion (month), 8.39
Letters, 14.5,9; 20.5; 21.2–4,53,59,72; 33.29;
  36.15; 42.262–3; 44.22,31; 46 A7, and
  n.5; 62.8; 65.27; 80 *passim*; 92.3
Liberation of Athens (287), 11.31; 55.12–40
Loans of public funds, 89.12,23–30 (Delphi)
Loos (month), 48.84; 104.1

Machimoi, 101.215–16, and n.14; 103.19–20
Maimakterion (month), 59.10
Mastroi, 46 A1,5 (Rhodes); 89.17, and n.3
  (Delphi)
Medimnos, *see* Glossary
Mercenaries, 5 I 5, IV 5; 37.60; 55.19–21; 61
  n.1; 68.12
Metageitnion (month), 4.5; 56.4
Molpoi (Miletos), 25.1, and n.1. *See also*
  Stephanephoros
Mysteries of the Maiden, 7.5

Naval station, 21.54 (Seleucid)
Neopoioi, 1.15 (Ephesos); 17.50, and n.7
  (Priene)
Neos Dionysos (epithet of Ptolemaios XII),
  110.8–9
Nesiarch, 92.3, and n.3
Nikator (epithet of Seleukos I), 32.2. *See also*
  Glossary
Nomes, 39 C; 94.3–4; 97.5; 101.115,258
Non-Greeks, 10.7, and n.4; 17.6; 68.44
  (dependents of cities)

Oaths, 22 *passim*; 28 *passim*; 37 *passim*;
  56.46,48,84–92; 68.40; 77.5–30
Occupation of Piraeus, 11.35–6; 13.30; 14.14;
  55.16; 67.10–16
Oikonomos, 1.20, and n.8; Egypt, 101 *passim*
Oligarchy (at Athens), 11.48–50, and n.11;
  55.81, and n.14
Oracles: Delphi, 30.5–10,11,18,23; Dodona,
  46 C116
Overseer (of Delphi), 69.5–6

Pachon (month), 110.11
Panemos (month), 8.26
Pantheos (month), 32.9
Paroikoi, 100.29, and n.10
Pay for military service, 17.18; 28.28–31
Peace and Friendship, 37.40
Peplos, 11.15; 55.67
Peritios (month), 19.3; 54.2
Persecution: of Alexandrian intellectuals, 105;
  of Jews, 42 *passim*; 43 *passim*
Petitions, 42.258,262
Phamenoth (month), 111.2
Philadelphos (epithet): of Laodike of
  Kommagene, 48.5; of Ptolemaıos II and

169

IV. Index of subjects and terms

Philadelphos (*cont.*)
  Arsinoe II, 93.11; 94.10,18; 103.38; of
  Ptolemaios XII, 110.10. *See also* Glossary
Philanthropa, 43 *passim*; 103.9–20; 107
Philhellene (epithet of Antiochos I of
  Kommagene), 48.3
Philometor (epithet), 48.6–7 (of Antiochos
  VIII); 111.1 (of Ptolemaios XV)
Philopator (epithet), 103,3–5 (of Ptolemaios
  IV and Arsinoe III); 111.1 (of Kleopatra
  VII); 111.1 (of Ptolemaios XV)
Philoromaios (epithet of Antiochos I of
  Kommagene), 48.2
Philosophy, 59.10; 76
Phratry, 6.34 (Athens); 20.20 (Ilion). *See also*
  Glossary
Phylarchs, 56.86 (Athens)
Piracy, 26.33–44; 31.11–15
Poitropios (month), 89.37
Polemarch, 62.1,32 (Chios)
Pollution, 28.25–7
Poseideon (month), 55.7
Praetor, 75.16; 80.41,50
Priests: of Alexander, 98 III 21; 100.4; 102.1–3;
  103.4; of Antiochos I, 10.19; 15.25,26; of
  Athena Lindia, 46 A11, D96–7;
  Egyptian, 97.10; 103 *passim*; 108.14;
  111.2–3; of Hestia, 73.45; rodbearers,
  93.11–12; of Seleucid Kings, 32.2–6
Priestesses, 10.19; 13.5–6; 15.20,26; 92.8
  (Kanephoros of Arsinoe II)
Probouloi, 89.21, and n.4 (Delphi)
Proconsul, 80.55,64
Proedroi, 4.8; 6.5–6; 11.5–6,52; 13.6–7;
  55.8–9,86–7; 56.5–6; 59.10. *See also*
  Glossary
Property of a God, 72 *passim* (Sarapis)
Proskynesis, 7
Prostatai, 36.20–1, and n.4 (Iasos)
Provinces (Roman), 80.54.5,64–5 (Achaia)
Proxenoi, 20.14–15; 64 *passim*; 69.13; 70 *passim*;
  82.13,23,25; 84.3. *See also* Glossary
Prytaneion, 2.39 (Miletos); 6.34–5 (Athens)
Prytanis: Alexandria, 93.11; Antioch in Persis,
  32.10; Athens, 6.46; Miletos, 2.20, and
  n.8; 40 I 1; 80.29; Pergamon, 83.1–2;
  Rhodes, 46 D100. *See also* Glossary
Prytany, 4.2; 6.3,4; 11.1,4; 13.2,6; 55.5,8;
  56.2–4; 59.10
Public Register, 8.27
Pyanopsion (month), 37.90

Raids, 16 *passim*; 17 *passim* (Galatian); 68 *passim*
  (Thracian); 77.14 (barbarian)
Ransom, 14.15–16, and n.5; 16.111; 19.15;
  37.69; 68.19–33
Rebellions, 15.5–6; 29.149; 51 A; 83.5;

101.220–2, and n.15; 103.19–28; 106.16,
  and n.7
Royal
  agents, 42.261 (Seleucid)
  land, in Egypt, 92 *passim*; 101.210–13;
    107.209; 108.38; Seleucid, 21.41; 24.2
  monopolies, 101.88–118 (textiles)
  peasants, 19 *passim*; 21.46; 24.8–9
    (Seleucid); 101.42–63 (Egypt)
  revenues, 96.3,6; 101.118–34,168–74;
    107.210 (Egypt)

Sacred
  ambassadors, 26.3–5,45–50, and n.2;
    32.65–77; 55.56–62,69,73; 62.4,27–9;
    87.11; 92
  animals, 107.177–9
  heralds, 62.21 (Chios); 71.31 (Elateia)
  truce, 33.27,57
Sacrificers of the tribes (Priene), 10.25
Sanctuaries, 2 *passim*; 9.3; 17.48; 19 *passim*;
  21.10,16, and n.2; 24.30–5; 26.5,45;
  38.56–7; 46 A2,10; 47.7; 49 A4, and n.4;
  71.8; 72.7; 75.9,25; 87.11,23; 100.37;
  102 *passim*; 111.6,27
Sarapieion, 102.14 (Delos)
Satrapies, 21.28–9; 98 III 10,20; 99.16–17
  (Seleucid)
Savior, 19.25; 33.52–3; 41.2; 53.5, and n.5. *See
  also* Soter
Scribes (village), 101.45 (Egypt)
Scrutiny of Civic Honors, 6.49–50; 55 n.15;
  61.6–8
Secretaries: Aitolian League, 31.3; Antioch in
  Persis, 32.7–9; Athens, 4.4.27; 6.53;
  11.68; 13.4; 55.6–7; 56.42–3,64–5;
  59.11; Chersonesos, 77.9; Macedon,
  66 A8; Rhodes, 46 A8
Security officials, 40 I 1; 80.29 (Miletos)
Senate, 75.16; 80.35,51
Sitologoi, 101.127
Six Years Truce, 12.13, and nn.3,7
Slavery, 35.144; 54 *passim* (manumission);
  65.31, and n.4
Soldiers' equipment, 28.33–4
Soter (epithet), 32.3 (of Antiochos I); 53 n.5
  (India); 92.28,44; 99.3; 103.4,38 (epithet
  of Ptolemaios I and Berenike I). *See also*
  Glossary
Speirarchs, 66 B12,17
Sphinx, 7.24
Stasis, 5 I 2
Stater, *see* Glossary
Statues: of gods, 5 IV 15; 48.28–63; 102.10; of
  private individuals, 6.38,45; 11.63;
  40 II 13; 47; 56 nn.2,7; 74; 76; 78; 79;
  111.28; of rulers, 2.32; 10.15; 15 n.10;

V. Index of translated passages

V. Index of translated passages